FAITH IN NATION

FAITH IN

Exclusionary Origins of Nationalism

NATION

ANTHONY W. MARX

OXFORD
UNIVERSITY PRESS

2003

OXFORD
UNIVERSITY PRESS

Oxford   New York
Auckland   Bangkok   Buenos Aires   Cape Town   Chennai
Dar es Salaam   Delhi   Hong Kong   Istanbul   Karachi   Kolkata
Kuala Lumpur   Madrid   Melbourne   Mexico City   Mumbai   Nairobi
São Paulo   Shanghai   Taipei   Tokyo   Toronto

Copyright © 2003 by Oxford University Press, Inc.

Published by Oxford University Press, Inc.
198 Madison Avenue, New York, New York 10016

www.oup.com

Oxford is a registered trademark of Oxford University Press

Library of Congress Cataloging-in-Publication Data
Marx, Anthony W.
    Faith in nation : exclusionary origins of nationalism / by Anthony W. Marx.
    p. cm.
    ISBN 0-19-515482-7
    1. Nationalism—Philosophy. 2. Religion—Europe—History. I. Title.
    JC311 .M3465 2003
    320.54'094—dc21   2002022449

9 8 7 6 5 4 3 2

Printed in the United States of America
on acid-free paper

TO JOSHUA AND ANNA CLAIRE

PREFACE

Few descriptions of the past have been as idealized as traditional accounts of the origins of Western nationalism. As a product of the eighteenth-century revolutions, initial European nationalism was lauded as a liberal form of mass political engagement and allegiance to the secular power of emerging states, consistent with popular rule. Accordingly, its birth was announced with the representation, rights, and toleration of England's constitutional monarchy and its banner the "liberty, equality and fraternity" of the French Revolution against absolutism. Nationalism in the West thus supposedly emerged as a unifying mass sentiment and participation. Specifically, it is usually portrayed as popular cohesion and loyalty to a state or inspiring efforts to build a state that conforms to such solidarity. And such solidarity has been conventionally described and celebrated as tending toward inclusion within a territorial political unit. Though some groups may not have enjoyed equal treatment as members of these nations, such exclusion was often ignored or described as temporary or tangential to an overriding tendency toward inclusion.

This Whiggish triumphalism was an inheritance of the purported founding of nationalism in the West during the Enlightenment, with nationalism seen as the quintessential expression of inclusive tolerance. And this image was then often reinforced by a distinction between the West's "civic" nationalism and illiberal "ethnic" nationalism that emerged later or elsewhere: the conflict-ridden and exclusionary efforts at non-Western or more recent nation-building, as in eastern Europe or Africa, have been denigrated and distinguished from the Western experience. As the central organizing principle of modern politics, nationalism was thus dichotomized between a noble Western invention and an ignoble non-Western imitation.

Even as this self-serving distinction of inclusive Western solidarity and others' violent exclusions has come under increasing scholarly criticism, it retains its hold on the popular Western imagination. There is no denying that new or resurgent efforts to consolidate nation-states have often been violent and exclusionary. And as we have painfully witnessed at the dawn of this millennium, non-Western efforts to challenge the existing dynamics of the nation-state system and to build regional, cultural, or global alternatives to it have also been violent and sought solidarity on the basis of antagonism. Both of these seemingly contradictory trends—to consolidate late-emerging nationalism or to move beyond it—impel further analysis of nationalism. If we are to grapple with the continued resonance of the nation-state, reject it, or replace it, we must understand what nationalism is and how it did and does develop. But the convention that the West's own initial experiences with nationalism followed a path consistently distinct from more recent developments, still stands in the way of a more complete understanding.

Hagiography of the West should be put aside, or at least be subject to further critical analysis, if we are to seriously inquire into what nationalism is and how it has emerged or been challenged. If western Europe was where nationalism developed in its earliest and supposedly inclusive "civic" form, then that is where the accuracy of this image would have to be assessed and where this "civic" path and motivation would be clearest. Or, put negatively, to argue that nationalism did not emerge as consistently liberal, comparative logic suggests that the formative role of exclusions would have to be evident where the supposedly inclusive path had been forged. Either way, we must understand these early Western experiences if we are to have an accurate picture of whether or not nationalism has been or can be built inclusively even today. The alternative view of nationalism built on the basis of exclusions should be tested against the hardest cases, where a civic founding was purportedly enjoyed. And if there is counterevidence, then we must move beyond discredited conventional accounts to show when, where, how, and why early nationalism was built through exclusions. Only then can we account for varying patterns of civic inclusion or exclusion or reject such distinctions as falsely self-serving.

This essay on initial core experiences of Western nationalism is designed to pursue these analytic concerns. Accordingly, I have confronted the long cherished consensus and conventions of Western historiography, and then tried to build an alternative unbound by limitations that implicitly accept the iconography of a civic founding or by the custom of beginning analysis where such inclusion was supposedly embraced. Instead, I have purposely peered behind established analysis to look for the earlier foundations of nation-building to determine when and how popular engagement with or against state authority began. I argue that the roots of modern nationalism and its centrality to politics go back a half millennium, if not further. This has pushed my analysis back at least two centuries earlier than most conventional accounts. And there is abundant evidence of nationalist engagement combined with exclusions under particular circumstances in this earlier period. From this evidence, then, comes my argument about the process of nation formation.

If inclusive nationalism was built on a foundation of earlier exclusion, then that later consolidation cannot be understood without reference to such earlier processes too often forgotten or seen as irrelevant. If my assertion is true, then we will have to finally abandon the image of a Western "civic" founding distinct from illiberal nationalism elsewhere. Celebrants of the West as inclusive, liberal, or civic long resisted having this image so questioned or besmirched, and I do not, therefore, expect that further disturbing the pool of history, stirring up the mud at the bottom, will be appreciated by those who still enjoy self-congratulation or facile denigration of others.

This rethinking of the origins of Western nationalism presented itself as a follow-up to my own earlier work bringing into question the conventional wisdom of nationalism as inclusive. In a previous study, I challenged the idealized image of that modern experience at nation-building assumed to have most closely followed the supposedly civic, Western tradition. In the United States, nationalism was forged not as inclusively as liberal hagiography would suggest. Rather than a tangential element in our own nation-building, the purposeful and long-maintained exclusionary policies regarding African-Americans were central to the process of uniting whites across regional antagonisms as a nation. Immigrants were more readily included in the nation than were resident blacks.

Nor did I find this pattern of exclusionary nationalism unique to the

United States. In this regard, and despite other significant differences, the forging of the American nation was more similar to that of South Africa than we like to admit. In both countries, appeasement was practised in dealing with conflicts among whites, and unity was reinforced on the basis of racist exclusions. Even Brazil, a country that did not legally encode racial exclusions of the sort mandated in the United States or South Africa, nonetheless forged national unity amid informal socio-economic discrimination against the descendants of slaves.

Nationalism need not have been—indeed was not—produced in the same way in different periods or places. But it seems odd that nationalism in the modern era has often been forged by exclusion while earlier Western nationalism was so consistently portrayed as having been built inclusively. And my own suspicions were raised further by what we increasingly recognize as a false image of American national inclusion. If Americans have inaccurately depicted a seamless process of integration, perhaps the self-congratulatory European image of its own earlier inclusiveness might be equally inaccurate. If modern, popular solidarity has emerged or proven easier to build on the basis of exclusion—that somehow this process reflected some basic aspect of how humans forge collectivities—then had earlier and supposedly more noble and inclusive processes tapped into a more liberal form of human motivation? Were the original nation-builders of "the West" somehow guided by "the better angels of their nature," if not actually better? Or perhaps this image of a tolerant past, against which the present is found wanting, is not only false but misdirects analysis of our current or future predicaments. Others have already launched such a critique, though I aim to go further in constructing an alternative analysis based on a review of relevant history.

As W. H. Auden wrote, we can only learn "to approach the Future as a friend, without a wardrobe of excuses" if we are honest about our past. It is to this ideal that my short exercise in comparative history is committed.

Pursuing that ideal, what follows is a selective examination of Western nationalism at its emergence, when the populace became engaged with secular powers and increasingly loyal (or actively opposed) to state institutions and authority. I focus on the pressures and processes that created such nationalism, when and where it emerged, why and how it was built, and how it set the course for later developments, including liberalism and democracy. My primary cases are early modern France and England, and to a lesser extent Spain, with all three then great powers making initial attempts to impose central authority from above and manage popular loyalties from below. Although these three cannot pretend to cover all western European experiences, they are core cases in the history of nationalism, with significant commonalities and revealing divergence among them. Other important cases might have been added to this comparison, much as my case studies might also have been extended further back into history when elements of national identity were starting to take shape. While I acknowledge these limitations, I hope that my particular geographic and temporal focus will prove suggestive.

The basic building blocks of this essay are a set of intertwined historical narratives. I have constructed these narratives by drawing on an array of documents from the period and from leading secondary sources, particularly those to which scholars of these cases and the period make repeated reference. Much of the resulting narratives are conventional but necessary for filling out the argument. Some aspects of these histories are more contested. Particularly in those instances I have attempted to check references and documents against each other before reaching any conclusions, while drawing attention to ongoing disputes of interpretation.

I could have organized my analysis in any one of several ways. It might have been easier on me and the reader to present three distinct historical cases as such, but I concluded that presenting three separate case studies would give the appearance of "potted" narratives and perhaps be seen as conventional or distorted, either way hiding the analytic argument. Alternatively I might have employed a purely conceptual organization, jumping between relevant aspects of history. I feared that such a format would confuse readers not intimately familiar with the history of the cases and result in an overly simplistic polemic. I have chosen instead a somewhat less conventional organization, constructing chapters around a combination of conceptual themes and relevant narratives. I hope that this approach will both clarify my argument about the development of nationalism and show how this development proceeded in each case history.

Retaining separate case sections within each chapter is consistent with the argument I present and should help with exposition. If nationalism is a collective sentiment tied to the object of an existing or emergent state, then such political institutions comprise the unit of analysis within which nationalism develops and should be examined. As I will argue, nationalism potentially ties masses to elites within states. The development of these ties is crucial for consolidating state power that requires popular allegiance. This outcome of mass cohesion and state loyalty was deeply contested, provoking conflict over whether such power should be consolidated and by whom it should be held and to what ends. This is the basic stuff of politics, and indeed we cannot understand nationalism if we ignore those conflicts that challenged national unity and which nationalism was designed or refined in order to contain. But these dynamics emerged within (and between) existing or emerging state structures, and the consolidation of states was a central part of those processes.

While I have therefore retained distinct case histories within each chapter, my inquiry is then fleshed out through comparative analytic history, bearing in mind the strengths and weaknesses of that form. In particular I seek to explicate causal mechanisms drawn from comparison, and accordingly my historical summaries highlight and categorize those particular events and processes most relevant to my argument, as is true—if less obviously so—of more traditional narratives. But, unlike such accounts, I am not attempting to be exhaustive but rather selective and suggestive. The result falls somewhere in that treacherous ground between the heuristic of relatively ahistorical social science models and the illumination of deeply historical single-case or comparative studies.

This approach, with its occasional distortions and all of its unconventional implications, can be justified by the important patterns of difference, similarity, and interaction that can emerge. I hope that the costs, the resulting selectivity and breaks in the historical narrative, are worthwhile for clarifying such patterns that undergird my analytic argument and that it will be clear that such analysis can emerge only through comparison. At the least, the results should provoke further debate and reconsideration of assumptions about Western inclusion and tolerance that too long remained unchallenged.

At the same time, if intolerant exclusion was central to bolstering early popular cohesion and then loyalty to states as the basis of nationalism, we must be careful not to assume such outcomes were either necessary or constant even in those cases. The political imperative for popular cohesion or loyalty to states emerged fitfully and often unintentionally, in an era when nation-states did not yet exist. But elites and commoners did gradually perceive the need to, and recurrently sought to, shape, protect, and legitimate state authority, facing various choices about how to do so and reacting to changing conditions. The uncertainty and agency involved in their decisions will be most evident by concentrating on such moments of choice. And as we shall see, on particular occasions the choice was made to attempt greater inclusion, or at least grudging coexistence, all the more notable in a distrustful age when even the word "tolerance" was often pejorative. We should not be too quick to denigrate such early efforts at inclusion just because they may have been later reversed or appear less than complete or conscious when compared with modern standards of liberalism. Only by examining the actual constraints and choices made by actors can we avoid the "presentism" of such ahistorical judgment.

In thinking about the dangers of such a retrospective reading of history, I am reminded again of San Clemente in Rome. There, a twelfth-century basilica is built upon a fourth-century early Christian church, itself built over the site of a first-century AD temple or meeting house. The modern visitor, descending through these three levels, can see how the present has literally been built upon the past. There is at least one shaft that cuts through all the layers. If you stand at the top, looking down from the perspective of the modern, all below is obscured in darkness. Instead, if you stand on the lowest historical level and look up, all levels are illuminated from above. The trick is to allow the light of the present to clarify the ancient levels but also to see that light from the perspective of the ancients, not to be blinded by it or drawn to it only in a way that obscures where the long dead lived and how they understood themselves and their situations.

Informed by this historical perspective, my argument seeks to illuminate the perspective and actions of the early moderns and to explicate causal patterns without assuming a mechanical or teleological process. I examine both varying elite strategies at the time for resisting challengers, gaining or holding power, and mass participation either harnessed by elites or directed against them. If much of "social history is history with politics left out," then I am here endeavoring to combine elite and popular history to illuminate important and linked developments in both. Indeed, nationalism is precisely where and how power politics and passions from above and below explosively came together, potentially forging collective cohesion. But if that cohesion was often forged in response to conflict and on the basis of exclusion, this would counter later claims of a liberal or inclusive founding. We would then be left with a different understanding of the formation of nationalism in the West, and a different starting point from which to assess the inheritances of the past that still trouble us.

ACKNOWLEDGMENTS

I am indebted for the advice and comments provided by colleagues at Columbia University: Karen Barkey, Peter Johnson, Ira Katznelson, Alfred Stepan, Charles Tilly, and Yosef Yerushalmi. And I am similarly appreciative for the suggestions and assistance of colleagues elsewhere: David Bell, Dan Chirot, Thomas Ertman, Philip S. Gorski, David Hebb, Mack P. Holt, Juan Linz, Keith Luria, Alex Motyl, Katherine Newman, Anthony Smith, Jay Smith, Dale Van Kley, and anonymous reviewers.

I am also grateful for the financial support for this project provided by a John Simon Guggenheim Memorial Foundation fellowship, a National Endowment for the Humanities fellowship at the National Humanities Center, and a George A. and Eliza Gardner Howard Foundation fellowship.

It has also been a pleasure to have the advice and assistance of my colleagues at Oxford University Press, most notably Dedi Felman and Niko Pfund.

Finally, I am most grateful for the support and encouragement provided by my friends and family, especially to Karen and to our children. It is to Joshua and Anna Claire that this book is dedicated.

CONTENTS

FAITH IN NATION

HISTORY AND ARGUMENTS
"Substance in Our Enmities"

1

As first light broke on New Year's Day of 1492, Christian forces entered and took Granada, completing the reconquest of Spain from the Moors. Six days later, the newly captured Alhambra palace of the Moors was admired by Queen Isabella and King Ferdinand. Their marriage twenty-three years earlier had aligned the major Spanish kingdoms for the first time and after long civil wars, making reconquest possible. On March 30, 1492, Ferdinand and Isabella signed an order expelling another distinct but less foreign group, the Jews, extending and bringing to climax an Inquisition over which the monarchs had been granted control by the pope fourteen years earlier. The year 1492 also saw the printing of the first vernacular grammar book in Spain, under royal approval. And on April 17 of that momentous year, the king and queen dedicated a portion of their new resources to the voyage of Christopher Columbus in search of a western route to India. Columbus departed on August 3 and on October 12 sighted land in what we now know to be the West Indies.

Within this ten-month period, a consolidating Spanish state had expelled its Moorish rulers, moved further toward religious unity, begun to spread linguistic homogeneity, and projected itself globally. This was truly a New World, at home and abroad, marking the start at midmillennium of Europe's emergence into the early modern era. Ferdinand and Isabella were no doubt mindful of the sea change. One can imagine that the experience of entering the ornate Alhambra filled Spain's monarchs with a sense of awe—not only at the majesty of the place, but at the task of fully inhabiting the palaces of state, building and directing their new powers to construct a state of matching grandeur.

The dramatic events of 1492 signal the conflation of royal challenges and social processes that would reshape the Old World. Large-scale states were being built upon smaller units in order to spread control and to repel or prevent invasions from earlier consolidated empires, whether by the Moors from the south or the Ottomans to the east. Wary of domestic or foreign challengers, monarchs pursued policies that often had the effect of centralizing rule, drawing resources from early capitalism in order to harness that growth and to project it into further trade and then imperialism of the New World. Local conflicts within emergent states had to be contained to ensure the spread of markets, direct rule, collection of revenues, and the provision of armed forces to protect those states and their markets. The development of vernacular printing would help to spread cohesion and mass political engagement, though linguistic and other forms of heterogeneity long remained within state territories. And religious differences had to be confronted if greater cohesion or unity of the populace was to be achieved.

The coincidence of events in 1492 was indeed remarkable, though we should not make too much of it as the initiation of a seamless process of consolidating state power and popular cohesion. Spain itself would indeed suffer major reversals in the generations to come. Rather than emerge fully as a prototype of early efforts toward nationalism, Spain may instead demonstrate how premature and then exhausted or distracted elite machinations left domestic popular cohesion undeveloped. But even Spain's failures should remind us that for the large-scale political units of emerging states to function efficiently required a widespread belief among the populace that such rule is legitimate and should be observed. Grand palaces are not enough for effective rule of unitary states without such popular allegiance. A preeminent challenge for the new states emerging out of the Old World was that such widespread popular belief and cohesion, or for that matter any mass political engagement with the state, was lacking.

If anything, early efforts at state preservation or consolidation laid bare the dilemma of forging a complimentary popular allegiance. As institutionalized political authority grows, it claims a monopoly on the legitimate use of force, bringing the imperative for wider allegiance but also making such cohesion in some ways less likely. Direct rule draws together under single authority a greater diversity of peoples with varying backgrounds, languages, interests, and experiences, often before central authority has the tools or power to encourage cohesion. Constant reliance on force to achieve such popular support was unworkable and inefficient in large-scale polities, even under absolutism. And consolidating centralized rule often provoked local resistance, while the spread of vernacular language through printing often spread further discord. Thus, state-building began before the emergence of matching popular allegiance, making the latter achievement both more difficult and more imperative. The potentially mutually reinforcing processes of state-building and of growing popular support for states were not a foregone conclusion, either separately or together.

The lack of popular support for states evident in resistance to centralization heightened elite interests in resolving such internal conflict, creating greater popular cohesion, and in achieving domestic peace. Rulers so challenged would benefit most directly from reinforcing internal loyalty to diminish conflict and reinforce their authority and military power. In contrast, the localized populace had a competing interest in avoiding state centralization, domination, and taxes. But the balance between mass resistance or support for the central state shifted over time and place. Commoners also gradually perceived an interest in resolving internal conflict, to avoid violence or foreign domination and ensure their own peaceful prosperity. Indeed, the potential complimentarity of interest in centralization from above and below added to the growing impetus for achieving domestic cohesion and stability.

It is this dynamic between state elites and the populace that emerged as central to modern political development. As state elites took central stage in the political drama, they found that they needed a "supporting actor," the masses speaking with a more unified voice. The absence of that interlocutor, how it fitfully began to appear and then the problems posed by miscues in the resulting dialogue, would produce a new form of political drama.

Toward Nationalism: Explication and Specification

If states emerged as centralizing political authority before rulers enjoyed widespread popular allegiance, then the lack of such cohesion and continued internal conflict posed a problem for consolidating direct rule. And those who challenged or sought to replace such rule also needed more unified popular support, which was often absent. The envisioned solution to this dilemma has a name—nationalism. This is the modern ideal of popular loyalty and obedience coinciding with the boundaries of political power, either institutionalized as states or asserted against those states. It is the collective soul envisioned as inhabiting and enlivening the political body, linking individuals en masse to the center.

Nationalism is here formally defined as a collective sentiment or identity, bounding and binding together those individuals who share a sense of large-scale political solidarity aimed at creating, legitimating, or challenging states. As such, nationalism is often perceived or justified by a sense of historical commonality which coheres a population within a territory and which demarcates those who belong and others who do not. According to Max Weber, such "a specific sentiment of solidarity . . . may be linked to memories of a common political destiny."[1] But such boundedness is not a historical given; instead, such cohesion must be and has been actively constructed by both elites and commoners. It may then be solidified as a fundamental political belief, inspiring and inspired by engagement with state authority. For nationalism as a particular collective sentiment and related discourse to become a historical force it must so refer to a state as an existing structure or potential object of engagement.

This definition of nationalism does not specify the locus of its initiation. It instead stipulates only that such a subjective collective sentiment or identity claim coincides with or refers to existing or emergent institutionalized state power.[2] Nationalism often inspires support for elites ruling a state, though its basis is not necessarily an elite ideology but rather a more widespread sentiment that may or may not be inspired by an elite or coincide with the interests of a particular elite.[3] Nor is it necessarily in opposition to such an authoritative elite, as Breuilly would have it.[4]

The emergence of states and of nations thus should not be conflated, though they are linked. Nationalism is the potential basis of popular legitimacy or expression of support for state power, and as such the two are tied by definition. But institutions of power and sentiments about such institutions are not the same, and in practice the relation between nation and state varies. Nationalism as a collective sentiment of bounded solidarity or identity may or may not be determined by the institutionalized power of states to which it is or seeks to be tied. It may exist among a populace before or without corresponding states being established, and then it may inspire the attempted creation or reconfiguration of such a state. Or states may emerge without such preexisting solidarity and then attempt to encourage such cohesion through rhetoric, selective allocation of rights or obligations, representative bodies, and similar policies or practices. When nationalism coincides with an existing state it provides legitimacy, spreading acceptance and support for the state's claim to a monopoly of coercion. When it does not coincide with a state, it de-legitimates, potentially threatening that state's coercive power. But whether as a sentiment inspiring state-building or justifying existing states, nationalism implies the ideal of a "nation-state" in which mass allegiance and institutional power coincide.

So defining nationalism as a mass sentiment for or against state power specifies our subject. If nationalism is not defined with reference to the state, then it would remain too vague a subject of analysis. As a category it might then refer to any mass political sentiment or solidarity, ranging from ethnicity or class to culture or regionalism. Not only is the definitional tie to states consistent with conventional understandings, but this linkage also contains and makes more explicable the category of nationalism. For instance, this definition generally excludes empires, in which political power is extended beyond state boundaries and often maintained more by force than consent. It also excludes popular mobilization on behalf of a unity or community within state territories, but without engagement with institutional, state-level politics. For instance, popular revolts against taxation that do not go further to uphold or gain state power do not qualify per se as nationalism. Nor do patriotism and mobilization to protect against foreign incursions by themselves qualify, thereby excluding early Greek defense against "barbarians," Chinese defense against the Manchu, or even France's Hundred Years War and the burst of "Frenchness" and resistance against the English led by Joan of Arc. Just as imperial rule can ultimately provoke nationalism, such international conflict and collective defense may also be related to national identity and often has helped to produce it, but such development remains contingent.[5]

So defined, nationalism should also not be confused with the collective action it may or may not inspire. The idea of solidarity which seeks self-determination in a state, or which is built to justify, reinforce, or challenge rule, may or may not produce collective outcomes under particular circumstances. Only when nationalism inspires such action does it become a historical force, but such action remains distinct from the sentiment or perceived imperative for it. To merge the two, as Hechter has recently advocated, limits analysis of the phenomenon of nationalism to the historical period when it becomes active and has been consolidated.[6] And conflating nationalism with collective action confuses definition with explanations of its outcomes. Instead, I define nationalism as the political sentiment of popular solidarity intended to coincide with states, distinct from analysis of its emergent causes and effects.

I am cognizant of the empirical difficulties posed by this definition of nationalism. "Collective sentiments" or claims of identity of any kind are notoriously difficult to document, and all the more so if we specify the requirement that such sentiments be held by an agent pursuing a particular objective. That is why so many analysts have instead defined nationalism as a set of explicit efforts to forge formal cohesion, evident in collective action. According to Hobsbawm, given the enormous difficulty of "discovering the sentiments of the illiterate" majority, we should not attempt to project nationalism onto their beliefs or define nationalism on that basis.[7] On the one hand, I resist this definitional move as overly top-down, with its focus on elite claimants, and insufficiently focused on popular beliefs, no matter how difficult to prove. On the other hand, I acknowledge that such beliefs may only become evident and subject to analysis once they are enunciated or acted upon.

While my definition of nationalism is then limiting in its connection to aspirations for or loyalty to states, it is also expansive in its inclusion of formative state-focused beliefs, claims, and actions all as evidence of nationalism. I agree with Gorski that "instead of drawing sharp distinctions between (formative) protonationalism and full developed nationalism . . . we (should) focus on variations in the intensity and scope of nationalist mobilization." These may begin with the spread of elite discourse and for an extended period produce what Mann describes as "only rudimentary protonations."[8] No doubt, this makes it harder to tell when nationalism emerges, before it inspires action. Nonetheless, even before full-blown nationalism is evident, we should and can look for evidence of mass sentiments and engagement with state-level authority as indications of emerging nationalism. Such evidence would range from popular rhetoric about state authority to mass participation in protests, riots, or wars that defend or challenge that authority but are not a result only of coercion or mercenary payments.

Nationalism so defined does not require fully developed homogenization or popular rule and democratic self-determination, which may and did develop later with the advent of more formal citizenship. The nation as a unit of emerging collective sentiment does not have to be so firmly or legally established nor egalitarian for nationalism to be evident. Nationalism can be expressed without an established nation, though such a unit is then envisioned or implied even in the rudimentary idea or loyalty to or against a state.[9]

These expansive definitional moves draw our attention to moments when the idea or imperative for nationalism began to emerge but was not yet consolidated. And western Europeans at midmillennium were confronted by precisely such a moment, with monarchs seeking to hold and build state power before their subjects had vested that power with popular loyalty and obedience. Instead, local differences and allegiances inherited from feudal land tenure and knightly service remained largely intact. Central state power just then being consolidated, albeit within still diverse "multiple kingdoms," could not and had not yet earned or built correspondingly centralized popular loyalty.[10] Institutional consolidation outpaced social cohesion. Smaller units, such as the kingdoms of Spain, were brought together, requiring resources drawn through taxation, needing to recruit armies and to impose order through law. But to be effective without constant resort to force, these processes required some degree of consent. The imperial strategy of "divide and rule" would not ensure such consent; unitary state-building required more cohesion or that mass sentiment that would become nationalism.

Already well before the late eighteenth century, centralizing rulers were concerned about the lack of popular allegiance and the reality of internal discord, and the populace had become engaged with the issue of state authority. Arguably, as soon as direct rule was being consolidated, with central authority eclipsing local lords' control over the masses, establishing loyalty of those masses to the center became a major political imperative.[11] Elites eager to consolidate their control of states, and to use that control to maintain social hierarchy, were forced into a give-and-take with the masses whose support and unity they needed. For all their differences, early modern monarchs faced a common challenge: their rule could not be protected or further consolidated without a corresponding popular allegiance that did not then exist. All were, more or less, state builders without nationalism in an era in which the very term "nation" had not yet achieved the salience it would later with the French Revolution. That the nation was not yet so salient was precisely their problem, to which they (and their opponents) directed much of their energies, sometimes consciously and sometimes not. To deny that there was such a thing as a nation in this early modern period misses the point. It did not exist and so had to be made, even if it was then turned against state elites.

Efforts to address the lack of popular cohesion would often only exacerbate it, with increasing efforts to consolidate centralized rule re-sisted as such. That resistance and resulting conflict often coincided with emerging religious tensions, reflecting differences of faith amid refor-mation. And such religious tensions were also manipulated or aggravated by elites eager to use emerging passions of faith as a basis for building their authority or challenging that of others. Economic disparities and interests, including the incentive to plunder the wealth of opposing fac-tions, further exacerbated conflict. In other words, the lack of popular cohesion evident in conflict constrained central authority, and any efforts to address this constraint—and to achieve greater popular cohesion—would take shape and be shaped by the reality of this conflict. Thus, focusing on early attempts to cohere elite and mass allegiances, before that cohesion was consolidated as nations, confronts us with the reality of a disconnect experienced and addressed by the early moderns.

This would suggest an explosion of concern with what would become nationalism began with the greater consolidation of central authority as absolutism, roughly two centuries before the French Revolution. That revolution and the Enlightenment that helped inspire it, do suggest an important historical break. But I am arguing here that the processes of political modernism so demarcated had their roots in the early modern period, diminishing the analytic divide between these ages. Just because the terms and form of mass engagement with state authority changed does not mean that we should discard all evidence of earlier engagement as irrelevant relics. Arguably, "premodern national consciousness was more like modern nationalism than the modernists have allowed."[12] Or at the least, the early modern set the stage for attempts at greater nation and state congruence in the modern era.

On the one hand, this is not to deny that there were even earlier roots of nationalism, for instance, as reflected in distinct cultures, lan-guage groups, stereotypes, or cohesion forged by international conflict or animosity, already emerging in the middle ages, as Adrian Hastings demonstrates. Nor does it suggest that national unity was completed in the early modern period, as Eugen Weber reminds us.[13] But it does suggest that the consolidation of state power in the early modern era did bring the issue of nationalism to the fore, justifying my focus here on this particular era.

This reasoning challenges the consensus as to the timing of the initial emergence of nationalism in the late eighteenth century, or it at least argues for greater attention to the earlier foundations of this process.

Hobsbawm argues against any such earlier nationalism either existing or (at least) being evident. Anderson similarly dates "the dawn of the age of nationalism" in the eighteenth century, arguing that it is distinct from and replaced earlier "religious modes of thought" and absolutism. Both share with Haas the assumption that the modernizing influences of literacy, urbanization, and economic development are necessary for producing or making evident the diffusion of nationalism beyond a narrow elite.[14] But just because it may be difficult to see or produce does not mean that earlier nationalism did not exist and should not preclude our search for evidence thereof. This search is made all the more difficult in that what was then most evident was the lack of any such binding sentiment amid ongoing local resistance and internal conflict. Both state authorities and the populace were painfully aware of this lack, suffering from the absence of mass solidarity that would diminish conflict and allow for further state-building and prosperity. Any explanation of the rise of what would become nationalism has to account for how this lack of uniformity amid conflicting loyalties was turned into a basis for cohesion.

So defining nationalism and specifying when it began also suggests those cases in which nation-building in the West first emerged as a political project and which should then be the most relevant subject of analysis designed to explain this early political development. Building effective state consolidation required not only centralized control over territory and resources but also capacity to mobilize and regulate the populace. This combined imperative was less evident in city-states (mobilizing and regulating but with little territory or resources) or empires (controlling territory and resources without mass mobilization).[15] Imperial rulers to the east and European colonizers would later find coercion insufficient and then also use combinations of persuasion and bargaining to bolster loyalty to their direct (or even indirect) rule.[16] But these instances of imperial consolidation fall outside the focus here on initial nation-building within unitary states. The relatively late emergence of centralized states, and of popular engagement therewith, in Italy, Germany, or elsewhere on the continent also place these cases more outside the category of initial experiences with nation-building.[17] Nor were the same dynamics at work in Ireland, the Low Countries, or Scandinavia, where politics was more shaped and identities imposed by external forces. Of course, analysis of these or other cases would also be relevant and useful, though for reasons above they are not the focus of my more limited efforts. Instead, I focus on early and autonomous imperatives for combining institutional power and mass support, here restricted as such to the Great Powers of the Atlantic seaboard: Spain, France, and England.[18]

These core cases have informed the convention of a "civic" founding of Western nationalism, and so any challenge to that convention must confront these cases. But within these cases, outcomes would also vary as much as attempted solutions and techniques to build and direct popular loyalty, with such variation itself requiring and refining explanation. Some monarchs would succeed greatly, in particular Elizabeth of England and Henri IV of France. Others would face rising counter-loyalties, fail, and fall, such as Charles I and James II of England. Most would do the best they could, often resorting to ignoble means, such as those employed to some degree by James I or more so by William and Mary of England and Catherine de' Medici and her sons in France. But all were confronted by the difficult challenge to forge popular loyalty and to diminish local resistance or conflict. This imperative would eventually become pervasive as the system of nation-states spread, though my focus here remains on initial attempts at resolution.

▨ Assessing Explanations

Definitions of nationalism must be distinguished from arguments about how it is built; explication should not be confused with explanation.[19] But definitions also set the terms for explanation, in specifying what is to be explained. By defining nationalism as a collective identity or sentiment of support for or against the state, potentially evident before its more consolidated form, I am similarly expanding what is to be explained. Any account for the rise of such nationalism must elucidate the early indications and causes of such sentiment. The context of this development must then be consistent with and incorporated into the explanation. And that context in early modern Europe included a lack of prior popular cohesion and significant conflict over whether the institutionalized state would be centralized and by whom it would be controlled. That the forging of such nationalism was a dilemma—at least in early modern western European great powers—runs counter to any explanation assuming that such solidarity preexists, in which case states would not have faced the challenge of countering diversity and internal conflict.

But states have seemingly been built as institutional expressions of prior homogeneity or allegiance. The traditional idea of such an established civil solidarity giving rise to states goes back at least to Rousseau, who described a nationalist "act of association [that] creates an artificial and collective body" or polity.[20] Various recent analysts have agreed that such a prior sentiment gives rise to forms of state rule.[21] And that collective sentiment has often been assumed as having been based on a particular preexisting group solidarity of ethnicity, seen as a supposedly ascriptive category of shared ancestry and culture.[22] In other words, nationalism was equated with "descent-based" ethnicity and with political units built accordingly as homogenous.[23] As described by John Stuart Mill, even nonethnic "fellow feelings" should and did then demarcate "the boundaries of government."[24]

The fundamental problem with this orthodoxy is that it assumes the prior existence of self-conscious, homogenous units of allegiance. But even when there is some such common cultural sentiment within a populace, this does not necessarily bring political cohesion. And amid diversity such unifying group consciousness is instead often absent and then constructed by elites or commoners, using selective evocations of history to project or impose an image of prior legitimacy, and purposefully forgetting inconvenient images or experiences of past or present internal division.[25] The images of a common identity and unifying "ethnicity" were instead only gradually invented, constructed, and reinforced, often purposefully to bolster social cohesion precisely because it was lacking.[26] Ethnicity or other forms of unity were not so fixed nor so firmly established as to be the necessary or only basis of state-building.[27] Instead, diversity remained or grew within large-scale polities, with the political incorporation of new territory, peoples, immigrants, or factions into states, threatening political unity.[28]

The recent work of Liah Greenfeld demonstrates both that the explanation of nationalism based on prior cohesion continues to be advocated and that even in a less ascriptive version it still faulters. She argues that the "collective solidarity" of nationalism emerges when a population "is perceived as essentially homogenous," with any "crisis of identity" thereby resolved.[29] Accordingly, nationalism first emerged in England, where it was ushered in by Protestantism but was then quickly replaced by "the consciousness of one's dignity as an individual." Greenfeld thus suggests that the emergence of nationalism rested upon prior unity, and as such it cannot account for or incorporate the ongoing conflict between Protestantism and Catholicism or within Protestantism, challenging unity. Similarly, her account of French nationalism suggests that bloody religious conflicts there did not represent any lack of united support for the crown, and again that such conflict was increasingly irrelevant to nationalism.[30] Greenfeld does then move beyond a strictly ascriptive explanation of nationalism, but her argument that it emerged united on the basis of elite ideas and aggregated individual support thereof is both idealistic and inaccurate in its denial of ongoing internal group conflict to be resolved.

If prior social cohesion is rarely so fixed or apparent as to form the prior basis for a nation seeking a state, then theories based on this assumption are so challenged or incomplete. The "problem" of building national cohesion cannot then be assumed away, at least for western Europe torn by internal conflicts.

Consolidating institutional state power is always contingent upon also building popular cohesion and loyalty, but in western Europe the former proved easier or more straightforward than the latter. Popular allegiance to centralized authority could not be taken for granted. Amid ongoing diversity and conflict within states, such cohesion did not pre-exist as cultural homogeneity or as ethnic cohesion based on supposed blood ties. In the absence of more cohering objective factors, "a living and active corporate will" had to be constructed.[31] And it was the emergent state authorities that had a leading interest in this project, even if they did not yet have the capacity for its achievement. Most notably, France and Britain, "often considered models of effective state formation ... bargained directly with their subject populations for massive taxes, military service and cooperation ... [promoting] popular identification with state ends." To build this identification in the absence of more objective homogeneity, "a community's sense of uniqueness" and sameness had to be projected from or onto the center.[32] Spain's relative failure to build such coherence after the burst of state activism in 1492, or the conflicts that tore England and France, reaffirm the import and uncertainty of this project.

Ongoing conflicts refute the argument that nationalism preexisted in early modern western Europe, but we should not be too quick to conclude that there was no early modern impetus for such nationalism or that it began to emerge only much later. That nationalism was not primordial or evident before state centralization does not mean that it could or did only begin to emerge after that centralization was completed. If we take seriously that early modern rulers (or their challengers) had an interest in beginning to reinforce, harness, or even create national cohesion from below to bolster their power, then we are still left to explain how such solidarity began to emerge or was built. And various explanations for this process have been developed to fill the void left by rejecting the prior orthodoxy of nationalism as preexisting or primordial. According to those explanations, nationalism was instead the result of social processes that forged solidarity on the basis of networks of shared communication or interests. But the timing and conflictual context of early emergent interest in nationalism has troubling implications for these society-based explanations for how this was attempted or achieved.

One important possibility is that the nation emerged as a sort of literary trope, out of the spontaneous sense of simultaneous existence and cohesion engendered by shared language and texts. This process would have begun with the spread of capitalism, with trading requiring a shared language, and with the spread of a printed vernacular diminishing linguistic diversity while encouraging a sense of shared experience and commonality, with the masses thereby brought into political history. The result has been described by Benedict Anderson as an "imagined community," by Homi Bhabha as a common "narration," by Deutsch as "communication," and by Habermas as solidarity and legitimation based on a consensus made possible by common language.[33] These arguments share with the liberal tradition the assumption that early social/national cohesion requires no institutional action; there is no state action necessary to encourage the process of community cohesion or loyalty. But at the same time, these arguments move beyond the earlier tendency to fall back on ethnicity as the purportedly fixed basis of such prior cohesion. For instance, according to Benedict Anderson, "from the start the nation was conceived in language, not in blood."[34]

Thinking about the early modern context in which the imperative for nationalism first emerged helps to assess such arguments about the role of language and communication. Certainly any collective sentiment or sense of large-scale solidarity such as nationalism does rest upon the possibility of interaction and communication among those who share or develop that sentiment. And nationalism was often spread by shared language and then printed mass communication, beyond face-to-face interaction, though as Weber notes this did not always "suffice" to build solidarity. Even more problematic, the limits and content of such communication also cut against or constrained such solidarity. Not only was the spread of common language, literacy, newspapers, and books incomplete when early modern European states and societies began to build toward nationalism, but it remained incomplete even later.[35] The diversity of language within those emergent states meant that spreading verbal communication or literacy could have had the opposite effect, reinforcing local or ethnic differences. We cannot then simply assume that nationalism was a direct outcome of communication and literacy, for the transmission of ideas was not so pervasive nor as unifying as its form would imply or become.

There is an even more profound problem with the "imagined communities" approach to explaining nationalism, made evident by the timing and context of early efforts at gaining mass political cohesion. Anderson and others assume that spreading communication brings inclusive solidarity, but amid religious, elite, and economic conflicts this was not possible and did not emerge in early modern Europe. Indeed, the content or messages so spread were often divisive rather than necessarily unifying.[36] It was precisely this problem that impelled efforts to spread some greater mass cohesion. But the "imagined communities" approach is silent on the crucial issue of resolving conflict exacerbated by spreading communication, and it suggests no agency or institution interested in or capable of resolving such conflict. If the resolution to internal conflict came with choices for selective inclusion in what would become the nation, this approach cannot explain how such exclusions were decided upon or who enforced them. Anderson does acknowledge that exclusions were relevant, as exclusion from the center inspired Creole nationalism, but such "hatred of the Other" for Anderson refers only to external antagonisms. On the subject of resolving internal conflicts he remains silent.[37] Put differently, if nationalism is defined as mass sentiment engaged with state power, and not all of the masses can be or want to be included, then any explanation of nationalism must allow and account for how such choices about membership in the nation are made amid conflict.

On a more general level, Anderson's "imagined community" ignores the central role of states in demarcating which particular community emerged and coincided with political institutions. As such, his approach does not fully distinguish nationalism from any other large-scale sentiment of cohesion. Anderson does note that the particular community of the nation is distinguished by being "both inherently limited and sovereign," but he does not explain how language and literacy produced this distinction.[38] As such, "the imagined community" may be generally relevant for explaining cohesion but is not adequate for explaining the more particular form of cohesion as a nation. That nationalism would become the primary form of such an imagined community should not be read backward to explain this outcome.

Another society-based explanation for the rise of nationalism places greater emphasis on the latter component of the emergence of "print capitalism." Accordingly, nationalism was the result of growing market relations forging networks of trade and resulting solidarity. According to Gellner, capitalism requires unity and cultural homogeneity—for instance, to ensure an available labor force able to read and follow instructions in a common language—suggesting economic imperatives as explanation for national solidarity.[39] And certainly such structural explanations are reinforced by comparative history, for instance with early development of a market economy in England helping to forge solidarity there, contrasted with the economic backwardness and lack of solidarity in Spain.[40] There can be no doubt then that economic development did contribute to the consolidation of nationalism.

But again we are faced with difficulties in applying such a society-based explanation to the emergence of nationalism in early modern Europe. Arguing that capitalism produced nationalism cannot account for any early forms of nationalism that emerged before capitalism was consolidated, and instead must deny the possibility of any such preindustrial nationalism. Nor can such a functionalist explanation of nationalism account for "its binding or passionate attraction."[41] Such passions, initial interests, and efforts to spread political cohesion significantly predated such economic development. Indeed, capitalism did often develop in the absence of cultural homogeneity, and it also forged networks across culture and as such cannot alone account for the emergence of national units. And even the early spread of capitalism and trade, which would later produce larger scale, incorporating markets, initially also generated early forms of class struggles that had to be resolved politically, at least as much as it spread domestic cohesion.[42] Later industrializing states had the capacity to head off such conflict and to encourage cohesion through schooling (and other means), but earlier on they did not, and yet mass engagement with states was evident.

Pushing back in time our focus on the emergence of nationalism thus raises challenges to the causal role of modernizing social developments such as spreading language, literacy, and industrialization. Yes, these developments did contribute to the rise of nationalism and were essential components of its later consolidation. It would go too far to advocate "expunging the hidden remnants of modernization theory from the theory of nationalism."[43] But that critical instinct is on the mark if we are to take seriously and seek to explain the early emergence of nationalism before such modernization took hold. Too narrow a focus on a particular historical period, a bias in favor of modernity, or the difficulties of analyzing the premodern should not blind us to the foundational processes occurring before literacy, efforts to legitimize capitalism, or industrialization. Nationalism that began to take shape before the Enlightenment, the spread of secularizing consciousness or related social processes, cannot be explained by those factors.

Not only were modernizing social forces too weak to produce national cohesion in early modern states but also initially these forces may have the opposite effect of reinforcing differences. Popular cohesion matching the large scale of states often rests upon an image of shared, unique culture.[44] But the same economic and literary developments that empowered and potentially allowed for the solidarity of the masses in early modern Europe were also seen as fostering subnational or cultural differences.[45] The early imperative to build national cohesion came not only from power above needing to reach down but also encountered assertions from below, fed by linguistic and economic developments having initially centrifugal effects. Even militarism could have been and was turned against the central authorities that sought to harness the same manpower into national armies.[46]

Thus, the social processes of rising cultural and economic activity, vernacular language, printing, and armed force, which could bring the populace into larger scale political cohesion, could and did also present the opposing possibility of dissolution. Cultural or economic identities often did not coincide with or bolster nationalism within political boundaries. Those so long illiterate, isolated, and disengaged were becoming less so, just as growing centralized authority began to recognize the need for their involvement and cooperation. But the masses' engagement was often divisive and as uncertain as was the consolidation of centralized rule. The retrospective assumption that modernization brought cohesion within a national will and established polity remained contingent. What Renan described as "the daily plebiscite" of nationalism, with individuals deciding about where their loyalties lay on an ongoing basis, remained unresolved.[47] Local differences long remained salient. Suspicions and superstitions fed by plague and poverty exploded into recidivist fears. Europe was not yet free of its Dark Age.

Searching for the roots of nationalism before the processes of spreading vernacular, literacy, or industrialization had spread cohesion refocuses our attention onto less spontaneous social forces. Instead of being the basis for state-seeking, collective sentiments of loyalty were often encouraged by states, elites, and others. Indeed, "nationalizing states" are more common than preexisting nations forming states, and this was

FAITH IN NATION

the case in early modern western Europe. Political units formed out of warfare and with an interest in raising revenues then faced the imperative of containing discord, encouraging or channeling allegiance with images of nationalism, thereby integrating the masses into the polity. Analysts focusing on later, modern nationalism, such as Hobsbawm, Tilly, and Mann, have argued that the state did play this essential role.[48] But as central state power was being consolidated in early modern Europe, that emergent authority already had a growing interest in building such loyalty and obedience, in turn provoking resistance. These processes toward nationalism are increasingly evident two centuries before their full blossoming with the French Revolution.

One way to think about early modern popular allegiances is that the masses then perceived themselves to be members of varying "imagined communities," but these did not neatly overlap with political boundaries. These divergent communities reflected culture, language, and then most prominently faith, as well as class interests and estates. But amid conflict within and between such communities, imagination by itself did not effectively bind the masses, and it certainly did not bound them within units coinciding with state boundaries. Such coincidence would only emerge through explicitly political processes, drawing borders of community through efforts from above and below Only then would international and domestic solidarities, linkages, and conflicts be partially resolved, with faith and secular identities reinforcing each other within particularist communities of nationalism.

Early central state authority had to and did so act for itself to try to bound and forge the beginnings of nationalism, with nation and state being consolidated contemporaneously. The debate about whether states came before nation or nation before states is arguably resolved with the alternative that the two processes were linked and emerged together, at least in the core of western Europe. State and nation were made together, or institutions and corresponding sentiments of allegiance were built together, fitfully combined. With increasing but still incomplete consciousness, state actors sought to channel rising popular political engagement, itself the result of social developments. On occasion such engagement was turned against the state. But with some degree of state authority evident before nationhood, states often took the lead in making nations, or at least attempted to do so.

Even linguistic or economic explanations of the consolidation of nationalism have had to incorporate the role of the state in shaping these processes. State authorities helped to spread literacy but also constrained its spread, limited or sought to control the content of messages. Anderson himself adds in revision to his earlier analysis that how the "imagined community" was so imagined was largely determined by official histories and mappings.[49] Nor did capitalism, even in its later development, by itself spread nationalism, depending instead on state-run schools to spread cohesion and language, making the expansion of market relations possible. And a central mechanism for encouraging such solidarity was the institution of early forms of citizenship, with emergent states granting membership and rights in order to encourage internal cohesion and allegiance. These processes were necessarily bounded or exclusionary, with states playing a leading role in demarcating who was included.

An irony emerges here. Our search for the roots of nationalism directs our attention to the role of state authority, which later built solidarity before social processes could have or did have this result by themselves. But in the earlier period when this process arguably began, such state authority was weaker, not yet reinforced by modernization processes. States may have sought to use the spread of language or literacy to also spread loyalty, controlling the messages spread accordingly, but literacy itself was limited and the state's power to spread or control it were also limited. States had an interest in encouraging the spread of the market in order to provide revenues, but again capacity in this regard was slow to develop. Schooling would later help spread vernacular, literacy, employability, and cohesion, but early modern states were not yet able to mount or control pervasive formal education, even with an increasing number of schools founded.[50] And the very notion of citizenship had yet to be refined, with state authorities unsure of its meaning, even as they became aware of its centrality. Some analysts have instead suggested that popular cohesion was spread before the eighteenth century by the imposition of elite ideology, military service, or legal courts.[51] But states and elites were not then capable of so effectively imposing nationalism top-down on their own, nor can any such explanation account for the vehemence and divisiveness of that popular solidarity that did emerge.

It is precisely this conundrum that drove the early process of a combined effort at state- and nation-building. When both state and nation were weak, state authorities had evident political and economic interests in building or demarcating both together, in a combined effort. That they were unsure and ill equipped to do so only heightened the imperative to build both state capacity and national cohesion. And again, those who instead sought to challenge and gain state power found that they also could not assume popular support. Neither ideas nor rules of solidarity could be dictated or imposed, nor did cohesion emerge then out of literacy or economic development. To meet the imperative of bounded mass cohesion, early state rulers or their opponents would have to find other means that could be turned to this end, in effect forced to meet their increasingly engaged and discordant populace halfway. They would discover such possibilities only through varying choices, attempts, and unforeseen consequences that would reveal what might be binding. But before we turn to the historical process of this discovery, we can lay out the logic of how conflict could be turned to cohesion.

Schematics of Exclusion as the Basis of Unity

Given the failings of past attempts, what is needed is an explanation of emergent nationalism that takes seriously the role of dominant structures, popular belief, ongoing conflict, and exclusion, without falling into an essentialist assumption of fixed ethnic cohesion. Currently popular theories of nationalism and related allocations of citizenship rights have largely ignored early developments in this direction and fail to fully account for them. Those theories have tended to assume universal inclusion, at least eventually, with exclusions often described as mere lags in the provision of rights. But such omissions and exclusions may not be mere lags but instead purposeful, with exclusion of some "other" not as accidents but instead crucially employed in an attempt to solder core coalitions among those included. Nationalism may not then emerge as an imagined community of inclusion, a sort of literary trope, or an institutionalized process toward inclusion propelled by economic development and modernization. Instead, nationalism is often exclusive, with such exclusion emerging in fits and starts but encouraged or enforced to serve the explicit requirements for solidifying core loyalty to the nation.

Before fleshing out the processes and implications of forging nationalism on the basis of conflicts and exclusions, we need a brief description of the schematics of this process, for which I draw upon recent theoretical advances to explicate how unity can be based on exclusion of a particular "other" group so demarcated. As in all such schematics, not all the fine points of the analysis are included here, and a somewhat exaggerated sense of purposefulness is employed to make the argument clear. And contrary to the current tendency to construct or use theories narrowly within only one methodological approach, I am instead erring on the side of theoretical inclusiveness in the hope of drawing together varying approaches to show how these contribute to a more complete explanation.

The key to my argument is that in instances of internal discord, selective domestic exclusion often was encouraged or encoded to heal past or threatened disunity. State elites (or their opponents) might then attempt solutions or make deals en route to nation-building, selecting whom to include, reward, and encourage loyalty from. They could thereby identify and bind the core constituency of and as the nation, selecting, aggravating, and playing off established antagonisms against some other group thereby excluded. That core constituency so demarcated and reinforced might itself change over time, according to shifting challenges and alliances. Put more generally, state-building laid the groundwork for varying identifications and strategic exclusions, which then bolstered early national solidarity, thereby resolving conflict and either unexpectedly or purposefully allowing for preservation and further centralization of states.

This argument can be presented in its more formal elements, even though these tend toward a simplifying functionalist logic. States are institutions claiming a legitimate monopoly of coercion and rule. To achieve that monopoly, states are often not faced with a dyadic issue of imposing their rule over an already unified society but instead face more complex challenges, with "the sovereign" facing competing or antagonistic groups. To avoid being disempowered or defeated by those competing groups aligning, the state may forge an alliance with one group, which is solidified by the exclusion of a different group from specified rights and reinforced prejudice of that other. A more manageable form of rule is enforced by such state action. Or, as recently described, states needing a minimum of support but reluctant to meet the needs of competing groups unable to coordinate their demands can solidify their support by transgressing the rights of one group to the advantage of the other group.[52] To achieve a modicum of required homogeneity, "relational" identities are replaced by exclusionary "categorical" ones.[53] Opponents seeking to gain popular support and state power may follow a similar logic. The result is a form of nationalism akin to the economic theory of the club, in which public goods are selectively allocated and protected from outsiders.[54]

Simplifying schematic arguments can be as misleading as they are useful, so it should help to rephrase the above argument in different terms. Once we reject the assumption of preexisting cohesion, nationalism of all may not be possible amid long-standing or emergent internal antagonisms. In such instances, state elites or other political actors may learn to encourage the support of a key constituency by acceding to its prejudices, often using that particular prejudice that can unify the key constituency itself otherwise divided by other antagonisms. By maintaining legal boundaries and excluding an internal "other" as a common enemy, state and other leaders encourage the cohesion and support of those included, focusing tangible benefits and reinforced by symbolic manipulations. This allocation process is at the heart of politics.

Demarcating, demonizing, and depriving "outsiders" found within provides a referent that can further unify and solidify the support of the "in-group."[55] Selective exclusion may thus serve the interests of avoiding or containing internal conflicts, where social cleavages make more inclusive unity of all impossible or difficult to achieve. It is not surprising then that nationalism "is not a shapeless free-floating unspecific unfocused feeling ... Its object is normally only too sharply defined, as the love of certain categories of people, and the detestation of others," with that love and detestation working together.[56] Or as Stinchcombe concludes, nationalism "is a wish to suppress internal divisions within the nation and to define people outside the group as untrustworthy as allies and implacably evil as enemies ... It is on the one hand a generous spirit of identification ... a love of compatriots ... But it is on the other hand a spirit of distrust of the potential treason of any opposition within the group and a hatred of strangers."[57]

This argument about the exclusionary basis of nationalism is informed by earlier analysis suggesting a similar process. Croser demonstrated that conflict and its resolution through exclusion can forge group cohesion more generally, and Armstrong applied such reasoning to nationalism.[58] Carl Schmitt argued that political competition solidifies friends and enemies, with "every human being symbolically a combatant." To legitimate state rule requires cohesion of those included as a nation, against some other. As Schmitt argued, "as long as the state is a political entity this requirement for internal peace compels it in critical situations to decide also upon its domestic enemy.... The high points of politics are simultaneously the moments in which the enemy is, in concrete reality, recognized as the enemy."[59]

Such macro theorizing about how nationalism can be encouraged through exclusion may also be reinforced by reference to analysis on the micro level, about how individuals think about their collective loyalties. Indeed, there may be innate predispositions toward such selective inclusion and exclusion. A rich tradition of psychological theories and experimentation has demonstrated that individual loyalty to any in-group is solidified by discrimination against an out-group, with the demarcation of an "other" giving a sense of common characteristics or fate to the core.[60] The actual basis of the category of those excluded may reflect what Freud too dismissively called "the narcissism of minor differences."[61] To augment core cohesion, often a scapegoat is selected precisely because it is present, visible, and powerless to resist and therefore useful for displacing aggression from some faction of the in-group too powerful to exclude. Purportedly minor differences are often thus magnified by elites and/or commoners eager to build cohesion. Such psychological tendencies suggest that humans may be naturally inclined to discriminate and to join together against a scapegoat, adding a powerful individual impetus to collective or strategic efforts to exclude.

Resulting organized exclusion is then often (though not always) designed or has the effect of encouraging the unity and allegiance of those included. Such exclusion is evident in informal discrimination, state policies of citizenship, forced assimilation, expulsion, or eradication. This process certainly builds upon the "habitus" of psychological and historical social dispositions constraining the state, most notably "the primordial tacit contract whereby they define 'us' as opposed to 'them.' "[62] The result combines Marxism's traditional focus on self-interest and strategic calculations with the symbolic power of historically determined but seemingly natural "habitus."[63] And as Bourdieu notes, precisely when antagonisms threaten to go out of control, to threaten the state itself, more rigid or legal codification is more likely. Such codifications then "minimize ambiguity . . . making clear cuts" upon which sufficient state support can be built. Moments of such boundary codification are then the moments in which nationalism is crystallized.[64]

To reiterate, the emergence of nationalism can be explained according to the logic of exclusionary cohesion. And this logic has apparently often been put into practice. Distinctive groups, so perceived, were often unwilling to be joined. And elites did not then consistently incorporate all potential internal constituents but instead often excluded some, contrary to the presumed imperative for pervasive unity or ethnic homogeneity. Ethnic subgroups have been retained as victims or expelled. Citizenship rights have often been allocated selectively, not universally. The franchise has been limited. The imagined community has been so constrained; fellow feelings and loyalty have been contained. Nationalism has been internally exclusive—for instance, according to cleavages of ethnicity, race, gender, class, or religion. Such difference has been institutionalized and reified within and by states, contrary to the assumption that states sought to unify all within. As Brubaker suggests, nationalism has been institutionalized in particular forms, as "a practical and bounded category or contingent event."[65]

Turning Religious Passions to Nationalism

Thus far we have discussed in general terms what nationalism is—when, where, and how the imperative for building such cohesion may have emerged. But contrary to functionalist logic, the "need" for such collective sentiment or the possible paths by which it was forged do not alone explain whether and how it actually did emerge. To this we now turn, and to make this move we need to first specify the particular form of social closure and target of exclusion that could be employed as a basis of selective cohesion.

In the emerging great powers of early modern Europe, religion involved symbols, stories, theologies, and even cosmologies, but it was also the primary basis of mass belief and solidarity. Faith provided both a template for popular engagement, which state rulers or their opponents sought to emulate in the secular realm, and the only existing basis for such actual engagement. According to Lewis Namier, "religion is a sixteenth century word for nationalism," or it at least served as the potential cement for what would become nationalism.[66] That the social bonds of religion could or would be used as the basis of national cohesion is not surprising, for faith was then the most pervasive form of identity among the populace whose loyalty was sought by state rulers or their opponents. Before the enervating effects disparaged by Karl Marx, "religion as the opiate of the masses" could and did bond. Its salience before state consolidation only added to its perceived power as a form of cohesion that states or opponents could attempt to mimic, deploy, or harness.

But religion should not and could not be conflated with early modern nationalism, not least because identities of faith did not coincide with secular boundaries of state. Before Reformation, Catholicism was relatively universal, drawing allegiances across boundaries and away from state rulers toward Rome. And within states, there remained groups of different religions, further complicating any direct link from faith to nation. Then with Reformation, Catholic unity itself came apart amid violent conflict, within states and between them. Rising Protestantism was tied to increasing print capitalism, as Anderson notes, but the result was to aggravate conflict more than to forge inclusive communities.[67] Rather than religious conflict feeding into unifying political loyalties, instead it cut against them, with competing elites using or aggravating sectarianism to support or challenge central rulers. Differences of faith both coincided with and cut across other distinctions and sources of conflict threatening emerging state authority.

While religion was strongly felt among the masses, as it became more torn by conflict it also served as a potential and then actual basis for political engagement from below within a distinct community, a requirement for nationalism. But not only did faith not neatly coincide with state boundaries within which nationalism would emerge but religious passions were not fixed or primordial, nor were they neatly functional in their political impact. Instead, conflict enraged religious passions and also pulled them in varying directions. In the process, faith became politicized and increasingly relevant to state- and nation-building. As Schmitt suggests in terms of the outcome of this process, "a religious community which wages war against members of other religious communities . . . is already more than a religious community; it is a political community."[68] Though how such a religiously informed and enflamed political cohesion would be turned into the particular community of nationalism remained contingent.

The possibility of faith emerging as a crutch for building or bounding community and national unity emerged most forcefully amid religious and related divisions. Monarchs and other elites then faced a set of choices about how to resolve this problem. As the narratives that follow will demonstrate, no one choice was predetermined, nor were such choices made finally and fixedly at any one moment. Indeed, what appears as choice was often wavering and unintentional, certainly in terms of outcomes. Context, structure, individual preferences, and happenstance led to particular attempts, with results then assessed and adjustments made. The overriding elite imperative for achieving popular loyalty and obedience remained amid varying attempts judged and refined against this purpose and mass actions.

In at least one general sense, Spain differed from France and England. In Spain, the populace remained relatively united within Catholicism, but in the absence of violent religious conflict faith also remained largely that and was not effectively engaged as a basis for secular nationalism. Relative homogeneity did not bring comparable political cohesion. The state did exclude heretics through the Inquisition, but this process was institutionalized, did not fully engage mass passions, was relatively peaceful, and then ended and lost any possibility of further establishing coherence among the populace once the Jews, conversos, and Moors were expelled. These victims had been very much a part of this society, but once they were defined and excluded as foreigners, antagonism against them lost much of its force. There then remained few if any internal heretics against which further popular cohesion might have been built. In contrast, France and England were more similar to each other in the level of mass violent conflict over ongoing internal religious differences, which did engage and cohere the populace. Conflict cohered. Religion was thereby turned into a basis for selective and secular allegiance, though again with important differences as to how this was achieved.

As pursued at the time by England and France, one alternative path to secular cohesion was to attempt to diminish religious conflict with moderation and relative tolerance. Elizabeth I and Charles II of England, and even more so Henri IV of France, stand out for their attempts to pursue this noble path, though even they were constantly on the defensive against religious purists. Their own lapses into sectarianism or the later reversals of enacted civility should not diminish our acknowledging the impressive efforts at coexistence in a period of general intolerance. And that such relative toleration was even attempted and then reversed reinforces the uncertainty and choice as to such policy.

Less inspiring or weaker monarchs and elites attempted a different solution, though also amid some uncertainty, choice, and variation. To channel divisive religious zeal into national unity or more distinctly binding cleavages often meant harnessing that divisiveness. If religious unity was no more established than cultural or other forms of early national cohesion, then perhaps religious factional coherence would do. Indeed, the passion unleashed by doctrinal conflict was precisely the sort of strong identity that states sought to bolster for their own ends. There was a possibility of huge proportions hiding there, for instance as embraced by France's Catholic nobles and then Catherine de' Medici after her own earlier pragmatism had failed to bring unity or peace. Their choice of using and channeling intolerance to bolster secular loyalties not only reflected elites' own sectarianism but was made all the more attractive by the powerful and binding popular salience generated by violent conflict. Volatility and bloodshed cohered loyalties that monarchs and others sought to direct toward their own interests and support. Religious division thus made impossible inclusive unity, but at the same time it provided a powerful alternative of building selective nationalism. Exclusion was most effectively directed against internal heretics, all the more binding than antagonism against international enemies, which sometimes co-incided with internal antagonisms but also shifted with the diplomacy of foreign alliances.

This suggests a somewhat different relation between religion and nationalism in France than has been recently suggested. Analysts agree that popular loyalty to the French crown had earlier been bolstered by Catholicism, as indicated by the faithfulness of Joan of Arc and her followers, and would then serve as a basis for nationalism. But David Bell and others argue that nationalism in France emerged later after the wave of religious conflict had receded into more unity and therefore was not an exclusionary process per se.[69] I will argue that it was that earlier conflict which forged such unity, albeit purposefully cohered by sectarianism. In that sense, I also disagree with Greenfeld that "Frenchness was (then) dissociating itself from Catholicism."[70] The eras of passionate religious conflict and of emergent nationalism were not so distinct.

The use of religious sectarianism to build nationalism was more wavering and is even more hotly contested in the literature on England. Greenfeld acknowledges that "nationalism (was) sanctioned by religion," but then, to justify that "the religious idiom . . . was soon cast away," she largely ignores the religious aspect of ongoing conflicts.[71] Such conflicts are more fully incorporated into the alternative view that "anti-Catholicism, then, was an ideology that promoted national cohesion, countering, though not submerging, the kingdom's political divisions and tensions."[72] Linda Colley is the leading advocate of this latter view, though she focuses on the eighteenth and nineteenth centuries and even then is criticized for implying an overly "uniform" anti-popish feeling and for downplaying sometimes violent divisions among Protestants.[73] Her critics conclude that antipopery remained a "frequently contested terrain . . . an anxious aspiration, rather than as a triumphal description."[74] But even as a wavering aspiration, unity on the basis of anti-Catholicism would prove powerful.

In part, such uncertainties about embracing sectarianism reflected fears among rulers and elites that impassioned mass anger threatened the anarchy of internal antagonisms exploding beyond control. Yet the general trend to embrace sectarianism suggests that in such conflict leading political actors also saw the glimmer of a powerful tool for its resolution, worth the risks—or saw no alternative at the time. Choosing to encourage and channel internal discord as a basis of selective cohesion often proved too tempting to pass up, even as it unleashed passions that would not then be easily controlled or contained. Elites, fearing that domestic conflict would threaten their power, sought a basis for building popular cohesion, and they understood, as Yeats reminds us, "there is more substance in our enmities than in our love."[75]

The monarchs and elites of early modern Europe foresaw and recurrently embraced the awful insight of the later poet. Reflecting their own sectarian passions, they often sided with one domestic religious faction against another as the basis for building and channeling loyalty based on confessional passions. When successful, they would then seek to solidify and enforce a religious sect as unitary, excluding others, as a basis for increasing cohesion. Resulting cultural identifications were then turned to secular obedience, albeit indirectly. But as much as this process served secular aims, its basis and its power remained religion itself, for nothing matched the salience of faith. And that salience was forged and reinforced by the confluence of religious discord and contests for political power, with authority ultimately bolstered by exclusionary forms of faith, reinforced by enmity and encoded in nation.

⫸ Excavating History and Revising Memory

If this argument is right and can be sustained, how is it that the basis of early nationalism has been forgotten, with the curtain of historical consensus drawn to hide the embarrassment of an ignoble, exclusionary past as if irrelevant? In part, "familiarity has bred a forgetfulness of origins," though this argument is not sufficient.[76] Nationalism is all about more purposeful manipulation of memory. According to Kedourie, "nationalists make use of the past in order to subvert the present," but they may even more profoundly subvert the past in order to create the present.[77] Or as Renan more directly reminds us, "forgetting, I would even go so far as to say historical error, is a crucial factor in the creation of a nation . . . Indeed, historical inquiry brings to light deeds of violence which took place at the origin of all political formations . . . Unity is always effected by means of brutality . . . Yet the essence of a nation is that all individuals have many things in common, and also that they have forgotten many things . . . [E]very French citizen has to have forgotten the massacre of Saint Bartholomew."[78] Indeed, earlier conflicts or exclusions would eventually lead to victim groups' efforts to resemble insiders and to become part of the nation, thereby contributing to both the image of inclusion and to historical forgetfulness.

Nations drink at the fountain of Lethe, clearing their memories, be-

fore their rebirth in the Hades of modernity. To forge "large-scale solidarity" requires "the social capital" of "a heroic past," codifying a "family memory" of unity that rests upon purposeful amnesia of those deadly
quarrels that tore apart the unit at its formation.[79] Nationalism does rest
on common memory, but that memory is selective, with projections of
unity often dependent on mutual forgetting. On its face, such forgetting
would appear to contradict the imperative to encourage and use conflictual exclusions to forge national unity. But what appears contradictory
is not. Instead, unity has been forged amid conflict by exclusion, and
then once forged, the exclusions used to that end have been forgotten
to reinforce unity thereafter.

Elites have purposefully encoded or advocated such selective amnesia. In the aftermath of religious wars in France, in 1570 the King's
Edict of Saint-Germain declares: "First, that the remembrance of all things
past on both parts, for and since the beginnings of the troubles . . . shall
remain as wholly quenched and appeased, as things that never happened." And even after the massacre of St. Bartholomew, the Royal Edict
of Union, from Rouen in July 1588, proclaims that "to render the present
union permanent and lasting . . . we intend for ever to bury the memory
of past troubles and divisions."[80] In 1660, Charles II paved the way for
his return to the throne of England lost by his executed father with the
Declaration of Breda, seeking to "awaken all men to a desire and longing
that those wounds which have so many years together been kept bleeding
may be bound up . . . we desiring and ordaining that henceforward all
notes of discord, separation and difference of parties be utterly abolished
among all our subjects, whom we invite to and conjure to a perfect union
among themselves." And again, in the Act of Indemnity and Oblivion
of that year, the populace was commanded "to bury all seeds of future
discords and remembrance."[81]

Later analysts have also seemingly conspired in this amnesia, either
to accord with their own nationalism or as reflecting undue adherence
to accepted periods of study. The historians' consensus of nationalism
starting not with those earlier violent religious conflicts but instead with
later liberal inclusiveness, seemingly abides by royal edicts of purposeful
forgetting. "The religious idiom in which initially the national ideals had
been expressed was soon cast away," by royal edict, popular amnesia
and historical editing.[82] But such casting away of inconvenient memory
must not be allowed to obscure the role of such sectarian conflict in
forging secular solidarity and instead reaffirms the role of both the conflict
and the forgetting.

FAITH IN NATION

Selective amnesia was not just fatuously ordered by rulers or evident in the periodization of historical studies but has also been relevant for and in popular processes. If national cohesion could not be built on common blood and culture given past divisions, then at least it had to eventually forget the blood spilled in those divisions. Myths of common past glory and unifying sacrifice pushed aside the reality of prior internal conflict, forging the image of a coherent unit that history and historians could then take for granted. Not just monarchs but also others seeking to forge national loyalty and to contain internal divisions understood well the need and the power of such selective remembrance. And their success is indicated by later popular narratives describing nationalism as long-standing homogeneity, even primordial unity. Inconvenient facts, of Englishmen or Frenchmen having killed each other in violent quarrels, were expunged from the collective history of core nationalism as anti-quarian, irrelevant, or inconsequential. For instance, the crucial role of antagonism against the Irish Catholics in solidifying the English as a Protestant nation was later subordinated to the image of a United Kingdom, even if never fully abandoned.

The Enlightenment image of a more civic nationalism and liberal order eclipsed the memory of exclusion. Liberal individualism brought "the negation of the political," in particular the denial of conflict and its resolution.[83] Shifts toward more inclusive political orders were in turn so legitimated, with past (or remaining) exclusions marginalized or forgotten as inconsistent. What began amid exclusion can and did become more inclusive or civic, for these are not distinct paths, but to do so the later civic order forgot its ignoble origins and remaining flaws.

As I will argue later, both the establishment of national unity through exclusion and the forgetting of this ignoble past were essential ingredients also in the ultimate emergence of Western democracy. National unity is a necessary precondition to democracy, for it establishes the boundaries of the community to which citizenship and rights are then accorded, without which democracy is impossible. And the birth of nationalism was related to the political baptism of the lower classes whose empow-erment helped bring democracy, with both nationalism and democracy thereby relatively and impressively inclusive. But this greater conver-gence and inclusion, which Greenfeld argues was already evident at the birth of nationalism in England, came only later with the consolidation of both nation and democracy.

The tradition of dating the birth of nationalism with that of de-mocracy falsely conflates the two, not only diminishing their analytic distinctiveness but also making it harder to account for the prior rise of nationalism as a precondition to democracy. Thus, Barrington Moore's implication that England developed democracy without or before nationalism (with the latter more a product of later fascism elsewhere) ignores the early modern impetus for national cohesion prior to and as a basis for democracy.[84] That such cohesion was built on the basis of conflict and illiberal exclusions was forgotten, allowing the liberal image of inclusiveness undergirding later democracy to take hold. The formative stage of liberalism, when the selective boundaries of membership in the national community were imposed, was forgotten in order to reinforce the then established unit. But that political imperative for forgetting should not blind us to the analytic necessity to remember.

The conflict-ridden and exclusionary roots of nationalism must be rediscovered, not only to explain its emergence but also if we are to understand the legacies of that process. Building unity to contain conflict and by excluding a religious or social faction within deprived emergent states of particular peoples and their skills and provided resources seized in the process. Nationalism demarcated against foreign enemies was reinforced by depriving rights, property, or residency to heretical traitors from within, aggravating the international tensions associated with the rise of nation-states. And, the manner and timing in which internal conflicts were resolved did then shape the forms of state building, governance, and social provisions to come. Only after exclusion had forged unity could central state power be further consolidated and liberal democracy founded, with unity taken for granted. Despite denials, exclusion and denigration of "others" both within and without would also create a template for later discriminatory unity and for disparagement of colonial subjects and others on the periphery. Repetition of this exclusionary process would and still does feed ongoing antagonisms and conflict.

We cannot then account for what came later if we do not assess the reality of these early processes. The foundations on which we did and still do build must be excavated if we are to account for the structures built thereon.

AMASSING STATE AND GATHERING STORM

"Brute Blood of the Air"

Allegiance or obedience to political authority, which cannot practically be forced upon each individual, typically rests upon some constructed image of sameness. People are usually willing to sacrifice their money, lives, or liberty only to those with whom they feel a bond of similarity. Perhaps that bond is easier to imagine and forge in a small local community where similarities and mutuality of interest are more self-evident, although in such circumstances differences and distrust are also more immediately evident. But if the basis of cohesion and obedience is somewhat uncertain even in local settings, it becomes more so in larger contexts where supposed compatriots do not even know each other and where there is greater diversity. This is the quintessential political dilemma faced by every large-scale polity.

Europe in the fifteenth and early sixteenth centuries had not yet faced this dilemma. Strong states did not yet exist as larger scale, effective units requiring matching popular cohesion. Preindustrial economies were still largely based on localized agriculture. And power had long been held locally by nobles only loosely connected to monarchs, with central authority remaining weak. That authority was challenged by recurrent civil wars, pitting nobles against each other and against the crown, and by foreign powers. State bureaucracy was underdeveloped, with limited ability to draw taxes or to raise armies. Currency or legal systems had not yet fully developed. And the populace remained largely isolated, more conscious of their ties to local lords, parishes, and town markets than to larger-scale political or economic units. That isolation was reinforced by linguistic variation, with printing in vernacular languages that would later help to spread an image of larger community just starting to appear.

By the end of the sixteenth century, western Europe would look very different. Centralizing states had gained strength, with unifying monarchs challenging resistance from local lords, raising taxes to pay for domestic armies used to contain civil wars and to expel remaining foreigners. This allowed for the expansion of authority by officials and legal regimes, and the expansion of currencies and markets. Spreading state authority and printing also diminished local isolation, raising the possibility of larger-scale identifications. The institutional and structural underpinnings of such a shift toward centralized identifications were largely in place, if not yet filled out by engagement and allegiance from below.

With this emergence of centralized states, the Atlantic seaboard powers of early modern Europe would confront the dilemma that their states were built without nations. Direct rule and authority were constructed from above over local units of loyalty drawn together into larger polities, without a corresponding scale of popular allegiance. The absence of such cohesion limited the ability of rulers to project their authority to enforce law, wage war, or ensure stability needed for economic advance and revenue collection. Both state authorities and the populace were painfully aware of this lack, suffering from the absence of mass solidarity that would diminish conflict and allow for further state-building and prosperity. Building cohesion emerged as a major imperative.

The stage for meeting this imperative was set by those early rulers who sought to eliminate the intermediary powers between the monarchy and the people.[1] According to John Elliott, the supremacy of absolutist monarchs was projected as "the perfect embodiment of the national will," with pageant and ceremony used "to assert what [was] not taken for granted."[2] In other words, absolutism was at least as much a "myth" as a reality; it "did not automatically create order; it was a theory to combat disorder . . . absolutism was always in the making but never made."[3] Instead, the ideal of absolute sovereignty had to be reinforced by establishing authority, a minimum of popular loyalty and obedience, or the beginnings of nationalism. Contrary to Perry Anderson, absolutism did not then emerge as an alliance of crown and nobility simply dominating the peasants and merchants but instead sought to appease or win over the commoners. As suggested by Norbert Elias, absolutism emerged as "a balancing act; no king could face down a whole society."[4] Efforts to build increasingly absolute institutional power depended then upon building corresponding cohesion that was also as absolute as possible.

State-level interest in overcoming internal conflict was further reinforced by international relations. As suggested by Tilly, early modern states were consolidated by warfare against each other, such wars themselves impelled rulers to gain popular loyalty in order to recruit armies, and international antagonism encouraged domestic loyalty.[5] International relations also had less direct effects. Monarchs seeing the benefit of popular loyalty for their competitors sought to emulate it, and masses were inspired or provoked to engage with political power when they saw foreigners doing so. The idea of nationalism not yet fully formed spread across borders, as historical waves of interest encouraged or forced the adoption of such rhetoric in places where diversity precluded inclusive forms of nationalism. The international Reformation would add to this spread of particularistic identities counter to prior universalism. In addition, the early modern explosion of global economic competition and later of slavery may have reinforced images of national distinctiveness and cohesion.

But the imperative for nation-building arose at least as strongly from within, or more accurately from its domestic absence. Arguably, the most dramatic and ongoing threat to the early modern consolidation—and even the existence—of states was posed and symbolized by recurring civil wars, the most extreme expression of a lack of popular obedience or cohesion. Conflicts between emergent states did not cease by any means, but fighting such wars increased pressure to reduce internal conflict that made states more vulnerable to foreign enemies. More dramatically, earlier peace accords and then the 1648 Treaty of Westphalia ended the Thirty Years War—a series of conflicts between Catholics and Protestants, France and Spain, Hapsburg rulers and subjects, mercenaries and princes—and reinforced the emerging state system. As a result, internal conflict came to the fore, as any challenge to state authority that had to be met. England and France were notably torn from within by such challenges during the sixteenth and seventeenth centuries.

State-building did not and could not then proceed smoothly. To consolidate centralization required asserting or imposing authority over local power-holders or factions that were not inclined to cooperate. Longstanding local solidarities resented threats to their autonomy, as did nobles. As the efforts of monarchs began to pay dividends of increasing power and authority, that consolidation also came with increasing resistance and difficulties. As power at the center grew, so did the temptations to challenge or wrest it. State power had begun to reach down and engage local elites and the populace, and it found a fierceness of resistance there, reinforced by economic disputes. Meeting the challenges of such internal resistance would then become the primary imperative of rulers seeking absolutism, as understood by those rulers, elites, and opponents. To solve this problem, an obvious solution was for state elites to look for some existing form of widespread mass sentiment that might be channeled toward a positive engagement with the state.

In early modern Europe, there was only one such form of collective sentiment that had widespread salience among the people, religion. According to Max Weber, faith about God and the next world inspired behavior "oriented to this world" and understandings thereof. It determined "man's attitude towards the world," providing meaning and cause for all suffering or fortune, life and death, and "the dynamics of interest." The peasant majority in particular, otherwise disengaged or isolated from larger social forces, looked to faith both for salvation and to explain the "organic processes and natural events" on which they were dependent. The institutionalized form of such faith, the church, also provided the model and chief "bases of authority" through charismatic leadership, tradition, and institutional power.[6] The church was the one large-scale institution the populace believed in and participated in regularly and the primary far-reaching network and source of communication with the world within and beyond the local community. The salience of faith was evident in regular practices, including Mass, and in the passionate explosions of pilgrimages and crusades.

Before confessional identity could be merged or converted into more secular cohesion, religion more immediately reinforced the earlier, institutional process of state-building. As described by Gorski, both church and state "constructed new mechanisms of moral regulation (for example, inquisitions, visitations, consistories) and social control (for example, schools, poorhouses, hospitals). Neither purely religious nor strictly political, these institutions were rather *res mixtae* in which church and state interpenetrated one another to varying degrees. Nonetheless, these institutions could be and eventually were absorbed and appropriated by the state. Confessionalism thus forged a new 'infrastructure of power,' by which the state began to effectively penetrate social life for the first time."[7] Indeed, for long periods of time church and state were difficult to distinguish, for instance with rulers seen as intermediaries between God and his people.[8]

This institutional convergence of church and state did not guarantee that a corresponding link between religious and secular identity could be achieved directly. Confessionalism established horizontal community and solidarity of the sort that might become nationalism, with secular powers later eager to encourage this transference. But this shift was not automatic, as religious belief itself constrained secularization. While faith was the most salient form of popular identity and widespread authority in early modern Europe, its reach and impact were for a long time more limited to spiritual or social concerns. No less powerful for being so, religion was for most people and most of the time not politicized, remaining in major respects "other-worldly." And religious social ties remained largely local; its everyday practice "was not so much a symbol to underscore the bond between an individual and God as the bond between the communicants themselves."[9] According to Kishlansky, "the parish was the pimary unit of self-identification."[10] Accordingly, faith would not be easily or fully subsumed or conflated with large-scale emergent nationalism. Instead, in important ways religion long remained "a serious rival to secular nationalism."[11]

For religious linkages to become secularized and expanded beyond local ties, they had to be reformulated into a basis of distinctive cultural identity. To the degree that faith did instill such collective identity, that identity could then be embraced by states as a basis for loyalty or obedience. That this process might work in both directions—with religious identity secularized by states, and states shaped by religion—furthered the potential convergence. And religious images of "a chosen people" were precisely the form of uniqueness and solidarity that was sought for nationalism. Confessionalism demarcated community as a form of "social closure" akin to that of nationalism, itself later described as a "civic religion."[12] England would ultimately be described "as new Israel." And "France, the devoted daughter of the Catholic Church, graduated to become the mother of her people," building upon faith.[13] But these outcomes remained to be found or consolidated and were not a foregone conclusion. As long as Catholicism largely retained homogeneity and was unchallenged by alternative faiths, and the authority of the church was also unchallenged, religion remained both universalistic and on the pragmatic level, largely an issue of local community.

Rather than religious identity leading to national cohesion, then, it had instead the opposite effect. Reformation and vernacular bibles would ultimately help replace Catholic universalism with more particularistic identities akin to nationalism, but the more immediate result was conflict.[14] With Latin Christendom coming apart by 1500, the early modern European states were notable precisely for their internal religious schisms, reinforced by international tensions. Achieving religious unity was envisioned as a basis for national unity, much as "the preservation of religious unity was essential for survival of the state itself." But the 1555 ideal of *cuius regio eius religio,* or what the Treaty of Westphalia would later codify as a unity of monarchy, faith, and law, remained increasingly challenged. The problem for Europe was the lack of fit between "national versus religious interests, when not the same." Religious passions could not be directly turned into passionate loyalty for the state or for a unifying social movement, as that rising religious passion was more often divisive. In other words, passion for faith and for the state did not neatly overlap and could not simply be merged, in the context of religious schisms and even civil wars. European states would seek "compensation for religious division in the common bonds of nationality," though that nationalism was also seen as only possible by building upon religion, which remained an arena of conflict more than unity.[15]

This problem of religious division impeding inclusive national solidarity did help to solve the prior "problem" of spiritualism, localism, and political disengagement. Religious conformity is often as complacent as other forms of homogeneity, whereas religious sectarianism against alternatives tends to be more enflaming. A chosen people are all the more inspired by their election and cohered when under threat, much as the cohesion of any group is solidified by conflict with some out-group. "When confessional escalated into armed struggle and civil war . . . it established new organizational and ideological bonds between the elites and the populace."[16] In other words, only with conflicts over religious faith and authority did religion emerge as a more secular identity that might be harnessed as a means to bolster or challenge political authority. Only when faith came unstuck did its power to provide large-scale political coherence emerge.

The imperative for greater mass solidarity then emerged in the context of religious division that politicized faith through conflict but also furthered the imperative for resolution of that conflict. Civil wars were a response to economic differences and growing centralized power, with competing nobles vying for the prize of that power and resisting absolutism, drawing in the populace to fight. And these contests for power were exacerbated by confessional disputes, pitting the adherents of Rome and of Geneva against one another in an apocalyptic conflict. As described by Paul Kennedy, "national and dynastic rivalries had now fused with religious zeal to make men fight on where earlier they might have been inclined to compromise."[17] Elites aggravated and manipulated these religious disputes for their own purposes.

Rivalries were "overlaid with a new layer of hatred and suspicion," exacerbating and pulling in the religious passions of elites and populace still uncertain about their nationalism but claiming certainty of faith. Amid such rancor, fear of apocalyptic discord, division of faith and over power, there could be no "lasting peace" nor effective absolutist centralization.[18] Thus, rather than religion becoming a basis for unifying cohesion, as it moved beyond more spiritual or local concerns to more secular cohesion, it instead worked against efforts to unify. At least in France and England, the most salient form of social solidarity thereby began to engage the populace in resistance, making it even more difficult for monarchs to ensure obedience or loyalty. State-building provoked just the opposite to nation-building, with religious discord making national unity both more difficult and more pressing to achieve.

In an age of intolerance, the masses were "so caught up, so mastered by the brute blood of the air" that also infected their rulers.[19] But as conflict grew, the building blocks for its possible resolution also began to emerge. While sectarianism brought rising tensions, it also politicized religion, forging and solidifying distinctive identities. And conflict in itself made clear that disputed issues of faith could not be isolated from issues of political power, suggesting a potential but selective merger of faith and politics. But before that merger would or could be consolidated, the first steps were an increase in state power, conflict, and popular engagement within divisive religious identities. That engagement would only later be redirected more fully into issues of authority, but it was the prior and conflictual process of state and identity consolidation that set the stage.

◤ Spain: Consolidating Kingdoms and Empire

If the imperative for widespread popular allegiance emerged with the consolidation of a centralizing state, then our analysis must begin with that prior process. Such a more unified Spanish state would emerge during the sixteenth century as the earliest great power of Europe, drawing resources from its holdings in the Americas.

Just over a century earlier, this relative explosion of central state power was anything but a forgone conclusion. Amid the ravages of the

Black Death, there was no order, no single currency, tax, or legal system. For most of the fifteenth century there was not even such a thing as Spain, with that territory of Hispania instead ruled by smaller kingdoms, themselves of uncertain strength. The most developed of these kingdoms, Castile, had its own strong internal solidarity and distinctness but had also been torn by the "anarchy" of competing aristocrats and by civil war from 1366 to 1369. There "the King was little more than a puppet of which rival factions sought to gain possession in order to cover their ambitions with a cloak of legality, and those which failed to secure his person treated his authority with contempt, or . . . as an excuse for rebellion." The next strongest kingdom, Aragon, was itself divided into three competing principalities and a set of well-entrenched estates, suffering tensions between king and oligarchs, peasants and lords, rival families, and its own civil war in 1462–1471. Throughout, "the condition of the common people can readily be imagined in this perpetual strife between warlike, ambitious and unprincipled nobles . . . The land was desolated . . . there was neither law nor justice save that of arms . . . the roads were unsafe . . . Disorder reigned supreme and all-pervading."[20]

Change in the international situation provided an opportunity for establishing a more pervasive institutional order in Hispania. The end of the Hundred Years War and then renewed tensions with France led to rising interest in a defensive alliance between the two largest kingdoms, Castile and Aragon. This alliance was consolidated with the wedding in 1469 of two cousins, the heirs to the two thrones, Isabella of Castile and Ferdinand of Aragon. They shared power in a partnership deepened by marital affection, even as they each retained authority over separate reigns and Spain remained wavering between "centralization and regionalism."[21]

The considerable talents and energies of the newly joined monarchs were applied to state-building, in a context of continued disorder. Ferdinand and Isabella sought to gain control over police forces, to suppress restive nobles and rebellions aimed at resisting further centralization.[22] On at least one occasion, the queen herself rode through the night in order to negotiate with potentially rebellious local notables. And on the international front, the monarchs challenged the pope for control over the Inquisition, the only national-level institution then existent (which was wrested from Rome's control in 1478).[23] By the time of her death in 1504, Isabella would refer to "absolute royal power" seven times in her last will, a testament to both her and her spouse's endeavor to create such authority, and perhaps the need to insist on it more than it had been established.[24]

While consolidation of central authority remained incomplete, renewed efforts to throw off Moorish rule provided a crucible for self-determination, unifying efforts against a foreign enemy. There had been early antagonisms against the Moors at home, as against Jews, and dramatic crusades against the infidel abroad. But to some extent, the long-standing presence of the Moors had been accommodated, with the lack of animosity evident in the celebration of "El Cid" who had "fought frequently in the service of the Mohammedan princes."[25] That accommodation of the Moors had largely evaporated when "the fall of Constantinople in 1453 revived the crusading enthusiasm of Christendom," provoking a renewal of efforts at "reconquista" at least of Iberia from the Moors.[26] The combined forces of the still distinct Spanish monarchies were then able to take advantage of divisions and treachery among the Moors to defeat them, culminating in the final taking of Granada in 1492. There is a dispute as to the financial consequences of this victory, whether the cost to the royal treasury of the military operation was worth the benefits.[27] But there can be no dispute as to the benefit for building further coordination of the kingdoms emerging from the successful effort to rid the peninsula of infidel rule.

Ferdinand and Isabella were sure in their efforts to build a joined sovereignty and to end foreign threats to their rule, both as crucial steps toward state-building. But they were less confident about nation-building as a complimentary process, while the potentially binding effects of antagonism against the Moors diminished after reconquest. For instance, the monarchs were uncertain about allowing or using printed communication to further unify their subjects. The printing process had arrived in Spain in 1473, the first bible in Catalan was printed in 1478, and in 1492 the monarchs did permit the printing of the first vernacular grammar book, published in Castile. But they sought to contain further expansions of printing in the vernacular, insisting that any printing of a book be officially licensed, and forbidding the reading of scripture in the vernacular. Indeed, the Catalan bible was quickly suppressed and the first translation of the bible into Castilian did not come until 1569, a century after the arrival of printing.[28] Fearful of empowering the masses with greater access to knowledge and ideas, the use of print to spread an "imagined community" was officially constrained. Institutional consolidation was embraced by the center, while a corresponding consolidation of common popular identity was not, establishing a pattern that would persist in Spain.

At its very start, the Spanish state proved hesitant about nation-building, which it feared might be turned against the center to instead reinforce the multiple kingdoms and solidarities reflected in local ver-naculars. The result by the dawn of the sixteenth century was that "Fer-dinand and Isabella created Spain . . . They had united two Crowns, but had not even tentatively embarked on the much more arduous task of uniting two peoples . . . (with) the beginnings of a corporate identity . . . [They] had laid the foundations for a unitary state in the only sense in which that was possible in the circumstances of the fifteenth century . . . (though) administrative, linguistic and cultural barriers remained."[29] There was as yet no discussion of large-scale nationalism other than a growing desire to manage affairs together, no "habit of unity . . . Span-iards still saw themselves as various nations . . . (with) national con-sciousness still [but] half awake." This is not to suggest that Ferdinand and Isabella were uninterested in harnessing the support of their subjects, in particular to win the allegiance of urban dwellers who might otherwise align with rebellious nobles. But "royalism" would be a more accurate term than "nationalism" for this effort to spread obedience.[30]

For all the monarchs' hesitant efforts toward building cohesion, the one form of identification that could be said to unite their subjects was the Catholic faith. But that faith had long been more spiritual than po-litically cohering, even as it remained the strongest basis for any "con-cessions to the common welfare."[31] Non-Catholic or converted descen-dants of the Moors and Jews remained, but internal religious differences would continue to be more limited than elsewhere. With the Reformation yet to come, there were not any Protestants dividing Spanish Christen-dom, and there would be few even later (though many more within the inherited Hapsburg lands). Diversity remained in the secular realm and between Christians and others, but not as a matter of sectarian conflict or engagement among believers. Instead, political allegiances remained more focused on regionalism that divided Catholics.

Having been incompletely unified internally by the marriage be-tween Isabella of Castile and Ferdinand of Aragon, the Spanish state then returned to an even looser confederation of regional powers after the death of the queen in 1504. And that confederation was then torn by turmoil over succession, a recurring problem for monarchies, and re-lations between the kingdoms. Aragon upheld its king, the widower Fer-dinand, while Castile favored Ferdinand and Isabella's daughter Joanna and her husband, the Hapsburg Philip. But when Philip died in 1506, Joanna lost her tenuous grip on sanity and thereafter kept out of sight and power. The dispute over succession ended only in 1516 with the death of King Ferdinand, leaving no child from his second marriage who might otherwise have ruled over a separate kingdom. This circumstance brought to power over an again unified Spain the young Charles V, son of Joanna and Philip, grandson of Ferdinand and Isabella.

While the coming to power of Charles helped to resolve the disputes within Spain, it also brought to power a monarch unsuited to command domestic allegiance. Charles had grown up outside of Spain; he had been raised effectively as an orphan from the age of six when his father died and his mother became mentally incapacitated. When a flotilla of ships finally returned him to Spain in 1517, a storm forced a landing near the village of Villaviciosa, where the populace assumed a foreign invasion had landed. And in a way, it had. The Cortes had to request that Charles learn Spanish, and local powers resented the efforts by the monarch to bolster centralized rule and the heavy tax burden imposed to pay for those efforts. Notably, in 1520–1521 the Comuneros in the heartland of Castile revolted.[32] Tensions within the Iberian peninsula were further exacerbated by the commercial rivalry between Spain and Portugal. As a result, Charles's hold over Spain would only become more tenuous, if officially maintained.

Intertwined royal ancestry within a transnational dynastic system then also brought Spain an astonishingly large and loosely organized empire, exacerbating the diversity of royal holdings and diluting royal authority at home as it spread it beyond. Through his father, Charles was heir to the Hapsburg lands, in addition to three other large inheritances. In 1519 Holy Roman Emperor Maximillian died, and Charles, as his grandson, thus had a claim to that imperial throne. As a result, Spain became more fully enmeshed in the dynastic struggles that had plagued Europe since Charlemagne, extending from medieval into the early modern times. To resolve uncertainty and win lands, Charles expended nearly a half-million gulden bribing the Holy Roman Electors to choose him as emperor. The electors obliged, in part to resist an alliance of the pope and French crown, the latter also seeking to add the imperial title.[33]

In gaining the empire, Charles also added tremendous further obligations for which he was ill suited and which made cohesion of the enlarged populace under his rule even more unlikely. A Catholic, he now ruled over Germany, in which by 1522 a growing portion of the population had become Protestant. Amid varying approaches to religion among the principalities, Germany desperately needed religious toleration and a national consolidator. But when Charles finally met Luther at the Diet at Worms, he condemned Luther as a heretic, with Germany thereafter engulfed in civil wars. The Emperor had chosen to uphold his religion at the cost of antagonizing a large constituency and making more difficult the consolidation of imperial rule. The resulting conflict continued to distract Charles, with his extensive holding requiring constant attention and travel. During his reign, he traveled nine times to Germany, six times to Spain, four times to France, twice to Africa, and twice to England.[34]

Charles's Catholicism made his rule over a heterogeneous empire more difficult, but it also helped him retain a hold over devout Spain. In this sense, his reign was a period of Spanish consolidation, furthered by his son Philip. But at the same time, Charles remained an often absent ruler, distant in terms of both place and culture. If the crown remained too diluted in its global concerns to effectively build state power in Spain, the inquisition in Spain, reignited under Ferdinand and Isabella and continued under Philip, did help to hold together the Catholic population. But as we shall see, under Philip even the unifying effects of the Inquisition could not compensate for the centrifugal effects of an overly stretched royal authority.

As such, Spain remained an incomplete project. Centralized authority had begun to emerge, bolstered by and allowing for the expulsion of foreign rulers on the peninsula, but was torn by ongoing conflict and regional resistance. Authority still remained largely localized, or at least divided among the major kingdoms, with their own laws, armies, and taxes. Popular loyalty remained even more disparate, to the degree it was focused on political units at all. Most of the people whose descendants would become Spaniards did not yet think of themselves as such and often resisted efforts to force such coherence. The major potential focus of cohesion, widespread Catholic religious faith, remained largely "other worldly," not harnessed to the project of nation building. Catholic Spain did avoid religious schism within Christianity, with Protestantism infecting neither nobles nor crown. But such relative religious uniformity may have produced less secularized identity formation than elsewhere, and it certainly produced less conflict that elsewhere further forged and bounded secular identities more than in Spain. And resulting relative tranquility within came together with an extension of power without.

Spain was born prematurely large as an empire, which presented its own challenges to state and nation consolidation.

France: Refining and Splintering the Catholic Crown

If Spain was unpromising ground for nation-building, France in the early modern era appeared even less hospitable. With a population of 16 million in the sixteenth century, more than twice that of Spain, the sheer number of those who might be drawn together was staggering. And this populace's loyalties were—and would long remain—largely regional. Language was as centrifugal as in Spain, for despite considerable early pride in the French tongue used in Paris, it remained "not the language of France" (as there was no one) amid five principal languages and a great diversity of dialects. Nor could printing in vernaculars be expected to pull together communities, for among that roughly 90 percent of the population making up the peasantry, illiteracy was almost complete. And even if they could have read or spoken the same language, the people of France (as in Spain) would still not have had much interest in anything akin to nationalism. They were simply too busy trying to stay alive for such an abstract, inspirational notion; infant mortality was close to fifty percent and life expectancy for those who survived the first year of life remained very low, by some contested estimates as low as thirty years.[35]

Nor did the central state have the resources or capacity to build popular cohesion against these odds. At least after the collapse of Burgundy in 1477 there was a single dominant French state, unlike the rival Spanish kingdoms first aligned only under Ferdinand and Isabel. Minor monarchies remained in the peripheries but were increasingly subordinated to the crown officially based (though not always residing) in Paris. But this apparent advantage was chimerical, for at least the Spanish had relatively viable units to combine and reinforce each other. The French state, by contrast, had been torn by the Hundred Years War, a civil and international contest pitting feudal princes against each other vying for the crown, in which Francis himself was taken prisoner at Agincourt, and leaving that crown greatly weakened by its end in 1453. Much of the territory of the realm was restored, including much of the North, but the population, land, and economy were left decimated.

Even the basic stuff of state-building was left in disarray. Royal ritual and personal staff had increased, but even the geographic boundaries of the realm remained unclear. Royal taxation competed for payment from the peasantry against seigneurial dues and against dîme paid to the church.[36] In some ways, the war had contributed to state-building—ending knightly service, bringing the first regular army and countrywide taxes—but regionalism and administrative difficulties still allowed for little state centralization beyond the imposition of customs duties. The Paris-based monarchy was the only truly national institution, but it was not yet reinforced by extensive related structures or loyalty.[37]

The monarchy was however reinforced by its religious overlay. Indeed, the one thing that potentially united the peoples who would come to be known as French was their Catholicism, particularly after the expulsion of the Jews in 1394. And that religious link was concentrated in the monarchy, seen as divinely appointed, entitled "the most Christian king," recognized as such by the pope, and as indicated by the fleur de lys, the symbol shared by the French monarchy and the Virgin Mary. In France, "the fusion of Church and state was in the person of the monarch, who was bound by his office to protect the Catholic Church."[38] The king even supposedly had the miraculous power to heal upon his touch, though we cannot know how widely this and other rituals were believed. Still, the unity of monarch and faith was relatively strong (at least until the outbreak of the religious civil wars in the mid-sixteenth century), if not yet also reaching to a unity of law as aspired to by the Westphalianesque motto engraved in 1570 over the door of Paris's Hotel de Ville: "one King, one law, one faith."[39]

The century of relative peace following 1453 had provided the French crown an opportunity for renewed efforts at building toward absolutist power, refining those advances made during war and creating an institutional base to match and rule the spiritual. Already by 1438 French cathedral chapters could elect their own bishops and abbots. After an extended period of international tensions and conflicts with the pope, in 1516 the king became head of the Catholic Church in France, with power to nominate bishops and abbots, consistent with rising anti-Roman Gallicanism, a distinctly French church and identity. By the 1530s, Francis I was creating various national institutions and in 1539 mandating that all acts be written in French dialects, thereby attempting to match pervasive rules with the further spreading of more common language, though incomplete on both accounts.[40] Internal consolidation had been redoubled after the 1529 peace of Cambrai with Spain, which also freed Francis's two sons previously held hostage. The later death of the first son would ultimately bring to the throne the second as Henri II, who sought to build further on state advances.

For all their efforts, both Francis I and Henri II were still resisted by the locally entrenched power of the nobility. These aristocrats—including all their sons and not just the first born heir—had long enjoyed exemption from taxes in return for military or other state service. State offices were sold in order to make up revenues not gained by taxing the nobles, who continued to assert their privileges against the center.[41] Even those with state offices engaged in such assertions of local control or attempted to strengthen their control over the state.

Renewed conflict with Spain in the late 1550s did not make things any easier. The war effort required higher taxation, fueling inflation and discontent.[42] And the war did not go well, with the Spanish empire already encircling France and the prospect of a Spanish invasion from the Netherlands threatening Paris, spreading panic reinforced by famine and plague.[43] But despite its victories, Spain was under comparable stress, and with bankruptcy threatening both sides of the conflict, the monarchs negotiated an end to their hostilities with the treaty of Cateau-Cambrésis in 1559. At the same time, a treaty with England was signed. France, again at peace and under the vigorous leadership of Henri II, seemed poised for another round of consolidating central state power.

At this juncture, royal efforts had still not created anything like a fully absolutist state in France. Countrywide institutions were undeveloped, as was the economy. Monarchy was not as divided as it was in Spain, but its authority was no less challenged by local powers. Like its neighbor on the southern side of the Pyrenees, France then entered the early modern era as an emerging state. And the populace was largely disengaged, mindful of the crown only as a distant object of demands and fear and upholder of the faith. Anything resembling nationalism, or collective loyalty to the central state, was even less developed than the state itself, with the long wars having only partially encouraged a unifying spirit. France existed in name but not in extensive state structure, and even less in sentiment or common culture.

The one element of commonality, potentially linking populace to crown, was Catholicism, though even that faith existed more as an aspect of local community than as religious zeal directed centrally. Catholicism within and international conflicts without did provide some basis for popular coherence, but this remained largely localized, abstract, and untapped. Religion did inspire some mass fervor, indicated by a rising number of church processions in Paris by the mid-sixteenth century. But in some respects, the church was still itself underdeveloped, though institutional weaknesses of church and state did not diminish the link between the two.[44] Still, with the notable exception of the proclaimed sacrality of the king, Catholicism in France had remained largely unconcerned or unfocused on more secular issues beyond Gallican authority and local social ties.[45] For the populace, God was prayed to and the king's sacrality observed, but largely in spiritual terms rather than as an expression of political community. With the earlier expulsion of the Jews and others, relative homogeneity of Catholicism may have contributed to that unity of faith being taken for granted more than it served as a political bond to match growing state consolidation. Then, Catholic unity also came to be challenged, bringing more zealotry that merged political and religious conflict in a combustible and divisive mix.

The early to mid-sixteenth century saw an explosion of Protestantism, including within the top ranks of French society. There remains much dispute about which sectors of the populace began this trend, though it seems likely that new ideas about religion were first picked up by those more educated and by professionals and traders with international contacts. But from this initially small core, reformism took a somewhat surprising turn. Benefiting from his appeal as a French humanist, Calvin himself (and his deputies), "assiduously cultivated the favour of influential noblewomen," and those wives and mothers then often converted their husbands and sons. Already in 1534, Protestant broadsheets were posted throughout Paris, including on the door of the king's own bedchamber. Henri II became so concerned that he asked the pope to establish an inquisition for France. The pope did appoint three cardinals as inquisitors-general, though with little effect.[46] By 1559, between a third and a half of all nobles had joined the Protestant movement, and in that year they held their first national synod. Protestantism also spread further among commoners. In 1561, "there were 2,150 Huguenot congregations worshipping openly, with roughly two million adherents—something like 10 per cent of the population."[47]

This rapid emergence of a Protestant faction—and of the potential for conflict it raised—would seem to have had more to do with economics and politics than faith. In many local communities, Catholics and Protestants were able to pursue their faiths and live together in peace, suggesting a lack of popular religious fanaticism.[48] Montaigne ridiculed any sense of purely spiritual motivation for later conflict; those attracted "out of pure zeal to religion . . . could hardly . . . make one complete company of gens-d'armes."[49] Instead many of the noble converts were no doubt aware of the possibility that a reformation would bring to them property previously held by the Catholic Church, as it had recently in England.[50] But arguably Gallicanism made such a state-led reformation less likely. Rather than look to the crown to institute Reformation and confiscations, as it would across the Channel, the nobility embraced Protestantism as a form of resistance to the monarchy and possible enrichment. Religious sectarianism thus became a cover for noble rebellion against a crown seen as gaining too much central power and overly influenced by foreign alliances and interests, the latter symbolized by the Italian-born queen. Such a political motivation was also seen as consistent with Calvinism.[51]

By 1559, the French crown appeared to be gaining strength enough to combat its internal adversaries, including restive Huguenot nobles. In the century of relative peace since the Hundred Years War, monarchical power had been reinforced. Noble intrigues remained, but by the time of Henri II the monarch could and did effectively play off against each other the two leading rival factions.[52] On the international front, the Italian wars with Spain were ended, and an alliance between France and victorious Spain was cemented by the marriage between Henri II's daughter and Philip of Spain, who had earlier been widower of England's Mary and more recently spurned by Mary's half sister Elizabeth. Plans were laid for projecting French power, engaging in war to defend Catholic rule in Scotland and against the heretics in the Spanish-controlled Lowlands.

Henri II seemed poised to enjoy the fruits of state-building and a continental alliance, but then chance intervened. In July 1559, the French and Spanish were celebrating their treaty and alliance through marriage with traditional feasts, dances, and a tournament at the Tournelles palace in Paris. A vigorous forty-year-old, Henri himself participated in the games. The wooden lance of a jousting partner accidentally pierced the visor, the one open spot in the royal armor. A fragment of the lance entered the King's eye, infection spread, and ten days later the monarch was dead. The history of France turned on a splinter.

Of course, the outcome of contingency depends on the structural context. For France in the wake of Henri II's death, that context was one of state resources depleted by recent war, the rising potential for a religious schism, tensions between noble factions and the monarchy, and royal weakness at the center due to the happenstance of succession. The king left four sons, all young, so that much of royal authority passed to his wife, Catherine de' Medici, though she was herself barred from the crown by Salic law against a woman monarch. And as a woman, the queen's informal hold on power was precarious in an age in which female rulers often failed—think of Mary Tudor, Mary of Guise, and Mary Queen of Scots, with Elizabeth I of England the notable exception. Catherine was at further disadvantage as foreign-born, and her loyalty to France was suspect and arguably less strong than her passion for her children's interests.[53] Her and her sons' unexpected coming to power would unleash a set of power struggles and conflicts, in turn provoking remarkably vicious royal maneuvers to hold onto power.

The new king at age fifteen, Francis II, was already married to Mary of Scots, herself the niece of the cardinal of Lorraine and the duc de Guise, brothers heading one of the most prominent Catholic noble families of France. The Guise family used their new leverage to install their own allies in office and then to attack their political and religious rivals. They pressed the young king to increase arrests and executions for heresy, expedited by offering informers immunity and "a share in the properties confiscated from convicted heretics."[54] Not surprisingly, this attack raised the ire of another leading noble faction recently converted to Protestantism, headed by the Bourbon princes of the blood, Antoine of Navarre and Louis, Prince of Condé. In March 1560, Condé conspired to seize the king at Amboise and to also kill the Guise brothers there, all falsely rumored to be with the assistance of fellow Protestant England.[55]

The prospect of an ongoing conflict seemed imminent, pitting the four young Catholic sons of Henri II—whose number suggested a continued Valois hold on the throne—against the Protestant Bourbons next in line for the throne. To ensure peace and security, leaders of the third major noble faction, Constable Anne de Montmorency—supreme military officer of France—and his son, came to Paris. An amnesty was issued to ensure peace, but mob violence and slaughter continued, indicative of rising popular engagement.[56]

Thus, within eight months of the death of Henri II, France teetered on the abyss. Reflecting the frequent intermarriage of royals, the crown was held by a young man of half-foreign descent married into another half-foreign family, who pressed their advantage under the guise of Catholic purity at home (and for Scotland, under their niece Mary). Pushed to extreme defensiveness was the second family of France, the Bourbons, who had alienated themselves from the mainstream with Protestantism. This rivalry coincided with religious schism but remained more a political contest for power, with Calvinism itself forbidding formal rebellion.[57] Somewhat ambivalently in the middle were the Montmorency,

FAITH IN NATION

with the old Constable always loyal to the Valois crown but also rival to the crown's allies, the Guises. Reinforcing these family rivalries and religious divisions were the competing regional bases of each faction: Bourbons in the Southwest, Guise in the Northeast, and Montmorency central.[58] These overlapping religious, regional, and political tensions threatened to engage the populace in conflict and to tear the country apart.

The balance of power between the noble rivals shifted perilously back and forth. With the connivance of his weaker brother Antoine, Condé was arrested for his Amboise conspiracy. But before a trial, Francis II fell ill and died, again demonstrating the instability built into personalized rule. The crown would fall to his nine-year-old brother, Charles IX, who would clearly require a regent. By tradition, that position should have gone to Antoine of Navarre, bringing power to Condé's faction after all. But three days before Francis's death, Catherine de' Medici convinced the weak-willed Antoine, her second cousin, to renounce the regency, which she was awarded thereafter.[59] This woman, capable of spending the days while her first son lay on his deathbed looking after her own and other sons' power, would effectively rule France for a generation. Her own passionate defense and defensiveness for her remaining sons, inflamed by a sense of personal vulnerability, would help set fire to France.

The queen mother's initial pragmatism convinced her of one thing, in the words of her Spanish envoy at the time, that the conflict exploding around her "is more a matter of rebellion than of religion."[60] Certainly the machinations of the noble factions at the time appear more focused on power than on doctrinal schisms, with the two often not coinciding but instead dividing the leading families. Indeed, the pivotally placed Constable de Montmorency disagreed on religion with his three nephews, including the eldest, Gaspard de Coligny, who had recently converted to Protestantism. In addition, the Guises had Protestant clients, and the leading titular Protestant Antoine de Bourbon's brother Charles remained a Catholic Cardinal. Nor did economic interests pursued at the time neatly correspond with faith. Overall, then, "ambition and expediency among the princes, the magnates, and their followers made a mockery of religious ideals."[61]

If religious schism was indeed mere pretense for a struggle over centralized power, then resulting conflict could perhaps be resolved and compromised like any other factionalism, with mass engagement not yet strong enough to prevent compromise. Catherine embraced this logic, concluding that if neither of the two faiths were strong enough to wipe out the other, nor the state capable of fully repressing Protestantism, then the crown and her family could be strengthened only by appeasement and accommodation of both, if not by unifying them. Part of the trick was to ensure that elite machinations did not explode into further mass conflict. To diminish such discord that would weaken the state, she stressed commonality; "Frenchmen should not think of other Frenchmen as Turks . . . There should be brotherhood and love between them."[62] With the able assistance of chancellor L'Hospital, Catherine pursued unity then seen as possible without religious conformity. In 1561 she forced the Catholic Church to make payments to the state, thereby further diminishing its autonomy, and greeted leading Protestants at a conclave called to discuss a merger of faiths.[63]

Not everyone shared Catherine's pragmatic interest in compromise and conflict avoidance nor appreciated her efforts. As leader of the major noble Catholic faction, Guise was disgusted by the queen mother's toleration of the Huguenots and by her soliciting of advice from his rival Coligny. Guise accused Catherine of "drinking at two wells of religion," and indeed that was precisely what she was attempting to do in order to make peace and consolidate the power of her son.[64] As such, and despite her later intolerance, Catherine emerged as a founder of a movement aimed at a more secular state and avoiding further civil war that threatened that state, disparaged by zealots with the label "politique." According to the queen, religious difference should be accommodated just enough to meet the political interest in stable rule.[65]

Catherine and her son's initial attempts at appeasement and toleration were evident in royal edict. In January 1561, the king's lettres de cachet focused on "those matters most necessary for the maintenance of public peace . . . having taken the advice of our said lady and mother . . . ordain you most expressly to cease and desist from all prosecutions and pursuits . . . for the sake of religion." And the Edict of Saint-Germain, of 17 January 1562, began by acknowledging "what troubles and seditions are now in hand and are daily instigated and increased in our kingdom by the malice of the times and the diversity of opinions which reign in religion." Accordingly, the king ordered the return of churches seized by the Huguenots, but also "to keep our subjects in peace and concord, while awaiting for God to do us the grace to be able to reunite and restore them to the same sheep-fold," he ordered to "suspend and supersede the prohibitions and punishments . . . for preaching, prayers and other practices of their religion."[66] Parisians understood and resisted these acts as toleration of heresy and as effective granting of citizenship rights regardless of religious orthodoxy, winning a citywide exemption that lasted for more than thirty-five years.[67]

Officially mandated coexistence (outside of Paris) allowed for an expansion of Protestantism, or at least the public worship and acknowledgement of that faith. The very name "Huguenots" by some accounts came from the Tours vernacular for ghosts, signifying both the secretive and sinister nature of those who sneaked out at night to so worship. But under the new edicts, Protestant worship could occur in public and daytime, losing some of its stigma and gaining in popularity. By one estimate, nine-tenths of France was "infected" with some Huguenot presence by 1562, though the actual number of adherents probably remained close to two million.[68] Even a bishop converted. This significant shift of faith in itself suggests a growing level of mass engagement that could not long be ignored or contained but was instead fanned by elite conflict.

Appeasement of the Huguenots did not bring peace to the kingdom but just the contrary, inflaming the fears and jealousy of the larger and stronger Catholic faction. Aghast at the moves toward toleration, the leading Catholic nobles, duc de Guise, Constable Montmorency, and marshal Saint-André, had joined together in 1561 as the Triumvirate to defend Catholicism—if need be against the King himself. They even succeeded at gaining the support of the feckless Antoine de Bourbon and attempted to gain support from Philip of Spain. Catherine was forced to look for support and protection from the Huguenots, who in turn looked to Elizabeth of England for help; but none of these alternative links would prove as strong as those binding the Catholic forces.

Tensions then exploded. In March 1562, Guise came upon a Huguenot worship in Vassy, and in the ensuing fight up to seventy-four were massacred. Guise then marched on to Paris, taking the capital and forcing Catherine to accede to the Triumvirate's superior force and to recognize Condé and Coligny's pivotal failure to provide Protestant protection for the crown. Before this first religious war was over, Antoine and Saint-André were killed, Guise was assassinated (according to a recanted confession by the assassin, on order of Coligny, who denied it but confessed pleasure at the outcome), and Montmorency and Condé both captured.[69] Blood was in the water, and the superior force of the Catholics had been impressed upon the crown. And with this initial spurt of violence, factions had engaged popular support and participation, with the conflict beginning to move from elite maneuverings to social maelstrom.

To avoid further explosion, Charles issued the Edict of Amboise in

March 1563, imposing peace while acknowledging the rising level of discordant mass engagement. Concerned about "the growth of divergent ideas in religion . . . [and] seeing how the war was so damaging to the kingdom," the king ordered "that all occasions for these troubles, tumults and seditions should cease, and to reconcile and unite the wills of our subjects." The edict went on to ordain that "all injuries and offenses" should be forgotten, "as if they had not happened," to forbid any further "dispute, quarrel or contest together over religion," and to require that all "live peacefully together like brothers, friends and fellow citizens."[70] The queen mother meanwhile advised her son that to ensure such peace among their subjects, he had "to keep them merry and to occupy them with some exercise."[71] Under the cover of such peace, and as inspired by the experience of a tour of the provinces, Catherine and her son would then endeavor to build further centralized power, reducing "crime and disorder," reducing the authority of provincial governors, and even regulating printing.[72]

For all the talk of unity, forgiving, forgetting and building of evenhanded control, the Edict of Amboise ushered in a period of further resentment and restriction of the Huguenots. The edict itself had restricted Protestant worship except among the highest nobles and was amended by forbidding any such worship when and wherever the Court was in residence. Huguenots, feeling more repressed than tolerated, concluded that they would have to resist the crown and even challenged its legitimacy, precisely for the lack of popular allegiance. According to a 1564 pamphlet, when monarchs so "lose the love that they [their subjects] owe to them and when they abuse their authority . . . they are no longer kings but tyrants."[73] Contrary to Greenfeld's interpretation, Protestantism was thus attacking the monarchy itself, and accordingly would come to employ the early rhetoric of nationalism more than would the crown or Catholics who took their legitimacy more for granted.[74] But the Catholics also responded to increasing Protestant stridency. Even the restrictive edict was resented as too lenient by the Catholic majority, for instance, with Paris town criers reading the edict pelted with mud and forced to flee.[75]

Meanwhile, the crown itself appeared to be conspiring against the Protestants, most notably with Catherine and Charles meeting with Charles's sister Elizabeth, queen of Spain, at Bayonne in July 1565. At that meeting, Catherine was indeed pressed to end religious tolerance. France's Huguenots falsely assumed that an international Catholic alliance against them was thereby forged. Their fear of such an anti-

Protestant plot was reinforced the following year by the campaign of terror against heretics in the Lowlands, launched by Spanish forces under the command of Count Alba who had been the Spanish King's representative at Bayonne.[76]

Rising Protestant fears bred defensiveness and then further conflict. Seeing the tide turning against them, the Huguenots under Coligny laid siege to Paris and desperately plotted to seize the king at Meaux in 1567. The plot failed but clearly antagonized the queen mother, who then herself plotted to seize Coligny and Condé and ushered in renewed massive conflict. The year 1568 saw the start of the bloodiest and most savage religious war yet. On both sides, women and children were tortured, and mobs indulged in mass killings by the hundreds. Condé himself was shot in the back and killed after a battle. No compromise seemed possible. In July 1569, three Huguenots were hanged in Paris, where the house of one was torn down and replaced by a monument. That pyramid topped by a cross would come to signify the rising popular intolerance and fanaticism of Paris, if not of France as a whole.[77]

This terrible conflict inspired the crown to again seek peace through coexistence and to vainly appeal that the blood just spilled be forgotten. In August 1570, a second Edict of Saint-Germain stipulated "first, that the remembrance of all things past on both parts . . . shall remain as wholly quenched and appeased, as things that never happened." It went on to forbid all provocation or dispute and to call on all "to live peaceably together as brethren, friends and fellow citizens, upon pain that the offenders be punished as breakers of the peace."[78] This tack coincided with the resurgence of the "politiques," advocating realistic compromise to avoid further civil war and allowing for just enough religious coexistence to thereby preserve the kingdom in peace.[79] The queen mother again joined this trend, allowing for the return to court of Coligny, who insisted on the removal of the cross on the pyramid monument to intolerance. Coligny soon gained influence over the young king, shifting French foreign policy accordingly toward an alliance with Protestant England and against Catholic Spain and its campaign of terror against Protestants in the Low Countries.[80] There were even efforts to arrange a marriage between the king or his rival brother and Elizabeth of England, though she eventually declined. Rising accommodation would however culminate in the marriage of the king's sister Marguerite to the leading Protestant royal, King Henri de Navarre, son of the late Antoine.

For all these efforts at reconciliation, increasingly bloody internecine mass conflict tore France apart. Charles IX himself, in a 1571 speech to parlement, decried that "wherever I look in my kingdom, I see things misdirected, out of order . . . factions and partialities [that] permit no intrigues or practices [or] vices too repugnant."[81] Yet the king was understating the level of conflict, which posed "the single greatest threat to the French monarchy prior to the Revolution" two centuries later.[82] Between 1560 and 1572, ten major battles were fought throughout France. In just one street fight in Toulouse in 1562, an estimated 4,000 were killed. By 1581, according to one estimate, more than 750,000 were killed. While this number may be questioned, "it is clear that the massacres of this period were of a scale and intensity which was unmatched anywhere else in Europe."[83]

What remains striking is not just the scale of this violent conflict but also its mass base, for this was not so much a war of armies as it was a social maelstrom. According to one French pastor at the time, this "is not like other wars, for even the very poorest man has an interest in it, since we are fighting for freedom of conscience." Or, according to Etienne Pasquier in 1562, "there is nothing so much to fear in a Republic as civil war, nor among civil wars, as that which is fought in the name of religion." Unlike the dynastic wars of the fifteenth century or the noble revolts of the seventeenth, these wars "had a resonance among the common people . . . as crucial choices between truth and error, between salvation and damnation, between God's favor and impending wrath."[84] Self-serving elites had used religious propaganda to gain popular support, but that propaganda had a powerful effect on the masses who took the religious issues seriously. Religion quickly became politicized by elite conflicts and mass violence.

Inspired by rising religious fanaticism, the populace had become passionately engaged with issues of state, with that engagement then exploding beyond elite control. But rather than bolster the state as early nationalism, this engagement fed and was fed by discord that threatened to destroy the state and topple the crown.

England: Scepter Contesting Mitre

The development of central state power in England emerged more ambivalently than in Spain or France. The Norman monarchy had consolidated rule early but then had neither needed nor engaged in centralizing campaigns comparable to those in France, allowing for the consolidation of local powers. And in England such local governance centered on lords had developed without having to overcome earlier Roman authority structures. Those lords had further consolidated their rights against the crown with Magna Carta, described by Bishop Stubbs as "the first great public act of the nation," and then with financial reforms in 1311.[85] Constraints on the monarchy would be explicit even in the coronation oath "to confirm to the people of England the laws and customs to them granted."[86]

Especially under Edward III, thereafter the feudal monarchy had regained some strength in the context of less diversity—the English population was one-fourth the size of France—and weakened local lords. Those lords had been united by the external campaigns in France during the Hundred Years War, but in its aftermath they fought one another in the War of the Roses. With his victory over Richard III at Bosworth in 1485, Henry Tudor and his son later sought to further appease restive nobles in order to bolster their power. But with local authorities still strong, isolation from continental threats or conflicts afforded by the Channel "removed the need for a strong central government."[87] Further efforts to strengthen the crown under the Tudors and Stuarts had to work against powerful decentralization. Even as late as the Stuart age, the crown still lacked a professional bureaucracy, army, or police.[88]

With central state power still being built, England arguably enjoyed fewer barriers to popular cohesion than Spain or France, though the actual level of such cohesion remained low. There were no competing monarchies dividing loyalties within England per se. With the Jews having been expelled even earlier than in France, Catholicism was unchallenged, and the monarch was acknowledged to have divine right. And printing came early, arriving at Oxford in 1478, though the first daily newspaper was not printed in London until more than two centuries later (still almost a century earlier than in France). But while the spread of printing is assumed to have spread "imagined community," in England (as elsewhere) it would also spread discord, particularly later as "the bible became a battlefield" of disagreement over interpretation.[89] More immediately, the widespread plague had torn at the social fabric. Distrust and fear were further indicated by witch-crazes.[90]

Even the unifying effect of enmity against foreigners, in particular the French and to a lesser extent the Spanish, would take hold of the English populace more fully only in the eighteenth century.[91] In its earlier guise, even this seemingly clear focus of internal cohesion was blurred by the vagaries of personalized alliances—for instance with the peace established with the marriage of Henry VII's daughter to James IV of

Scotland and undone with Henry VIII's war on France and its Scottish allies. Enmity with Spain was diluted by the marriage of Henry VIII to Catherine of Aragon, reenflamed by his divorcing her, and alliance reestablished with the marriage between Henry's daughter Mary and the Spanish heir Philip. While commoners did on occasion attack foreigners, for instance with the riots in London of 1517, such tensions were perhaps more evidence of economic competition than xenophobic zeal.[92] Certainly the crown's shifting involvements did little to channel any popular international antagonism into national cohesion.

These varied alliances, like shifting domestic policies, were all designed by the Tudors to solidify their sovereignty and centralized control. Their aim was to contain civil conflicts, "disorder and lawlessness" that had earlier showed "weakness of the crown" and disrupted the realm.[93]

But in an age of monarchy, the stability of rule depended upon the uncertain fruits of royal marital alliances. Mary was born to Henry VIII in 1516, but a female heir was vulnerable to challengers. By 1525, when Queen Catherine had reached forty years of age, Henry concluded that she would not produce the male heir he sought, and within two years a crisis had exploded over the king's intention to divorce. Henry claimed that marriage to Catherine, who had been the widow of Henry's brother before, was a sin; according to Leviticus "if a man shall take his brother's wife, it is an unclean thing . . . they shall be childless." The monarch seems to have believed this imperative to end the marriage, though his intended second marriage to his mistress Anne Boleyn, herself the younger sister of a previous mistress, was perhaps just as much a sin.[94] But marrying Anne would accord with the king's new passion and bring the advantage of another chance at a son, the latter a justification of state more sure than competing impieties.

Religious ordering followed reasoning of state. When the then Spanish-controlled pope refused to allow divorce from Catherine, Henry divorced the pope, ending control from Rome and establishing himself in 1532 as head of the Church of England. This had certainly not been a forgone conclusion—Henry VIII had been declared "defender of the faith" by the pope only a decade before the rift.[95] But as the first European sovereign to break with Rome, Henry was pursuing the political imperatives to throw off foreign constraints on his power. The statute by which the king prohibited any appeals to Rome's authority would be seen as "the founding charter of English national self-sufficiency" or self-determination. His acts of 1532 and 1534 prohibited any "manner of appeals . . . to the Bishop of Rome" and the "payment of annates to the see of Pope." Thus ended a "double allegiance," with the state eclipsing a foreign-based church that had been seen as aligned with enemies in France and Spain, and whose taxes had long been resented.[96] Sir Thomas More was executed precisely for challenging that the crown had absolute sovereignty against the pope.

At issue in the Reformation were less spiritual matters but more secular concerns with the monopoly of power in state territory. A reluctant protestant in religious terms, Henry never claimed to have sacredotal powers, only administrative authority over the church. Indeed, the act enumerating the powers of the king as supreme head of the Church of England was explicitly justified "for the conservation of the peace, unity and tranquility of this realm."[97]

Advances toward greater state consolidation came not only by throwing off foreign intervention by the pope but also by diverting resources from Rome. Self-determination of authority also brought revenues used to reinforce that authority. The Catholic Church had owned close to a third of all land in England, much of it under wealthy abbeys such as St. Albans, itself under Cardinal Wolsey as absentee abbott. Dissolution of the monasteries under Reformation provided astonishing wealth to be redistributed, with large tracts of land given to the nobility thereby further tied to the crown by gratitude for this largesse. With one stone, Henry freed himself from the pope and used the result to buy elite loyalty at home. And at the same time, royal income more than doubled from the redirection of resources and taxes away from the church. Those revenues were used to further strengthen the state. By 1536, the crown was funding public works for the poor, again extending state reach and encouraging the loyalty of yet another section of the populace.[98]

While the break with Rome did help to build loyalty to the state among important constituencies, it remained primarily a conservative revolution from above, asserting national sovereignty more than it redirected spirituality. Certainly "in the absence of massive popular demands for religious change, the king took the initiative" in the Reformation.[99] But as such it was also resisted, at least by protest if not rebellion or unified Parliamentary resistance. When the state moved against the larger monastic houses and threatened to enclose their lands, in 1536 Catholic lords and peasants in Lincolnshire and then Yorkshire joined in a Pilgrimage of Grace. By 1540, these popular movements were defeated by force and the seizure of monasteries was largely completed.[100]

Amid some protest based on both faith and self-interest, Henry may have been uncertain about whether his people would follow him out of the Catholic Church. But unlike the age to follow, this was not yet a time of strong religious fervor, making it easy to achieve a break with a church already resented for its wealth, its distant clergy, and its foreign control. Most people saw the Reformation as an issue of authority over the church, of relatively little concern to them, leaving their personal religious practices largely intact. When they did resist, they were crushed, not so much on the basis of faith but reflecting the king's insistence that all "shall obeye . . . order muste be hadde."[101] As a matter of faith, "the Reformation sat as yet lightly on most Englishman's minds," while the crown was heavily invested in it primarily as a basis of asserting its power, and the nobility gained a self-interest in the church resources redistributed.[102] As resources captured by the state flowed from it and revenues to it, the monarchy under Henry gained considerable power.

Reformation seems to have initially had a stronger influence on state-building than on nation-building, as much as those would end up interconnected. A religious transformation brought forth for and by matters of state did not fundamentally alter the lack of connection between the populace and its rulers. Still, "rebellion to the Pope served a valuable function in the process of nation-building," diminishing conflicts between nobles and monarch, local and central powers, feudal and national interests. Turning the pope into the Antichrist would indeed help to strengthen national solidarity.[103] And the Reformation's translation of the bible into the vernacular did crucially set the stage for later mass communication, though initially focused on spiritual rather than political issues.[104] But these moves also brought resistance and conflict. The 1533 Act of Appeals asserts for the crown "unto whom a body politic, compact of all sorts and degrees of people divided in terms and by names of Spirituality and Temporality, be bounded and owe to bear next to God a natural and humble obedience."[105] But that unifying obedience remained to be forged, more than the Reformation from above had achieved.

Up to this juncture, state power was being centralized and reinforced through reformation, the latter largely imposed from above despite some resistance. Power remained less broadly challenged in the hands of successive monarchs, though this would also concentrate the issues of religion onto the monarchy. Instead of factions of various faith wrestling with each other and for support of the crown as in France, in England it would then be the crown itself that wavered in its faith. Certainly after Henry VIII, the rapid succession of monarchs of different faiths "brought home . . . the implications in practical terms of the crown's claim to supreme ecclesiastical jurisdiction."[106] The result was increasing conflict or the rising potential for it. Later, when the populace became aroused by the coinciding issues of religion and power, it would turn its anger on the crown itself as the locus of uncertainty and conflict. But even before such active mass engagement, the increasing politicization of religion would set the stage for massive turmoil to come.

The death of Henry VIII in 1547 after a thirty-eight-year reign brought to the throne a young boy of nine at a time of unsettled religious doctrine, an uneasy truce with France, and war in Scotland. Edward VI and his advisors sought to find resolution, with the 1549 Act of Uniformity mandating the first vernacular prayer book and allowing the clergy to marry, both of which proved more controversial than settling, and in 1550 making peace with France.[107] Then the young king's death in 1553 underscored the instability of royal rule, not so much for the short reign allowing for little policy consolidation but for the dramatic change that could come with succession.

The same royalism that had characterized the relatively peaceful start of religious change in England would quickly come back to haunt. If the Reformation had been justified in part by Henry's lack of a male heir, the short reign of that heir would then bring to the throne a queen who would pull England back toward Rome with a violent reversal. England would long be scarred by the memory of that jerk of the royal chain.

Unlike her younger half brother, in an equally short reign Mary left an indelible mark upon England. As the daughter of Henry's first queen, a Spanish Catholic, Mary had remained devoutly in that church, and she dedicated her reign to restoring papal obedience and reversing a Reformation that had unthroned her mother. But even if Protestantism remained limited and certainly its ascendance far from inevitable, undoing twenty years of rule was not easy, given the interests vested in the Reformation. The reformed liturgy, Books of Common Prayer, and allowance of clergy who had married were all withdrawn, and recently enriched nobles feared the next step would be restoration of the monastic properties. While that property was not taken, lives were. Around 300 men and women were burned at the stake, most infamously at Smithfield, and though this number was smaller than the victims of violence on the continent, it was unprecedented for England. A populace that had been largely indifferent about religious schisms was suddenly horrified by this carnage, with Protestant evangelists using the expansion of printing to spread the image of martyrdom. Fear spread among the upper classes that the attack on heresy would rise up the social ranks. Approximately 800 fled, including such dignitaries as the vice chancellors of both Oxford and Cambridge.[108]

Mary failed to bring England back into Rome's fold, with her efforts helping to accomplish just the opposite. The queen was motivated by her own strong faith, decrying "much false and erroneous doctrine hath been taught . . . swerved from the obedience of the See Apostolic and declined from the unity of Christ's Church."[109] But her zealotry arguably reinforced an emerging anti-Catholic vehemence that would last for centuries. It exploded almost immediately with riots in London against the renewal of Mass a month after Mary arrived in London. And this growing religious conflict coincided with an ethnocentric anti-Spanish sentiment based on the queen's ancestry, her marriage to the Spanish heir Philip, and dismay at the unfolding Iberian Inquisition. Indeed, the two themes came together under and after Mary, seen as both anti-Protestant and un-English, and thereby merging anti-Catholicism with gathering xenophobia.[110] Bloody Mary and the fires at Smithfield would become pivotal images for England, effectively destroying the remnants of her official religion and the Spanish alliance while feeding fears that would provoke violence.

The primary purveyor of these images was John Foxe in his *Book of Martyrs*, with its multiple editions, large print runs, and distribution in churches alongside the bible, seen as a miraculous boon for reformation. Foxe portrayed Mary as merciless, regardless of the comparatively small number of victims, with her tortures and burnings graphically described and pictured, and the martyrdom of ordinary people making her persecutions all the more salient.[111] The common folk were described as innocent victims, confused by a queen who happily acknowledged "that is not God's Word now, that was God's Word in my father's day." Her efforts to "bring in the Pope" were understood to threaten "the utter destruction of the realm," no better than aligning with the Turks.[112]

Foxe's intentions merged politics and religion, for he even dedicated the 1570 edition of his best-seller to Mary's successor, whom he hoped to further influence at least as much as Machiavelli would his prince. Indeed, Foxe saw Elizabeth's very survival under Mary as an indication of providence, hoping that under her rule, a new order would be established. In the 1570 edition, speaking not just to the monarch but to her subjects, Foxe made explicit that hope: "And if there cannot be an end of our disputing and condemning against an other, yet let there be a moderation in our affections ... No man liveth in that commonwealth where nothing is amiss. But yet because God hath so placed us Englishmen here in one commonwealth, also in one Church, as in one ship together, let us not mangle or divide the ship, which being divided perisheth ..."[113]

To head off that threat of divisive conflict, of the very destruction of England, would become the primary challenge and success for Elizabeth. Her initial Act of Supremacy avoided the rhetoric of religious truth used earlier by her half sister Mary, instead referring back to her father's efforts for "the utter extinguishment and putting away of all usurped and foreign powers ... restoring and uniting to the imperial crown of this realm the ancient jurisdictions, superiorities and preeminences to the same of right belonging."[114] And overall, her approach to ensuring this authority and unity was to maintain a moderate form of Protestantism without demanding or making war on her subjects to ensure unity of faith, thereby indeed avoiding the turmoil that was then engulfing the continent.

Remarkably in an era of forceful intolerance, Elizabeth refused that any of her subjects be "molested by an inquisition or examination of their consciences in causes of religion"; she sought not to "make windows in men's souls."[115] Accordingly, she balanced appointments in church and state between Mary's Catholics and Edward's Protestants and combined Protestant doctrine with Catholic organization of the church. She even elided the title of "Supreme Head of the Church" with an ambivalent "etc." and declared herself instead "Supreme Governor" of the church in England, thereby giving Catholics some leeway to accept her as monarch. Simply put, and impressively so, under Elizabeth "there was no heresy-hunting, no Inquisition, no burnings."[116]

Relatively pragmatic regarding religion, Elizabeth was less tolerant regarding challenges to her own secular authority. Catholicism was permitted as belief, if not as more threatening public worship, and only so long as all laws were observed. As her successor would write, "the late Queen of famous memory, never punished any Papist for religion" but only for "their owne Misbehavior."[117] In this regard, her pragmatism was contrasted with the growing fanaticism of the French crown against the Huguenots, with Elizabeth claiming that all prosecutions of Papists were for treason and not heresy. But in an age when political and religious issues and authority were so intertwined, this distinction was not always clear. For instance, Elizabeth made it treasonable to deny her supreme authority or to bring any papal bulls into her realm, prosecuting priests thereby for acts that the sovereign saw as political but they no doubt saw as required by their religion.[118] When she ordered the 1585 expulsion of the Jesuits and priests owing primary allegiance to the pope, she did so arguing that they had come "of purpose not only to withdraw her Highness' subjects from their obedience to her Majesty but also to stir up and move sedition, rebellion, and open hostility within her Highness' realms and dominions . . . to the utter ruin, desolation and overthrow of the whole realm."[119]

Indeed, over the course of her reign, Elizabeth's official tolerance tilted toward anti-Catholicism. She was pushed in that direction by returning Marian exiles, though she consistently justified her actions on the basis of need to ensure authority rather than any Protestant religious fervor. Her 1559 Act of Supremacy mandated that anyone not swearing to the queen's primary authority would be ineligible for office or university degrees. Attendance at Anglican weekly services was mandatory. Use of the Book of Common Prayer was required to ensure "uniformity."[120] Recusants were ordered to stay within five miles of their home, so as to be better controlled.[121] Catholics were forced to answer "the Bloody Question" of whether they would support her majesty in the event of an invasion by the pope or his allies, with the wrong answer bringing dire consequences. Over a hundred priests were executed, still ostensibly for such treason rather than religion. Many followers of Rome felt compelled to hide their faith, as suggested by the false theory that Shakespeare himself was a crypto-Catholic.

But Elizabeth faced a two-front religiously inspired challenge to her authority, not only from Catholics but also from Protestant Puritans. In the "hot house" of exile in Germany and Switzerland during Mary's reign, Protestant nobles and commoners had learned to be and to defend their right as "free intellectuals." They criticized Henry VIII as having "cared for no manner of religion" and for imposing a purely secular Reformation, and they decried Mary as one of the "enemies unto God."[122] And having drafted their own church constitutions while in exile, they had learned to challenge royal authority more generally. Calvinism had taught them "to claim the right of participation," forgoing the "otherworldliness" of religion, and they brought these views back home with them after Mary. Elizabeth was thus faced with a growing Puritan movement that demanded "a new integration of private men into the political order," and which as such challenged the monarch's monopoly over that order.[123] In effect, the Puritan movement brought a new image of legitimacy and level of popular engagement with political power from below. This movement would grow in the decades to come and ultimately cohere the nation, not as loyal to the crown but instead in resistance to Elizabeth's successors.

But while Puritanism grew from below, the primary threat to Elizabeth remained Catholicism, with its challenge to the monarch orchestrated from Rome, including a papal blessing for invasion of Ireland. Already by 1570, only twelve years into her forty-five-year reign, Elizabeth had been excommunicated by the pope, as had her father before her.[124] Not surprisingly, the pope did not stint in challenging Elizabeth's secular power but also attacked her on religious grounds, describing her as "the pretended Queen of England and the servant of crime . . . having seized the crown and monstrously usurped the place of supreme head of the Church in all England . . . Prohibiting with a strong hand the use of the true religion." Even those who "dare obey her orders, mandates and laws . . . we include in the like sentence of excommunication," thereby effectively expelling the majority of Englishmen together with their queen.[125]

Pope Pius V's strong-arming forced English Catholics to choose between their religion and their sovereign, unintentionally pushing England and Elizabeth toward greater religious conformity under Protestantism. Schisms within Protestantism and its own challenges to the monarch would emerge more forcefully only later. In the meantime, the crown, the church, and the nation of England all coincided, all the more so for the peoples' support having helped to ensure that Elizabeth would be spared by Mary and allowed to come to rule. Later, as John Foxe would conclude, Elizabeth came to symbolize "the link and identity between the Protestant and national causes."[126] Even "by the time the Queen died, no good Englishman could have defined his national identity without some mention of his distaste for Rome."[127]

The shift from more evenhandedness toward anti-Catholicism was evident too in international relations. In the early years of her reign, Elizabeth entertained the possibilities of marriages to Catholic royals, building alliances with Spain or France, succeeded in 1560 at negotiating the removal of the French from Scotland, and enjoyed Spanish resistance to her excommunication.[128] But the French persecutions of the Huguenots and Spanish terror under Alba against Protestants in the Low Countries made a balanced approach difficult to maintain. Those difficulties were then exacerbated with the arrival in England in 1568 of Mary Queen of Scots, widow of the French king and rival for the English throne. By the time Mary was executed in 1587 and the Spanish Armada defeated the following year, England had clearly set itself off as the Protestant alternative to the continent's Catholic powers.

International tensions further fanned English nationalism, which in turn fanned further tensions. Conflict would arise again in Ireland, reaffirming the complicating factor of relations within the British Isles, which would become potentially explosive in regard to Scotland. In the decade after the armada, Shakespeare's historical plays took a distinctively nationalist turn in glorifying England, reflecting popular trends. And already by 1589, Elizabeth was sending 35,000 pounds and a small army to bolster the hold on the French crown of the lapsed Protestant Henri IV, whose financial needs were evident in his reputation among his own troops for not being able to pay their salaries.[129]

It is the episode of Mary Queen of Scots that makes most explicit Elizabeth's travails, bringing together international and domestic issues. As the daughter of Scotland's James V and widow of the French king, Mary Stuart was the Catholic alternative to Elizabeth as England's monarch, recognized as the legitimate heir by the pope. And she was certainly eager to gain that throne, entertaining possibilities of assistance from France or Spain or domestic plots against her royal cousin, while duplicitously maintaining cordial relations with Elizabeth. England's Protestant majority was reasonably distrustful of this foreign Catholic schemer close at hand, all the more so after Mary was rumored to have arranged for the murder of her own husband, Darnley. Elizabeth still resisted popular pressure to eliminate this imminent threat to her throne, refusing to call Parliament when she knew it would demand execution.

But Mary was eventually caught by her own devices. For instance, evidence of her plotting against Elizabeth providentially blew back onto a ship from which it had been thrown. Thousands of English subjects signed the Bond of Association, swearing to resist any efforts at Mary's usurpation of the crown and celebrating the arrest of Mary's conspirators. Mary refused to recognize this popular resistance to her as "the true voice of the nation," continuing in her scheming until Elizabeth was forced to agree to her execution.[130] Again, it was the combined international and domestic threats of Mary's loyalty to the pope and her conspiracy against the crown and tranquility of the realm that led to her demise, not her religion per se.

Elizabeth's retained hold on the crown and her increasingly anti-Catholic drift were perhaps connected, but at least part of her strategy created uncertainties as to royal succession. The queen had refused to marry and thereby ensure the continuation of her line. She had been pressed to use a wedding to cement a continental alliance but had seen how the prior Queen Mary's tie to Philip of Spain had undermined popular support and fed uncertainties about the true "Englishness" of the royal. Her proposed marriage to the Austrian Archduke Charles was opposed by Leicester and others, ostensibly because of the Archdukes's Catholicism, and later a proposed match with the French heir Alençon was widely decried for threatening to bring "wildfire that all the seas could not quench."[131] Elizabeth preferred the flexibility of "virginal" spinsterhood, playing up and off possible alliances without being tied to any. But the result of neutral spinsterhood was the lack of an heir, raising the possibility of Mary's succession and the certain end of the Tudor line. As Elizabeth approached the close of her long realm, the succession was smoothed to the Stuart king of Scotland, bringing to the throne of England the son of the half-French Catholic Mary Queen of Scots, who was executed by the Protestant Queen Elizabeth and who had herself been spared by her Catholic half sister "Bloody" Queen Mary.

Before its end, Elizabeth's reign thus demonstrates that increasing state centralization and consolidation were challenged by related religious, international and personal tensions that had to be managed from above. While Elizabeth was largely successful at defeating these challenges, the English populace was rousing itself in a way that would later pose greater problems for her successors. Horrified by Mary's victims, Protestantism had become politicized in resistance and in exile. And then faith was further engaged and merged with politics, albeit initially in support of Elizabeth against Catholic threats, foreign and domestic, and notably within the British Isles. But the rising mass engagement inspired by religion and opposition to the pope's authority already showed signs of freeing itself from royal control or obedience. After all, it had emerged in opposition to Mary, a monarch who had tried to enforce a "foreign" religion, and would again unify in such opposition.

These western European experiences provide a benchmark to begin our analysis of early modern processes of state- and nation-building. In the late fifteenth and sixteenth centuries in Spain, France, and England, centralized states were being consolidated by monarchs seeking to gain power over local lords. Pressures for such centralization came from at least three fronts. The interest in removing or resisting foreign incursions, or international war more generally, required stronger states able to draw revenues to raise armies, with a ratchet effect retaining gains in this direction in the aftermath of actual or threatened conflict. Albeit with dramatic differences of economic development, increased capitalist activity both made resources for war more readily available and began to provide incentives for central authority able to manage such growth and contain internal tensions that might hamper it. And last, monarchs themselves had an interest in gaining further power and resources, or at least in containing threats to their power.

The early imperatives for state-building brought increased interest in forging popular allegiance, or at least obedience, though this imperative was initially muted and certainly lagged behind institutional consolidation of power. Emergent states showed some signs of an interest in popular loyalty, if only minimally to ensure stable rule. Elites needed sufficient legitimacy to draw armies and revenues and to contain conflict, but these processes remained as undeveloped as did state legitimacy. These internal conflicts, when they flared up, remained largely focused on local resistance to increased central authority. Nationalism per se remained weak, and conflicts were not yet consolidated into larger factions that might have been merged.

As with nationalism itself, literacy and economic development were as yet nascent, though there are indications that the emergence of these social developments was not foreseen by elites as necessarily promising cohesion. Emerging economic interests threatened to be divisive, with monarchs attempting to direct such interests to bolster their own authority, as with England's distribution of church wealth to its nobility. Linguistic diversity remained, with printing in the vernacular only beginning. And such printing and the spread of literacy was eyed warily by monarchs concerned about the possibility of its fanning discord more than bolstering cohesion, evident in royal limits and licenses.

The one potential basis for mass cohesion was religion, the legacy of a spirituality that until the French religious wars and Mary in England had remained largely a localized social bond. Except for resident nonbelievers, many of whom would be forced to leave or convert, the people of Spain and France had Catholicism in common. But as long as it remained a relatively unchallenged unity of faith, that unity remained largely concerned with matters of faith and not with power politics. Even England's Reformation, significant as it was in setting the stage for later developments, did not in itself engage the populace on a wide scale, albeit with some local protests crushed.

This initial lack of both secular nationalism and large-scale religious fervor were connected. Compared to what would come after, there was as no major, popular religious discord within Christendom that would inflame passions and direct those into politics, for or against the state. Ironically, the relative unity of religion meant that it was not engaged as a widespread political force that could have provided a basis for more political unity. Allegiance to God did not ensure allegiance to state. Only for the elites—crown and nobles—were the more institutional concerns and interests of church and state intertwined and contested. For most people, these contests were distant and of little concern, except as elites raised armies to fight their conflicts.

Politics then remained largely an issue of the upper crust, whose conflicts remained the stuff of the histories of the period and from which most people simply hoped to remain distant. The masses were not yet present on the historical stage in force. And with the majority so disengaged, nationalism was at most an inchoate idea and not yet a widespread social force. Centralization of rule proceeded more unilaterally from above.

Rising absolutism then brought forth a gathering storm of conflict, challenging state power. As power was more centralized it was also more shaken, with the populace becoming more directly engaged in disputes over power. Monarchs seeking to retain or increase their power were confronted by the reality that to consolidate the power of their state institutions also required building the loyalty of their followers, certainly among the nobility and to some extent beyond. But rather than enjoy cohesion, rulers increasingly faced challenges, exploding into civil war in France while more contained by shifting royal policies in England. This distinction in itself suggests more consolidated central power and a seemingly more loyal nobility in England. But England's relative civil tranquility also reflected the comparative lack of a religious schism pitting nobles against crown because of the way in which Reformation had initially tied the crown and nobility together. And by final contrast, Spain saw regional resistance but no comparable internal religious disputes, beyond its expulsion of Jews, Moors, and conversos. I will return to Spain, but now let us consider the implications of the more directly comparable French and English experiences.

In France, the challenge of rising discord and the imperative to bolster central power was confronted more starkly than in England. French royal power was held less surely by the unexpected succession of younger and weaker kings facing challenges from a nobility both seeking advantage in this weakness and itself divided by religious disputes. In contrast, England's monarchs governed with a surer hand, but in doing so also pulled the country in shifting directions of religion and international alliances. There, the nobility remained more unified in its self-interested Protestantism, reinforcing antagonism against the Catholic Mary but then consolidating the rule of her Protestant successors. The English crown thus remained stronger than the French, though that crown itself wavered in its religion with different occupants, finally enforcing Protestantism amid limited tolerance afforded by a stronger hold on power. In other words, rising religious disputes contributed to and demonstrated a weakening of the French crown more than the English, though in both managing such disputes was a major preoccupation of monarchs.

Different forms of conflict in both France and England brought mass engagement onto the political stage, though also in varying forms and levels. In France, this rising popular engagement fed division. Loyal to competing noble factions and religions, the French populace joined the fight with the dramatic violence of civil war. In Paris, the focal point of such engagement, the populace was frequently whipped into anti-Huguenot fervor that later coincided with loyalty to the crown as it moved in the same direction. In England, rising popular engagement was more unifying. In London in particular, mobs joined in attacks on Catholics during Mary's reign and thereafter, and then celebrated the emerging anti-Catholicism of her successors. Their engagement was reinforced by xenophobia and resentment of the pope, whose excommunication of Elizabeth and any who obeyed her effectively further unified popular support. Thus, while popular religious fervor fed by dispute further divided France, comparable religious fervor among the English brought them together toward an early nationalism merged with Protestantism.

And in both France and England, rising literacy and more mass communication bolstered popular engagement, though not necessarily with unifying effects. Preaching and pamphlets building the loyalty of Catholic and Protestant factions exacerbated discord in France more than it forged a unified "imagined community." In England, even more widespread communication had the opposite effect. The vernacular bible spread a sense of community, while Foxe's widely distributed diatribe against Papists and dire reminders of Mary's victims further forged Protestant unity. Even still, elites feared that the cost of such engagement through literacy would be anarchy. According to Dryden:

The Book thus put in every vulgar hand,
With each presumed he best could understand,
The Common rule was made the common prey
And at the mercy of the rabble lay.[132]

Literacy then had either a divisive or unifying tendency depending on the context and purposes to which it was applied.

The different levels of factionalization also relate to the question of memory and forgetting in this period. Torn by violent internal conflict and civil war, French authorities were early on committed to selective forgetting, mandating that memory of past conflict be abolished every time peace was fitfully restored. When engaged in peace, the monarchs understood that memory was an enemy, for it kept alive antagonism. By contrast, England's monarchs were more committed to retaining memory as a basis of unity. Elizabeth in particular understood the value of reminding her subjects of the threat of Papist plots and violence, in order to cohere unity. It was not an accident that she permitted the distribution of Foxe's history that was dedicated to her and that France had no comparably seminal and widely distributed recent history.

What then of Spain? There, significant regional and economic tensions emerged but did not explode as fully as elsewhere. Enjoying relative religious homogeneity, at least within the core constituency of believers, there emerged no comparable internal conflict nor a popular engagement fed by such conflict. Instead, official Spain's attention was increasingly drawn—or diluted—by the external interests of empire, a source of pride but also enervating of popular engagement and unity. As we shall see, the notable and dramatic exception to this outward focus and relative lack of religiously reinforced fanaticism was the inquisition.

We can then already see the emergence of telling similarities and differences in the consolidation of popular political identities and engagement, and these would set the stage for nationalizing possibilities to match or challenge centralizing state power. In France, where religious disputes and contests for political power were quickly merged and exploded into mass conflict, popular identities and political engagement were solidified as a result, though these exacerbated conflict rather than inspiring unifying cohesion. Popular participation in the religious wars is dramatic evidence of these developments. The English populace was less divided by religious passions and political power more firmly held by the crown, though that crown itself wavered in its religious impositions. The result was less conflict and possibly less popular engagement, or certainly less factionalization thereof, as evident in the lack of anything comparable to the French religious wars. And foreign relations reinforced English popular unity, for instance against Rome for excommunicating Elizabeth. By contrast again, Spain's populace remained more regionally focused and was less broadly engaged, neither whipped into fervor by internal religious schism nor as unified by foreign relations but instead distracted by imperial expansion. The initial result was the greatest degree of popular engagement in France (albeit divisive), less active engagement but more unity in England, and relatively little such engagement in Spain.

FOUNDING EXCLUSIONS

"Presences that Passion, Piety or Affection Knows"

3

State-building requires nation-building—at a minimum the containment or avoidance of civil war and conflict threatening the existence of the state, and beyond that to ensure obedience, tax compliance, or military service necessary for governance. Even federated states face these pragmatic requirements. Early aspirants to absolutist rule—and their opponents or competitors—gradually came to understand and acted upon this imperative for cohesion to make their authority effective and legitimate. Under their rule, institutional state power had become increasingly centralized, but further consolidation of that state power required engagement and support by the populace. To so tie elites and the masses emerged as a central political dilemma, with states then having relatively little capacity for achieving this goal. And this dilemma was not solved by spreading literacy or economic development, for these were both undeveloped and at least as divisive as unifying of the populace.

Ironically, consolidation of large-scale states heightens the imperative for popular cohesion but also makes such cohesion less likely. With the incorporation of more diverse peoples and greater centralized political power, that power is often fought over or resisted. In all three leading countries of western Europe, early modern monarchs faced substantial challenges to their authority, with the conflict over growing state power coming to a head. Spain had been rocked by local resistance fed by continued regional dispersion of power and loyalty. France was divided by noble factions competing for power and aligned to different faiths, exploding in the religious wars. England's crown was stronger after Reformation but was troubled by uncertainties of succession also inflamed by religion. The only powerful basis of mass engagement and potential cohesion then existent was religion, but as this form of collective sentiment became less localized or otherworldly, it became increasingly divisive. Rulers and others then faced the challenge and the possibility of turning faith into a basis for secular allegiance and somehow directing the passions unleashed by religious conflict into a basis for equally passionate but more unified support for or against state power.

Given such discord, centralizing allegiance could not be reinforced inclusively nor directly. And so, an indirect mechanism for channeling popular loyalty would be employed, bringing religious passions and identities thus consolidated into the service of absolutism—or its opponents. Political actors learned that exclusion of a group could serve to unify and cohere a sufficient core constituency to preserve the state and make it governable. Those seeking to consolidate centralized rule or to replace it might then pursue their own passions and interests in gaining popular support by embracing, exacerbating, or manipulating some form of cultural prejudice against an "out group" whose exclusion would unify a core. Then, strategy and prejudice would coincide to produce exclusive unity, pursued in a manner that linked state authorities (or pretenders) with the populace—thus the foundation of nationalism.

To consolidate their power and make governance possible and effective, elites embraced rising mass passions by encoding discriminatory laws enforcing those passions and cohering their supporters. In doing so, elites indulged their own passions. What Yeats described as the "presences that passion, piety or affection knows" threatened the established order to varying degrees and then was turned into a tool for reinforcing affection for that order or for reformulating it.[1]

In general terms, that states or their opponents accommodated mass passions, excluding one category of people to unify others in support, cannot in itself account for which group or category is so engaged. State elites or others may "piggyback" or "free ride" on social cleavages or prejudices that elites might share, using tradition as a resource in order to organize and utilize bias.[2] But in doing so elites must select among a variety of groups to subject to exclusion.[3] Passionate cleavages and exclusion on the basis of religion were not a foregone conclusion for either elites or the populace.

Rational choice and coalition theories suggest a possible answer as to why a particular group becomes the target of selective exclusion: alliances may be shaped by the imperative for establishing a coalition of minimum size necessary to win privileges, thereby ensuring that maximum benefits will be shared as narrowly as possible.[4] But individuals are not purely rational free agents able and willing to change and barter loyalties. Historically informed ideology or prejudice, or the "embeddedness" of identities, pose a constraint on viable coalitions.[5] The deeper the ideological or identity cleavage that emerges, the more a winning coalition will be determined by efforts to minimize such differences rather than being determined by minimum size. Background conditions shape the strategic perception of elites or commoners about what is rational, limiting the possible choices and bargains at moments of high tension. Thus, exclusionary outcomes are shaped by a combination of "rational" and historically determined calculations.

Such a schematic argument can be specified. Nationalizing states inherit and are faced with the legacies of prejudice or growing internal antagonisms, with such constraints on unified rule creating an imperative for state action. States or others may then act to purposefully exclude a category of people, with the result of encouraging the unity and allegiance of a core, forging a nation defined by those included. The particular category employed reflects the historical legacies of antagonism that posed the problem of internal discord, with an image of the past imposed on the present.[6] That past cleavage enforced and encouraging selective unity depends upon historical experience, ideology, and narratives informing impassioned and strategic debates among elites about what form of exclusion will heal pressing internal conflict within a core judged indispensable. Precisely because we are not all "geldings," as Gellner would have us cut off from our past, bias from our past could be reworked to shape exclusive nationalism.[7]

When a potential core constituency is divided by antagonism blocking essential national unity, exclusion according to that category of antagonism can be encoded to overcome that constraint and to selectively unify a core. The form of exclusion used to build national cohesion must then have sufficient torque to unify those key constituents otherwise in conflict or even at war with each other. In early modern Europe, religious exclusion had tremendous and unequalled torque, especially as directed against heretics found within. Such domestic antagonism was used accordingly as the basis of nationalism, cutting against regional or social divides. Minimizing coalition size was not determinant; building a workable coalition that was enforced by prejudice was. Institutional and selective nationalism then reified the category of exclusion, reinforcing assumptions or aspersions of difference. The result was an institutionalized coalition piggybacking on culture.[8]

Such exclusion occurs when a polity is threatened or divided, with solidarity potentially reinforced by distancing from or exclusion of an "other," whether that process is intentionally designed or discovered through trial and error. And once such a demarcation is reinforced, it becomes self-fulfilling in preserving the social order.[9] The conviction of difference may be socially constructed, but "in their effects they are real; this is the power of primordial arguments."[10] Informed by prejudice, interest groups manipulate culture to solve basic organizational problems and thereby achieve stability in which their interests can be met.[11]

Critics object that in such a supposedly "neo-primordialism" approach "the bedrock of essentialism is left intact."[12] But I am suggesting that while elites share and are constrained by popular beliefs, they then simplify, distort, and select among such beliefs to serve the purpose of unifying a core group.[13] Primordial imagery is not ascriptive but is what gives power to this process. That such prejudice or primordial imagery is contested or constructed does not diminish its power. Instead it is the image of such prejudice coming out of the past that ensures its salience and gives to elites such a powerful tool. In terms of the psychology of scapegoating, it is what makes the subject group "visible" and all the more vulnerable.[14] This argument explicitly borrows from and refines both cultural and instrumental approaches to explaining the particular group excluded to forge unity.

Culturalists argue that inherited or evolving meanings and beliefs about primordial ancestry and linkages have determined national units.[15] Even Karl Marx acknowledged that "the tradition of all the dead generations weighs like a nightmare on the brains of the living."[16] However, ideas that appear to come to us from the past change, as do their uses, and such change cannot be explained by some seemingly unchanging inheritance. Culture itself varies, and such variation cannot be explained by reference to only culture itself. For instance, religious identifications changed and were subject to varying forms of manipulation, either heightening or containing division, and therefore they were not fixed attributes determining outcomes. What was believed at the time to be primordial was not.

Instrumentalists build upon this critique, countering that tradition and belief are merely a resource for strategic calculations of interest. They reject cultural approaches as essentialism for implying an unchanging nature, and they focus instead on how different views are strategically pursued or enhanced for narrow advantage.[17] But beliefs and collectivities often persist even when they become costly rather than profitable.[18] Or, more fundamentally, basing analysis on rational calculations of interest takes for granted the preferences so acted upon. Such analysis ironically bends back toward primordialism in assuming that preferences are somehow historically fixed and knowable, as "comfortable."[19]

Rather than reject either form of argument, I prefer to use and combine aspects of both so as to account for varying motivations. Cultural and historically informed identities constrain and identify strategic options, foreclosing and disclosing possibilities at any time. Put differently, culture produces preferences that are then acted upon via rational calculation, or identities make some outcomes more likely.[20] Choice is conceived and interpreted according to past history.[21] As Thomas Schelling has argued, the coordination of such choices rests upon signaling and convergence, and that signaling often rests on prominent focal points.[22] Cultural and historical inheritances, such as religious faith, can provide such visible focal points as a crutch for coordination in its particular political form of nationalism. Religious sentiments are inherited from the past but then may change or be used selectively, with both elites and masses combining cultural vehemence with strategic action. Nationalism, or that sentiment that links mass engagement to elite controlled (or sought) institutional power, would then be a primary site for such combined motivation.

Those seeking greater popular allegiance and obedience to the state (or opposition to it), facing the imperative to build toward national cohesion, often found that amid conflict they could not do so easily or inclusively. They then fitfully embraced the logic of bolstering selective unity via exclusion, learning to focus that exclusion on heretics found within, resolving conflict accordingly. And to many at particular times, such sentiment felt "natural." Nationalism thus began to emerge by piggybacking on the passion of religious conflicts, which thereby cohered a core religious faith in the secular realm. Religion, both conflicts over it and exclusions accordingly, was then central to early nation-building as the most prominent collective sentiment or "focal point" of allegiance.

The sixteenth and seventeenth centuries saw the development of such efforts to gain popular support and bolster or reconfigure authority that used religious exclusion as its crutch. Implemented earlier by the somewhat weaker crown, Spain's inquisition against Jews, Moors, and conversos bolstered centralized institutional power and revenues while building a modicum of popular unity based on Catholic fanaticism. In France, religious passions emerged more from below, though fanned by noble factions and then embraced by the crown using antagonism against Huguenots to bolster its own position. And in England, the earlier elite-orchestrated Reformation solidified Protestantism led by the crown, with threats to that unity then turned by the populace against the crown as infected by popery. Particularly in France and England, religious passion informed and enflamed popular engagement, forging increasing cohesion based on sectarian fanaticism rather than civic inclusion. And in those cases, passions exploded from below and were directed against a present "other" found within, reinforcing popular engagement and cohesion more than would the top-down exclusion of heretics in Spain.

It is important to add that such victimization and scapegoating within was often tied to foreign antagonisms. International tensions reinforced internal exclusions, for instance, with those insiders suspected of being aligned with foreign enemies and heretics therefore being more likely subjects of internal exclusion. Amid overlapping international conflicts and internal divisions, rulers might then embrace one religious faction as opposed to another seen as traitorously linked by faith to outside adversaries. Thus, religious zeal could be tied to emerging national coherence, reinforced by international exposures and distrust. According to Wordsworth, "I travelled among unknown men, / In lands beyond the sea; / Nor, England! did I know till then / What love I bore to thee." The same logic could and was then applied domestically. What Kipling would call the "stranger within my gate" could be used to bind "men of my own stock" so demarcated.[23]

Instances of merged foreign and domestic antagonisms abound in the cases and period here discussed, mutually reinforcing emerging national solidarities, though there are also counterexamples. Spanish Catholics were united against North African Moors, Jews, and foreign Protestants, the latter including the rebellious Dutch. French Catholics were united against both Huguenots and English Protestants. English Protestants were united in turn against the French Catholics, especially during the conflicts of 1689–1815, though there remains disagreement among historians about whether this antagonism focused on the adversary's being foreign or of another faith. Certainly, English antagonism against Irish Catholics, fed by ongoing conflict, rumors of Irish plots, and the threat of Catholic incursions into England through the "back door" of Ireland, fed anti-Catholicism as both a domestic and foreign issue.[24] English politics was often so played out in Ireland. But in an era of shifting alliances, this pattern of coinciding internal and foreign antagonism was also contradicted, notably with the wars between France and Spain. Still, antagonism against a religion within and without did often coincide. And internal religious antagonisms and exclusions aimed at cohering domestic unity also enflamed international relations between countries with different official religions, though again with notable exceptions.

While international disputes significantly reinforced early efforts at internal nation-building through exclusion, I will seek to demonstrate that the imperative to resolve internal discord was more determinant of those efforts. Rulers came to understand that they could not effectively wage war or diplomacy if they were weakened within by civil or religious conflict, could not then recruit troops, be sure that those troops would remain loyal, and avoid challenges from a "third column" tied to external enemies. As we shall see, to avoid such difficulties and gain strength, monarchs sought to build national unity and loyalty through domestic religious exclusion. Activists from below did likewise. International antagonisms or exclusion of "foreigners" by themselves would not prove as binding within. Unity via exclusion of a group within would prove more popularly salient and effective, with antagonism against an internal enemy providing a more present and ongoing social glue.[25] In addition, given shifting international alliances and conflicts, we cannot assume that such foreign antagonisms by themselves were constant or that they determined the basis for internal loyalty and cohesion.

For all their differences, in these three countries a somewhat similar pattern began to emerge, forging mass identity and engagement from two different directions. Faith was becoming politicized, informing, and informed by mass identifications solidified all the more where conflict raged. And from the other direction, state authorities or their opponents sought to harness or channel those identifications toward more secular aims of holding or gaining power and popular support. These two processes would converge, in explosions of exclusionary cohesion. This conversion of mass and elite passions and interests would prove more or less effective in binding early national unity and would then later take different directions, in part dependent on whether popular engagement emerged more from below or was orchestrated from above. To begin with Spain, top-down efforts at exclusion would help to consolidate state rule but proved insufficient to forge matching domestic popular cohesion.

⫸ Spain: Authority by Inquisition

Efforts to solidify institutional power came early in Spain, begun already in the fifteenth century. With the marriage of the monarchs ruling over the two largest kingdoms, a more unified Spanish state came into existence. But that state continued to be threatened by civil conflict and by competing local authorities. To further build state power from above required greater subordination of the populace and a redirection of its loyalties toward the center. The Catholic faith provided one means of encouraging unity, although such unity was precluded by the presence of non-Catholics. But within such religious diversity was the possibility of its partial resolution.

The "problem" of religious diversity could be turned to advantage by elites building unity among Catholics and against others. Often Jews or converts were described as separate, alien, or enemy "nations," implying some unity of everyone else sharing "blood relationship . . . habit of unity" or faith. "To be sure, in the middle of the fifteenth century, Spain's national consciousness was still half awake . . . Nevertheless, it was groping for national identity. . . . A drive toward unification [came], along with demands for separation and exclusion." The result was a conflated and "obsessive concern with purity of the faith . . . with purity of blood."[26] This combination would conveniently lump together Jews and conversos as aliens in blood and race, distinguished from the "true" Catholics so unified.

The potentially binding antagonism against the Jews and conversos, was based on anti-Semitism against Europe's then largest domestic population of Jews. This hatred was linked to the image of difference and foreignness, itself connoting enmity reinforced by early Jewish cooperation with Moorish invaders.[27] But actually, it was the integration and loyalty of the Jews that was more apparent. Jews had long served as tax collectors and advisors and in other roles associated with royal finance, loyally serving the crown and seen as protected by it.[28] Such cooperation with the efforts to build state power, combined with relative wealth, helps to explain the popular hatred of the Jews, especially among the lower classes. This is not to suggest that those poorer Spaniards somehow demanded the Inquisition,[29] but it does suggest that the Inquisition's persecution of Jews or those popularly seen as associated with Jews might build upon popular antagonism and potentially redirect mass passions away from antistate toward pro-state sentiment. And to so reinforce its authority, the religiously inspired crown was perfectly willing to turn against its own previously loyal non-Catholic subjects.

The binding effects of anti-Semitism had long gained momentum as a social force, significantly predating the formal Inquisition. Already in 1212, Christian midwives were forbidden to attend to Jewish women in labor; in 1320 Jews were massacred in Aragon; and in 1371 Henry II of Castile ordered that all Jews (and Moors) wear a red circle badge on their left shoulder to mark them apart.[30] Panic over the plague and jealousy over wealth exploded into anti-Jewish riots in Castile, Catalonia, and Aragon in 1391.[31] Those riots and plagues had a particularly significant impact, reducing the Jewish population by a third and establishing a future pattern with the conversion of the chief rabbi of Burgos, who would become himself a leading anti-Semite as Paul de Burgos. In 1405 the separation of Jews was supplemented by harsher restrictions. The requirement that Jews wear badges was further enforced. Castile in 1412 formally excluded Jews from holding office, changing homes, engaging in certain trading, bearing arms, or hiring or eating with Christians. Anti-Jewish and anticonverso riots in Toledo in 1449 led to torture-induced confessions, property seizures, and the passage of laws requiring "purity of blood" to hold municipal office, thereby also excluding conversos.[32]

But with anti-Semitism as long-standing in Spain as elsewhere in Europe, this sentiment in itself cannot explain such an explosion of vindictiveness against them as the Inquisition in Spain in the late fifteenth century. Jews had been similarly excluded elsewhere—for instance, by inquisition and then expulsion in France and by expulsion in England in the thirteenth century, with anti-Semitism somewhat dissipating in those countries thereafter.

Why did anti-Semitism remain so strong in Spain? The most obvious explanation is that, unlike in France and England, in Spain the Jews remained present as domestic targets of antagonism in a period when state consolidation had proceeded far enough to indulge and channel such antagonism. What was particular to that time and place was the coming to power of Ferdinand and Isabella as joined monarchs, who would come to see the possible advantage to their state in institutionalizing this still vibrant anti-Semitism.

Spain's Jews expected just the opposite effect. Indeed, Jews had pressed for the royal marriage, believing that Ferdinand would ensure tolerance, given his (and later Isabella's) reliance on Jewish doctors and financiers and, astonishingly in retrospect, the king's supposedly own partial Jewish ancestry.[33] These were false hopes, for as Charles Henry Lea suggests, "the record of the time is one of the foulest of treachery," including the unproven accusation that both Ferdinand and Isabella gained their crowns as the result of each of their elder brothers being poisoned.[34] Alleged fratricide was a better indication of what was to come than were expectations of tolerance.

To impose order and combat heresy, Ferdinand and Isabella concluded that they needed a "more compact and centralized organization ... reducing to order the chaos resulting from the virtual anarchy of the preceding reigns."[35] As a result, the Inquisition would become the only tribunal or institution of any sort with authority over the still legally distinct monarchies of Spain. Indeed, by 1483 the Inquisition was governed by a new royal council, known as la Suprema, and administered by an inquisitor general, "the only individual in the peninsula [including the monarchs] whose writ extended over all of Spain." When Ferdinand died in 1516, it was the then inquisitor-general who temporarily held governing powers in the absence of the royal successor. By the end of the sixteenth century, the Inquisition's own roster of officials had grown considerably.[36]

Not only was the Inquisition itself the holder of tremendous centralized power; it also lent that power to further bolster the monarchical state that controlled it. "The Inquisition was the most effective instrument for subjugating to the crown all the subjects, in particular the nobility and the clergy, and completing the absolute power of the monarch ... by tightening the bonds that had just united the discordant provinces."[37]

In short, while Lea argues that there were no "political purposes" to the Inquisition and that its initiation was postponed for lack of centralizing authority, instead the Inquisition helped to build such authority.[38] This result may not have been fully foreseen or purposeful, but it was nonetheless significant and evident in retrospect. What apparently began more as an official exercise of antiheretical religious activism encouraged by the church had major political consequences. No less an analyst than Machiavelli himself noted that the "fame and glory ... and achievements" of Ferdinand, increasing "his standing and his control," were accomplished under "the cloak of religion ... a pious work of cruelty" used to keep "his subjects in a state of suspense and wonder."[39]

There remained resistance to the centralizing effects of Inquisition, but the power of that Inquisition was itself turned into an instrument against such local discord. Catalonia, for instance, had a long history of resisting the Inquisition's legal centralization and its use of Castilian, a "foreign" dialect, as did other regions that similarly resisted all such forms of centralization. To stabilize and consolidate power and to contain civil wars and regional conflicts, the monarchs "accepted an alliance with social forces" embedded in the Inquisition. For instance, in Castile "the appearance of the inquisitors was made possible because Isabella's supporters in the civil wars imposed their authority on the local elite." Where internal discord was high and central authority low, the Inquisition would become most active and feared, meeting what was seen as "national emergency." Indeed, there was a recurring coincidence of Inquisition with "attempts to gain political control after the chaos of the civil wars. [Ferdinand's] constant emphasis on the need for the Inquisition was clear Realpolitik."[40]

The Inquisition thus became a tool for building centralized state authority. This political use of the Inquisition arguably began with the granting in 1478 by the pope to the Spanish monarchs the power of appointment of priests as inquisitors, and later even of bishops. Two years later, the monarchs created the first of the Inquisition's tribunals to hear cases of "heretical depravity." And in 1483 Ferdinand and Isabella appointed the infamous Torquemada as inquisitor general over both Aragon and Castile. The final impetus came in 1485 when the Aragonese inquisitor, Arbues, was assassinated, allegedly by conversos, while kneeling in church, letting loose a torrent of anticonverso fervor that further strengthened the crown's hold over the process. Indeed, some analysts have suggested that the murder of Arbues was plotted by the monarchs to justify their control.[41] Regardless, the result was to reinforce royal authority over and through the Inquisition, "to forge the unity of the state" and of its subjects, curtailing dissent and overcoming feudal divisions.[42]

Consistent with such state-building, the Inquisition also became a source of further revenue collection. To an extent, such revenue gathering was in the narrow institutional interests of the Inquisition itself, for instance to pay the considerable expense of staging the spectacles of *auto de fé*. This narrow use gradually gave way to further state demands, for instance with revenues from the Inquisition of Valencia in 1486 used to pay for the fleet sent to Italy. Thus, the Inquisition helped to finance state power; confiscation of the riches of the Jews and conversos was an attractive means to augment a royal treasury depleted by war. Contemporary officials denied such crass motivation, lamenting "the harm and ill that could . . . affect our taxes and revenues," though they so protested too much. To the contrary, the Inquisition was generally a lucrative enterprise, with contemporaries noting that its victims "were burnt only for the money they had . . . they burn only the well-off." Or, in the even more colorful expression, "It is the goods that are the heretics," returned forcibly to the fold of the church.[43]

Indeed, the Inquisition as a source of revenues eventually brought criticism from unexpected quarters. By the time the Inquisition started exhuming corpses in order to try the deceased as heretics and thereby legally seize their estates, the revenue-gathering seemed to get out of hand. Already by 1482, the pope astonishingly concluded that "the Inquisition has for some time been moved not by zeal for the faith and salvation of souls, but by greed." The king continued to argue fatuously that despite "all the harm that might result to Our royal rights and revenues," he would continue to "place the service of Our Lord God before our own . . . all other interests put aside."[44] But this persistence of the king also placed him in opposition to the general direction of church policy. Papal orders and secular laws barred discrimination against converts so as to encourage further conversions extending the faith, but this was ignored. The focus on blood purity justified action against conversos as descendents of Jews, given that the Jews themselves were legally beyond the reach of an Inquisition to cleanse the Catholic faith only. And those conversos were also resented for their relative wealth and for the high social positions they had attained.[45]

Looking inward, the Inquisition became a tool for spreading centralized power; but looking outward it also became the basis for asserting domestic independence against papal authority. Ferdinand and Isabella set out to establish their autonomous hold over the Inquisition, disputing with the pope along the way and "habitually jealous of papal encroachments." By 1501 the king would declare about the Inquisition, "in fact it is all ours," signaling both autonomy and a growing assertion of the right to the "management of its own affairs." The related royal power to appoint all bishops was won in 1523.[46]

Begun as an expression of faith, the Inquisition then had bolstered centralizing power within the state and demarcated that power from foreign intervention, but it had also contributed to a limited assertion of early nationalism beyond these institutional forms. To exercise centralized and autonomous power, the monarchs needed the support of the commoners, in particular the urban masses who might otherwise be well positioned to rebel. Popular sentiment would have to be turned toward greater loyalty to the center, and the religious aspects of Inquisition provided a potential basis for this process. As fervent Catholics, Ferdinand and Isabella envisioned that "the nation be united in faith," though in reality "over much of Spain Christianity was still only a veneer."[47] In addition, not all in Spain could be so united in faith, even if they were ardent, as not all in Spain were of the same faith. To unify the core of Catholics, "others" would be excluded.

The imperative for unity through faith came to a climax with the single most dramatic episode of exclusion, the expulsion of Spain's Jews in 1492. Of the roughly 80,000 Jews then in the country, half refused to convert and were forced to sell their property for next to nothing and flee into a "pilgrimage of grief," subject to robbery and murder along the way.[48] The king himself wrote that he had been persuaded to expel the Jews because "Christians are endangered by contact . . . and we do so despite the great harm to ourselves, seeking and preferring the salvation of souls above our own profit." Indeed, expulsion of some of the richest people in Spain would seem to contradict the state's immediate self-interest, suggesting a greater passion or interest in achieving unity even at some financial cost. Modern analysts have disagreed about that cost, suggesting that revenue from taxing the Jews was less needed after the recapture of Granada or that expelling the Jews provided resources that helped to pay for that reconquest.[49]

Regardless of the immediate financial implications, there is no disagreement on the political benefits of the expulsion. The order for Jews to leave "had laid the foundations for a unitary state . . . [and] helped impose a unity which transcended administrative, linguistic, and cultural barriers, bringing together Spaniards of all races in common furtherance of a holy mission." Even Pope Alexander VI was impressed, granting to Ferdinand and Isabella the title of "Catholic Kings" in recognition of services, including this expulsion.[50]

As the institution of the crown and of the Inquisition came under stress, the impetus to further bolster central authority and to seek unity through exclusionary racial or religious purity remained. With Isabella's death in 1504, the union of the kingdoms came apart, as Castile was inherited as a separate kingdom by the incompetent Infanta Juana and her incapable foreign husband. The Inquisition also was divided by kingdoms, at least from 1507 until 1518.[51] But these institutional difficulties in no way dampened enthusiasm for exclusion, which was reinforced when in 1497 many Jews who had fled to Portugal returned (when Portugal also required conversion) and again with the demand for conversion of Mudejares in 1525–1526. Indeed, by the 1540s "the movement in favor of racial purity only gathered real momentum" particularly in the bitterly divided city of Toledo, where rival factions used accusations of impurity to gain power.[52] Before then, centralized power had been restored by the again united crown and Inquisition.

By the mid-sixteenth century, the inquisition had effectively contributed to the efforts of Spain's monarchs to reinforce their institutional power and their popular legitimacy. The inquisitors' countrywide authority had bolstered and unified the still divided royal authority of the kingdoms, providing resources along the way that were used for further assertions of royal power. Internal conflict had been more contained and, unlike elsewhere, no king was assassinated nor was there any religiously inspired dynastic conflict. The Inquisition's attacks on heretics had begun to solidify the popular unity of Spaniards, channeled thereby into greater allegiance to the crown as representative of that faith.

But for all its dramatic effects, Spain's Inquisition would remain more directed at building state authority from above and less binding of national solidarity from below. As we shall see, in comparison with France and England, Spain's exclusions were more fully orchestrated through the Inquisition, were directed against the unpure then largely expelled and absent, and were less bloody than a civil war would have been. In a sense, once Spain's Jews and conversos were expelled, anti-Semitism alone would not and likely could not continue to be the basis for further mass cohesion or passion. As earlier in France and England, with expulsion the passions of anti-Semitism dissipated somewhat. But unlike elsewhere, no other heretical group remained in Spain to become the new target of exclusion that might further bind the populace. Oddly, Spain's comparative peacefulness, relatively early exclusion, and resulting homogeneity left its populace less engaged, with homogeneity having just the opposite of the expected outcome.

 France: The Embrace of Fanaticism

While the Spanish Inquisition combined religious motivations with political effects, the religious wars of France in the sixteenth century added one further component even more dramatically, that of ongoing mass engagement emerging from below. As outcome and signal of that engagement, France's religious civil wars brought the masses into political contests with unprecedented violence. And while Spain's monarchs

FAITH IN NATION

sought to direct religious institutions from above to unify and end civil war, France's monarchs were unable to do so and instead provoked or engaged in civil war as an alternative, indirect, and violent path to greater unity. That unity would be forged in mass violence against a present internal enemy—the Huguenots—that would prove more binding than attacks on "foreign" Jews, who had already been expelled from France. Certainly antagonism against any group no longer present is less likely to be binding.

The unprecedented level of popular participation in France's conflicts was as evident as it was seemingly unstoppable. "Political struggle partly pursued in the name of religion" resulted in "the fusion of a political with a religious crisis . . . highly dangerous in that religion was, in all senses, a popular issue . . . capable of embroiling others in the quarrels of noblemen."[53] Disregarding the dangers of so enflaming the populace, mass engagement was spurred on by the venomous sermons of priests and pastors. Disputes were viewed as matters of truth and salvation, violence as purifying, and victims of such violence seen not as humans but as "vermin" or "devils." The coincidental rise of printing at the time only spread such venom, for books were still read as if they were scripture, lending authority to printed vilification. And if Catholics were particularly fanatical and violent, as particularly threatened by individual conversions to Protestantism and concerned with heresy and defilement, then as the majority in France they could engage their passion all the more. Catholic crowds were even known to regularly burn, drown, or dismember the corpses of heretics.[54] There can be no doubt that the people of France were directly engaged in these passionate times, having moved well beyond control or machinations from above.

Divisive popular engagement is destabilizing, and it fanned fears among France's rulers that they would lose control if they could not find a way to contain, unify, and hold the people's support. If domestic relations posed this threat, international relations seemed to offer a solution. In the words of Coligny, the chief proponent of this solution as he wrote to the king, "The conflicting humours of the French . . . caused by differences over religion could but indicate the likely ruin of your state . . . For this, there is nothing more suitable . . . [than] to undertake a foreign war in order to maintain peace at home. . . . there is no doubt that war with Spain will be easy to prosecute."[55] In other words, war with Spain would "avert or divert war in France." In this, Coligny shared the assumption of the more moderate Catholics "that the way to ensure internal peace was to follow a policy of religious toleration at home and sink domestic differences in a national war against the country's great rival, Spain."[56]

And the times provided a perfect opportunity for just such a war with Spain. In the Lowlands, held by the Spanish as part of the Hapsburg empire, a revolt of Protestant nationalists was raging. Alba seemed by 1571–1572 to be on the verge of defeating Nassau, as long as France did not intervene on behalf of the Protestants, as Coligny was urging Charles to do. And with the French king then very much under the influence of this Protestant noble, France appeared to be on the precipice of just such an intervention against its Catholic Spanish neighbor.

Even the queen mother seemed sympathetic to this international alignment, as a means of preserving the state of France intact and the rule of her family. Catherine de' Medici herself was accordingly described with the epithet "politique," and all such were defamed by Catholic fanatics as "more dangerous even than heretics." As further proof of her willingness to compromise with Protestants, Catherine agreed to marry off her daughter to the leading Protestant royal, Henri de Navarre, and try to arrange an alliance-building marriage with Elizabeth of England for her second surviving son (and, when that failed, her third surviving son).[57]

Countering this policy direction was Catherine's remaining concern that war with Spain would be costly if not disastrous for France and certainly not as "easy" as Coligny argued. Catherine was inclined to be wary of the power of Spain, which had held hostage her own former husband in his youth. And Spain was, after all, the most impressive military power of the day, having defeated the Ottomans in the naval battle of Lepanto only a year before, in 1571. Her fear of war with Spain had to be weighed against her fear of civil war within France, and the latter seemed perhaps more likely to undermine her ability and that of her sons to rule. In addition, she may have feared that if Charles followed the advice of Coligny to engage in war with Spain on the side of the Protestants, she would be further losing control over her eldest son to this new-found father figure.[58] Finally, Catherine may have suspected that the foreign-directed antagonism of an anti-Spanish campaign was less likely to cohere her people than would a royal embrace of domestic anti-Protestant passions inconsistent with an attack on Catholic neighbors.

Despite these concerns, France's crown appeared to be moving ahead toward a delicate arrangement of a pro-Protestant foreign policy and

FAITH IN NATION

tolerance toward Protestants at home. The wedding of Marguerite and Henri de Navarre was officiated on August 18. Charles had concluded that he would take "the great opportunity there is at present for some good enterprise for the liberty of the Low Countries, at present oppressed by the Spaniards," and a French invasion under Coligny was planned for the week of August 25.[59] Perhaps the French royal house was reassured in this choice by the Spanish loss of Brille to the rebellious Sea Beggars on April 1, and by France's signing of a treaty with Elizabeth on April 19. Catherine and her son were within days of a foreign and domestic gambit that risked the Catholic Church's recognition of a divine legitimacy of their throne as well as the loss of support by a Catholic majority population—particularly those in Paris who had never forgiven or forgotten Coligny's siege five years earlier.[60] The other continental Catholic powers also had much to lose if France proceeded against them, and they may have conspired in the events that followed.

The price of the gambit seemed too large to pay as it grew closer, and the queen mother apparently reversed herself even as the celebrations of her daughter's marriage to Henri were underway. Allegedly with Catherine's complicity, though this was never proven, on August 22 a hired assassin shot Coligny as the protestant admiral returned from the Louvre to rue Béthizy. But Coligny was not killed outright; he blamed his attack on his old enemy the Catholic duc de Guise and called on the king for justice. Still loyal to Coligny even then, the king himself initially agreed that "this wicked act stems from the enmity between [Coligny's] house and those of Guise. I shall give order that they not drag my subjects into their quarrels."[61] But with legions of sworn enemies together in Paris to celebrate a supposedly peacemaking marriage, the assassin's shot unleashed a torrent of suspicion and fear that seemed certain to cascade again to civil war. Whether or not the queen had herself been responsible for the incompetent assassination attempt, she now felt compelled to act in a way that would weaken her resurgent Protestant enemies before such a war came. By the next day she apparently had browbeaten her son, the king, to abandon Coligny and his plans for war with Spain—and to do much worse.

At the least, the events of August 24, 1572 in Paris were the low point for a mother's hospitality to her daughter's new kin and wedding guests. At the most, it is the day in which the infant nation of France was born, bound in blood. After that day's violence, there can be no denying that a large portion of the populace had become fully engaged in and, with the interests of state authority, enflamed by religious passions.

That the St. Bartholomew's Day Massacre began at all and when it did is explicable in terms of elite strategic imperatives. Perhaps, had the assassination of Coligny been quickly accomplished, the king might have punished its perpetrators and returned to his policies of tolerance.[62] But according to one contemporary analysis, Coligny's followers, angered by the attempted assassination, were plotting against the king. And the royal family in turn judged that "it would be best to finish the business and not lose the opportunity to avoid another civil war by slaughtering the Admiral and his followers." Or, according to another analyst of the time, if the king had instead acted against Guise, "the Protestants would have acted violently . . . Thus, on all sides he was reduced to extremities," and once Coligny was killed by Guise, "the king, who could not do otherwise, approved it as if it had been done on his orders, or at least pretended to."[63]

As such a "pre-emptive act of war," the massacre started as an or-chestrated event. It was begun on signal when the morning tocsin was rung at Saint-Germain l'Auxerrois next to the royal palace of the Louvre, with lists of victims prepared in advance and singling out wealthier Prot-estants. The victims "were not anonymous to their murderers. They were neighbors and acquaintances . . . Paris's Protestants were a marked peo-ple, a familiar enemy."[64] As a planned attack upon enemies in order to retain power or avoid or win civil war, the massacre was seen as a quintessential Machiavellian moment, in which the supposed influence of Machiavelli's writings over the Italian-born queen mother was the subject of speculation.[65]

But this strategic image cannot capture the intensity and extensive passion of this pivotal event. What was planned from above as "a specific strike against a few dozen Huguenot noblemen" quickly exploded be-yond such bounds into "a general massacre of all Protestants in the city" and then beyond.[66] The queen mother herself seemed suddenly to have indulged in fanaticism beyond narrow self-interest, and her passions then further inspired a popular wave of venom. Within several days, between two and four thousand were slaughtered in Paris; within weeks, at least another 4,000 or as many as 10,000 outside the capital, including many more than those listed by the authorities, lost their lives. "The event was a 'popular crime'—or 'the sword being given to the common people' "[67]

Once given to the populace, that sword would not soon be returned to its scabbard, for the people's furious passion was not merely strategic or functional and could not easily be contained. To the dismay of officials, even the King's command to halt the violence was ignored, overshadowed by Guise's earlier claim about the killings that "it is the king's command. . . . taken to mean that the king had commanded the death of all Huguenots, these words transformed private passion into public duty." And that passion reflected both religious hatred and more crass motivations of self-interest, for instance with Protestant wealth looted. In one noted occasion, a crowd cut off the hands of a Protestant woman in order to more quickly steal her gold bracelets. Even the duc de Guise was so surprised by the mass fury unleashed that he himself hid some Huguenots in his own house, providing "yet another piece of evidence that the massacre was never intended to encompass the mass of Parisian Protestants but . . . then got out of hand."[68]

This unanticipated explosion of popular fury frightened the elite, who just as quickly sought to contain it. The "misadventure" of the general massacre quickly gave way to the state imperative for a return to peace, to be expedited by the cooperation of the princes of the blood, Henri de Navarre and Condé, both of whom had been spared and who then privately converted to Catholicism.[69] The king himself cynically disclaimed responsibility for the massacre and pretended that peace could be easily restored: "The admiral's house was set upon . . . and others slain in divers places of the city. This was done with such fury that it has not been possible to remedy it as I would have wished . . . All this happened through a private quarrel . . . I had beforehand done all I could to pacify it, as everyone knows. The Edict of Pacification is not broken by all this and I want to maintain it more strictly than ever."[70] Four days later, the king revised that the violence had been caused by a plot against his royal person by Coligny, but he argued that this did not affect continued tolerance more generally. His edict incredibly proclaimed that Huguenots— or at least those still alive—"shall live under his protection . . . in as much safeguard as they did before," though they should refrain from assemblies in order to ensure "the tranquility of his realm."[71]

In the wake of such a bloodletting, restoring peace and coexistence was easier said than done. Concentrated in the south and west, Huguenots emerged more organized, if also more divided, and more rebellious against a king who had massacred them, for instance successfully countering the crown's army at La Rochelle. They resisted paying taxes, increasing the tax burden on the Catholic North and emptying the royal treasury. In effect "a new form of French Protestantism" had emerged, "one that was openly at war against the crown," in turn unifying Catholics with "a shared vision of a sacral monarchy" and as defenders of absolutism.[72] Religious passions and engagement with state authority had been violently merged. The effective division of France into warring factions exploded into four major battles and three sieges between 1572 and 1585.[73]

The reemergence of civil war attests to the renewed intolerance of the monarchy, its inability to repress and force religious conformity or political obedience, and its decision to instead bolster such obedience on the basis of fanaticism. Catherine herself had clearly abandoned any earlier efforts at coexistence or forgiveness, indulging her own passions. In 1574 she even had the pleasure to avenge the accidental death of her husband, capturing and executing in 1574 the same comte de Montgomery whose lance had killed Henri II.[74]

In a seemingly unrelated development, just before the St. Bartholomew's Day Massacre, the king of Poland died without an heir. The Polish diet was charged with electing a new sovereign who could maintain peace between the religious factions of that country. The diet sought such a sovereign who would both agree to limits on monarchical power and "keep the peace between ourselves and shed no blood." Astonishingly, on May 11, 1573, they elected the duke of Anjou, younger brother of a king who had sanctioned the massacre of Huguenots, and just then the prince himself was laying siege to those Huguenots at La Rochelle. In a show of absolute cynicism, Anjou withdrew the siege, returned to Paris, and accepted the Polish throne by agreeing to limit his own powers and maintain religious tolerance and peace.[75] To gain a throne—seemingly any throne—the duke would foreswear the absolutism and intolerance characterizing his own quickly forthcoming reign at home. But Anjou also hedged his bets, with his brother the king guaranteeing that Anjou's right to succession in France would not be lost by accepting the Polish crown.[76]

In May 1574 Charles IX died, and within days of hearing the news Anjou sneaked away from his Polish throne to return home as Henri III, claiming the French crown and embracing those principles to which he apparently was more truly committed. At first, what those principles would be—if any other than self-interest—were not clear. In 1576, the new king agreed to the Peace of Monsieur, aimed at appeasing Protestant rebels then led by the king's own remaining younger brother, Alençon. Henri III apologized for the massacre of four years earlier and "to take away all occasion of trouble and disagreement among our subjects, we have granted and do grant free open and general exercise of the Reformed Protestant Religion, through all cities and places of our realm."[77] And in 1581, the king granted special rights to Swiss Protestants as "semi-citizens."[78] But Henri III still remained tempted by the alternative impetus of encouraging unity through intolerance. For instance, he seemed to agree with the advice in 1577 that "it would be desirable for there to be only one religion among your subjects," and to implement such unity he agreed to become head of the "Catholic League" founded by Guise.[79]

By 1584, any impetus toward coexistence was gone. The king's younger brother had died, leaving the former Protestant Henri de Navarre as heir presumptive and in turn provoking further Catholic activism under a resurgent League to head off a heretical succession. The next year, Pope Sixtus V excommunicated the converted Navarre, and Henri III forbade all practices of Protestantism and denied succession to Navarre. The result was yet another religious civil war, the "War of the Three Henries" between the King and Guise versus Navarre, in which eight major battles and three sieges rocked France from 1585 to 1598.[80] In 1585 the king ordered that in his realm "there will be no practice of the new Reformed Protestant Religion but only that of the Catholic religion."[81] This intolerance was only further bolstered by the dismay among Catholics to the news in 1587 of the execution of Mary Queen of Scots. The following year, Catholic League extremists, "the Sixteen," took control of Paris for two years.[82]

By the late 1580s, France was fully torn by religious intolerance and economic disaster. The king himself then came to fear the growing power of the leading Catholic noble, Guise, who in 1588 was murdered in the presence of the king. Now the king found that "assassinating a cardinal of the church also brought the wrath of the entire Gallican church and Rome upon him." The next year the king himself was assassinated by a Catholic extremist fearful of compromise with Navarre, whom the king had sought to make more acceptable with a promised second conversion.[83] While Henri III had proclaimed his intention "for ever to bury the memory of past troubles and divisions," clearly those divisions instead buried him.[84] As summarized and predicted three years before in a poem:

> The Leaguers ask for everything,
> The King gives them everything,
> The Guisard deprives him of everything,
> The soldier ravages everything,
> The poor people bear everything,

The Queen mother arranges everything . . .
Religion covers everything . . .
And the devil in the end will take the lot.[85]

The poet captured the age, though his cynicism denies the powerful passions of religious faith and hatred which, rather than mere façade for strategic state-building, instead gave salience to elite and popular sentiment. Amid turbulent social and religious conflict engaging the populace, the crown sought and would benefit from "the imposition of authority and the maintenance of peace, law and order, without which government could not function and the monarchy might perish." To achieve this end, the weakened crown was willing to make deals with moderate Protestants but found that consolidating Catholicism alone could more surely provide for "the advance of royal authority in preference to ruin and anarchy."[86] And such sectarianism also accorded with the crown's own fanaticism and faithful self-righteousness, enflamed by the threats to it.

Combining passions and interests, eventually the religious wars and intolerance would become the basis for building absolutist power, as the poet suggested, with "religion covering everything."[87] Even the earlier more pragmatic Catherine de' Medici had acceded. She and her sons had been caught up in the popular passions of exclusion, which then exploded beyond control with an intensity of mass mobilization that the crown hoped to turn to support of itself. Catholic majority support for the crown was forged on the basis of attacks on the Huguenots, establishing a pattern of exclusionary popular cohesion that the next French king would find a powerful force to resist.

England: A Nation Roused against Heretical Tyranny

Across the channel from France, another merger of faith and nation was becoming evident, if with a different faith. According to Linda Colley, while English nationalism was largely an invention of the eighteenth century, already a century earlier Protestantism "gave them identity . . . A sense of Protestant unity did not always override social class . . . But to the questions: Who were the British, and did they even exist? Protestantism could supply a potent and effective answer, perhaps the only satisfactory answer possible . . . Protestantism was the foundation that made the invention of Great Britain possible," cutting across cultural and linguistic differences between English, Welsh, and Scots (some of whom remained Catholic), while reinforcing and being reinforced by antagonism against Irish Catholics. That Protestant unity is what ultimately made prosperity, state, and military power possible, or at least it would be widely perceived in that light.[88] Given a long-standing belief that "divisions of religion within a state were dangerous and usually led to upheaval and bloodshed," as they had under Mary, it is not surprising that religious unity would become the foundation for early images of national unity.[89]

The roots of this religious nationalism lay in the Reformation, even if it had not fully engaged popular passions. The authority of the pope, who was vilified thereafter as the Antichrist, had been rebuffed, thereby strengthening national self-determination. "The rebellion to the Pope served a valuable function in the process of nation-building," moving beyond the divisions of "aristocracy versus monarchy, localism versus centralism, feudal versus national interests," with all such "obstructions to unity [seen] as the malicious work of outsiders." By throwing off such foreign authority, the English hoped to achieve self-determination and unity for themselves, reinforced by the horror of Mary's attempts at counter-reformation.[90]

Setting apart the English nation as free of the foreign religious authority of the pope coincided with related antagonism against more secular foreign powers, those states retaining their papal connection. Just as "one of the main threats to the nation was the Catholic Church, nation-building meant anti-Catholicism," similarly threats came from other Catholic countries against which nation-building was further enforced. Indeed, the pope was falsely seen as commanding those powers, whether as having ordered the St. Bartholomew's Day Massacre in France or Philip of Spain to attack with his armada. This image of Catholic enemies was later reinforced by "the emergence of Louis XIV as the most powerful ruler in Europe and the self-styled champion of Catholicism," or for that matter closer-to-home antagonism with the Irish. As Linda Colley concludes, "in these circumstances of regular and violent contact with peoples who could so easily be seen as representing the Other, Protestantism was able to become a unifying and distinguishing bond as never before."[91]

For all this growing and nation-defining animosity against the Catholics, they could not all be eliminated or expelled, unlike the Jews in Spain and more like the remaining Protestants in France. Though England's Catholics probably numbered close to 60,000 by 1640, at the time estimates ran much higher, making expulsion seem impractical, and all the more so as up to one-fifth of the peerage were Papists.[92] Nor could all the Catholics in Ireland be expelled, resulting in ongoing conflict between "Old English" Catholics and "New English" Proestants there.[93] Of course, numbers by themselves were not decisive; "The fact that Protestantism was the religion of the overwhelming majority of the nation was not thought to provide any security. In [Parliamentary] debate members recalled how easily the nation had changed its religion at the bidding of the Tudor sovereigns" in the previous century.[94]

Relative lack of popular engagement over the prior religious conversion of the country helped to maintain elements of popular coexistence in social terms, though the vulnerability to fanaticism was evident in how comparable local tolerance in France had quickly deteriorated. In England's local communities there was still "little tension" and much intermarriage, and even those who "inveighed against Popery at court . . . might be on good terms with the few Catholics who lived near them, with whom they had ties of neighborliness and common social status and interests. Consciously or unconsciously, they distinguished between Popery as a malign political force and papists as people."[95] This is not to suggest there was no popular animosity, for in the years leading up to the Civil War there were indeed a series of panics and assaults on Catholics. Sometimes, such attacks were directed instead against "witches," with any form of heresy, non-conformity, or defect of blood seen as inviting of intolerance and treatment as scapegoats.[96] And such popular views and actions were becoming all the more pressing in a time of population growth and of property qualifications for the franchise reduced by inflation. As Plumb argues, "the perturbations of politics in seventeenth-century England, however, had called into being a wider political nation than [before], and one far less easy to control."[97]

Before control of the populace was so lost and religious conflicts and exclusions consolidated, Elizabeth's successor would emerge as a transitional figure. It might have seemed natural for James to pull England back toward the Catholicism of his executed mother. But he had not been raised by Mary and understood that his distance from her and her faith was the only route to the English crown and popular support. There was then no return to counter-reformation attempted from above, though James did attempt a limited coexistence with Catholics, much as had Elizabeth herself earlier on. And perhaps such evenhandedness was itself pragmatic for the first monarch of a combined England, Scotland, and Wales, who as a Stuart had greater historical and family links to Spain and to France and who was married to a Catholic, Anne of Denmark.

Indeed James had promised that like Elizabeth, "as for the Catholics I will neither persecute any that will be quiet and give but an outward obedience to the law, neither will I spare to advance any of them that will by good service worthily deserve it."[98] Following Elizabeth, James was another English-version "politique."

James's early feints toward coexistence had both theoretical and pragmatic underpinnings. In a 1610 speech to Parliament, he compared monarchism "to the Divine power. Kings are also compared to the fathers of families, for a king is truly *parens patriae*, the politic father of his people. And lastly, kings are compared to the head of this microcosm of the body of man."[99] Of course, any of these analogies emphasize the popular subordination to the monarchy, whether as divinity, head of the family, or head of the body politic. And James was conscious of the particular need for such common "allegiance" in a commonwealth "so long disordered and distracted."[100]

Principled commitment to resolving past disputes and to coexistence with remaining Catholics was then given further practical reinforcement to bolster international alliances. The king sought to arrange a useful marriage of his son to one of the Catholic royals from the continent. In 1623, James agreed to end the penal laws against Catholics in order to win for his son the Spanish infanta, though he failed on both accounts. Subsequent successful negotiations to join young Charles with Henrietta Maria of France brought English assistance in France's suppression of the Huguenots, liberty of worship for England's Catholics, and several prominent appointments at court for those Catholics.[101]

But these signals of pragmatic toleration were matched even at the very start of James's reign with contrary moves, which gained ascendancy over time. Already in 1604, the new monarch proclaimed that Catholics were "no way sufferable to remain in this kingdom" if they affirmed the "arrogant and ambitious Supremacy of their Head the Pope ... to have an imperial civil power over all kings."[102] Indeed, despite some reforms, the king was eager to assert his primacy, with more than five thousand convicted of being recusants in early 1605. Resulting desperation among Catholics led to the failed "gunpowder plot" by Guy Fawkes and his group of embittered Catholics who attempted to blow up the king in Parliament later that year. Suspicion grew that the whole Roman Church was behind the plot in some elaborate international conspiracy.[103] Now Catholicism would be associated with treason and attempted regicide, feeding popular antagonism and rising legal discrimination, even as the king resisted using the plot "as a license to hunt down Catholics."[104]

Despite some royal reticence, an avalanche of anti-Catholic legislation began with the 1606 act for repressing popish recusants. The "infection" of Catholicism was described as "dangerous to the Church and state," with those who refused to attend Anglican services or to take proper sacraments subject to fines if not worse. More than 5,000 would be convicted.[105] The harshest punishment was reserved for those whose religion was a pretext for foreign allegiances and treason, for as James wrote: "I confess I am loath to hang a priest only for religion sake . . . but if he refuse the oath of allegiance . . . I leave them to the law; it is no persecution but good justice."[106] Indeed, between 1607 and 1616, thirteen Catholic priests were executed, refusing even on the scaffold to take a required oath of allegiance to king over pope. And already by 1612 the keeper of Newgate described his jail as "rather a chapel . . . than a prison." Using earlier legislation, churchwardens were required to report recusants, fined if they failed to do so and rewarded if their reports led to convictions. The king could seize two-thirds of the land of those convicted. Later, Catholics were barred from coming to court, could not come within ten miles of London, could practice no profession nor hold any office, nor did the law recognize their marriages or transfers of land.[107]

Eager to avoid the same rising tensions evident on the continent and instead to ensure unity, the king became increasingly willing to voice his own anti-Catholicism, already evident in law. In 1626 he declared "that neither in matter of doctrine or discipline of the Church, nor in the government of the State, he will admit of the least innovation."[108] The juxtaposition of royal concern for popery connected to treason and discord was even more explicit two years later when the king declared his intention "not to suffer unnecessary disputations, altercations . . . which may nourish faction both in the Church and Commonwealth . . . these both curious and unhappy differences [shall] . . . be laid aside, and these disputes shut up."[109] Or in another declaration also of 1628, James stated his "full intention on our part to take away all ill understanding between us and our people . . . that nothing might be left for private fancies and innovations . . . to make up all breaches and rents in religion at home . . . and approaches against that foreign enemy."[110]

If James himself was increasingly intolerant of Papists and supportive of discriminatory legislation, with the rising influence of Puritan legislators Parliament itself was even more vigorous in this direction. For instance, the Commons Petition of December 1621 warns of an alliance between English Catholics and foreign "princes of the Popish religion," especially Spain. It argued that "for securing of our peace at home . . .

[and for] the honour and good of the Church and State . . . having kindled these affections truly devoted to your Majesty," further laws against recusants should be enacted, including the forced upbringing of Catholic children by Protestant schoolmasters."[111] By 1628, an increasingly powerful and assertive Parliament was warning His Majesty "of the great danger threatened to this Church and State, by . . . innovation of religion . . . Ireland is now almost wholly overspread with Popery . . . here in England we observe an extraordinary growth of Popery . . . whereby they have kindled such a fire of division in the very bowels of the State, as if not speedily extinguished, it is of itself sufficient to ruin." Such preying on "unstable minds" was the result of "suspension or negligence in execution of the laws against Popery" and the gains by Papists of "places of trust and authority," with the latter an ominous warning against those close to the king himself.[112] Publishers of Catholic influenced tracts were to be subject to "exemplary punishments." The Commons went so far as to argue that any advocates of popery "shall be reputed a capital enemy to this Kingdom."[113]

Parliamentary intolerance came together with further popular antagonism. The most obvious aggravation was the gunpowder plot itself, for nothing could be more provocative of anti-Catholicism than an attempt upon the combined symbols and leaders of the nation, king and Parliament in Westminster. This antagonism coincided with long-standing international enmity with the Catholic powers on the continent, which for the populace tended to outweigh any diplomatic niceties. For instance, the dramatic effort to negotiate marriage of the royal heir Charles to the Spanish infanta attempted in 1623 under the guidance of the Catholic-raised Buckingham, was seen as threatening Charles's own conversion. Its failure "was the occasion of nation-wide rejoicing." And this antagonism was reinforced yet again with the discovery in 1625 of a plot by priests to gain Spanish support for an invasion of Ireland, threatening England through its "back door." The successful negotiation in 1626 of a match between Charles and Henrietta Maria of France, with corresponding English concessions to Catholicism more generally, provoked strong opposition within Parliament and beyond.[114]

Rising popular participation and antagonism against a minority domestic group seen as aligned with foreign enemies is always a volatile mix, but in the England of the seventeenth century it was made all the more so by the particularities of its kings. With the head of state also the head of the church, religious nonconformity was also treason, surely the most popularly enraging of political crimes. And yet in England at mid-seventeenth century there was one further new complication: most prominent among the suspects of such treason would be the new head of state himself. Such suspicion of a monarch had already begun under James I, who had considered meeting with the pope, tried to marry his son to a Spanish princess, actually married him to the sister of France's Louis XIII, and in 1621 suspended penal laws against Catholicism. These popular suspicions would explode in the reign of Charles I, whose wife was openly Catholic, while the King considered a reunion with the pope and an alliance with Spain that was then fighting Dutch Protestants.[115] Resolving the conundrum of a seemingly treasonous and heretical monarch would be an insurmountable contradiction within the existing order, bringing revolution.

The turning of religious antagonism against the monarch himself arguably took hold first with popular distrust of Charles's French-born Catholic queen. In part, the problem lay with differences of perception, with the king appreciating the need for a peacekeeping alliance with France cemented through his marriage, which many in the country rejected as intrigue with enemies at the highest level. And that such an alliance was so suspect, what for earlier monarchs had gone unchallenged, suggests a new level of mass concern with such issues. This popular suspicion was fed further by the queen's bringing to court priests who actively converted others, and even an agent of the pope known to engage in regular conversation with Charles. But the simple fact of a foreign-born queen of a different faith, chosen after public celebration of the prior failure at a comparable Spanish match and with either match supposedly in violation of scripture, focused popular antagonism, especially in densely populated London.[116] That the queen and king would remain loyal to each other only further enraged popular animosity.[117]

With the queen as a focal point, suspicion of foreigners became increasingly of concern. Pincus argues that such antagonism against the French and their absolutist form of governance was ultimately the primary popular concern, more than suspicions of popery.[118] But foreign and religious antagonism was often inextricably merged, and the latter had already and would prove potentially explosive. As part of this mix, xenophobia remained focused also on the pope as antichrist and as foreign power, with his agent present in court, and even with the oath of allegiance required of clergy, including an ambiguous "etc." suspected of referring to the Holy Father. In addition, as Cromwell later argued, all Papists were seen as "Spaniolized," or linked to the greatest foreign enemy. And such linkage between domestic Catholics and foreign enemies was reinforced by the regular practice of English Catholics attending services at foreign embassys' chapels, where they were often attacked by mobs.[119] Even if those attacks were fanned by leaders and not fully spontaneous does not diminish their signaling of popular antagonism and the widespread perception that Catholicism was connected to treasonous intervention from outside.

Fear of Rome's influence was further enflamed by related domestic religious developments. The king was himself an advocate of the divine right of bishops and found personally appealing "high church Arminianism," which was opposed by a broad spectrum of Presbyterians and Independents in Parliament fearful of a counter-Reformation as under Mary. In 1633, the king elevated to Archbishop of Canterbury William Laud, a fellow Arminianist who favored more ceremony and whose reforms were seen as moves toward Catholicism. Laud himself saw those reforms as attempts to head off Catholicism, but he was offered a cardinalship by the pope, which he refused without diminishing the perception of his Roman leanings. Calvinist Scots rebelled in 1636 against Laud's forceful impositions and what they saw as moves toward restoration of the Mass. When Laud ordered the building of altar rails to reinforce authority and ceremony, these were seen as further moves back toward Roman hierarchy, distancing the clergy from the congregation. By 1639 army troops were getting drunk and pulling down these rails at local churches, as did congregationalists in 1641, further indicating popular engagement in the growing conflict.[120] This engagement in religious issues is not surprising given that attending weekly services was legally required, one-tenth of profits or produce were paid to the clergy, the pulpit was the major source of news or public announcements, and the church controlled publishing and education.[121]

The connection between foreign enemies and religious conflict came even closer to home with the Irish rebellion of 1641. This rebellion was described officially to Charles II twenty years later as "an unnatural insurrection . . . against your Majesty's royal father . . . [which] became a formed and almost national rebellion of the Irish papists." At the time, it was seen as a revolt in favor of Charles I against Parliament, confirming the latter's suspicion of royal tyranny, of a Catholic plot against the English people, and a popular perception of the Irish Catholics as foreign enemies.[122] With large numbers of English Protestants massacred, panic was stoked at the time by estimates of 40,000 dead, though probably the number was closer to 4,000. Retribution was fierce. The percentage of Irish land owned by Catholics would fall from 60 percent in 1641, at the outbreak of the revolt, to 20 percent in 1660, after the revolt's defeat.[123]

In part, numbers also tell the story. Increasing royal tolerance for Catholicism—or at least decreasing intolerance—is indicated by the number of executions for recusancy of priests and Catholic laity, which fell from 187 under Elizabeth and 26 under James to 3 under Charles by 1640.[124] This lack of prosecutions of Catholics fed popular perceptions that the crown was linked to the nation's enemies. In response, around 60,000 Puritans fled England after Laud's elevation, seeking to escape "the renewal of persecution by papistical bishops."[125]

With royal tolerance for Catholics and the king's own preference for religious practices increasingly similar to those of Rome, conflict emerged between Protestants over how to respond. Indeed, the civil war to come was a conflict among Protestants and not as much with Catholics per se, although anti-Catholic accusations and propaganda was a powerful rhetoric and crucially exacerbated the conflict. Those more inclined toward Puritanism feared and resented the king, whose growing power was seen as imposing a return toward Catholicism and a rejection of Elizabeth's earlier compromise. And the king's reliance on armed Irish Catholics against the Scots (and potentially against Parliament) reinforced those fears. Many opted for migration to escape his rule. Meanwhile, the king and his loyalists feared the increasingly radical drift of the Puritan critique of absolutism, merging religious and political disputes.

The passionate intensity of religious tension would become further enmeshed in the then growing political cleavage between monarchy and Parliament. While there were some powerful Catholic lords suspected of arming and plotting on behalf of the king, most were Protestant and resented the increasing power of the king and the tax burden placed on them, for instance by royal tax on port towns to pay for ships.[126] And such royal impositions were generally seen as unfairly ignoring Parliamentary power and as constraints on liberty. As described by one contemporary "Popery when encouraged by Government has always been dangerous to the liberties of the people." By 1640, rumors of conspiracy no longer focused on regicide but instead on popish plots against Parliament, increasingly seen as more legitimately representative of the nation.[127] And Parliament would act according to such fears, earlier refusing to pay for an army to quell the Scots, then impeaching Archbishop Laud and Thomas Wentworth, the earl of Strafford, before moving directly against the king.

A transition was clearly underway "from a situation where Popery was seen as the enemy of crown and nation, to one where Popery and the crown were seen as dangers to the Protestant nation."[128] That perceived threat of combined Catholicism and absolutism was increasingly resisted in Parliament, representing an ever more engaged populace and inspired by Puritan ideology to pursue "the art of opposition" nurtured by earlier resistance and exile under Mary.[129] This escalation of the conflict between crown and Parliament, and the aggravating role of rising popular antagonism against Catholic influence, is reflected in the historical documents.

At first, the focus of conflict was primarily on issues of religion, including a dispute on predestination, which apparently inflamed the populace even more than resistance to absolutism. But the two issues remained joined by royal imposition of resented tolerance. For instance, in 1640 the City of London—together with a mob—sent the Root and Branch Petition to Parliament, citing as grievances "the many schisms, errors and strange opinions which are in the Church . . . The growth of Popery . . . [s]etting images, crucifixes and conceits over them . . . Popery or Arminianism are countenanced, spared, and have much liberty; and from hence followed amongst others these dangerous consequences."[130] Commons would order that churches remove the eastern Communion tables, rails, crucifixes, and candlesticks and curtail bowing at the name of Jesus.[131]

Concerns over strictly religious issues quickly turned against the monarch as head of the church. Only a half year after the Roots and Branch Petition, a conference of Lords was turning attention to the dangerous religious influences close to the king, using the Ten Propositions to call upon "His Majesty to remove from him all such counsellors . . . furthering those courses contrary to religion, liberty, good government of the kingdom, and as have lately [sought] . . . to stir up division between him and his people." The queen herself was named as suspicious, the prince's education was preferred to be overseen by those "well-affected in religion," and "His Majesty be moved that he would be pleased to be very sparing in sending for Papists to Court."[132] At the same time, the king's instruments of absolutism were also challenged, with acts calling for the abolition of the courts of the Star Chamber and of the High Commission.[133] In a related protestation, the issues of popery and tyranny were explicitly joined, with the claim that "adherents to the See of Rome . . . endeavour to subvert the fundamental laws of England and Ireland, and to introduce the exercise of an arbitrary and tyrannical government."[134]

By the end of 1641, any remaining royal authority was wearing thin in Parliament, which presented its Grand Remonstrance to the king at Hampton Court on the first of December. The petition began politely, as "humbly present(ed) to your Majesty, without the least intention to lay any blemish on your royal person, but only to represent how your royal authority and trust have been abused, to the great prejudice and danger of your Majesty." The first issue taken up was the corruption and divisiveness of an "increase in Popery" of those close to the king, as contrasted with Parliament's own self-proclaimed interest "for preserving the peace and safety of the kingdom from the malicious designs of the popish party." They called upon the king "for uniting all such [of] your royal subjects together as join in the same fundamental truths against the Papists . . . to see his people united in ways of duty to him."[135] The petition warned of "a most dangerous division and chargeable preparation for war" to be avoided by so unifying against the Papists and ending their influence at court, which had been used "to further the interests of some foreign princes." The queen was again herself singled out. And the issues of religion were explicitly joined to "the restraints of the liberties of the subjects."[136]

For all the pretense of politeness, warnings to the king, and blaming heresy on those around him but not on him, the Grand Remonstrance widened the rift between crown and Parliament. The proposal to print the text of the Remonstrance, thereby publicizing the conflict, "led to uproar in the House, in which swords were drawn for the only recorded time in history."[137] The king responded to this printing that he was "very sensible of the disrespect" of such public condemnation. He went on to deny that there was any "wicked and malignant party prevalent in government" but nonetheless agreed to the need "for preserving the peace and safety of this kingdom from the design of the Popish party," and he proclaimed "the glory of God in the Protestant profession . . . our honour and that of the nation."[138] Indeed, the king also merged the issues of religion and unity, arguing that "the preservation of unity and peace . . . require[s] obedience to the laws and statutes ordained for the establishing of the true religion in this kingdom."[139] But Parliament responded with renewed attack, calling for controls over whom the King asked for counsel, chose to guard him, or arranged for his own son to marry. Parliament also called for ending any toleration of Catholics and revoking the vote of Catholic peers.[140]

The king himself had endeavored to assure his subjects of his own interest in religious unity to ensure peace and stability and in upholding the Church of England, but to little effect. Already in 1623, he had written that "there can be no friendship without union in religion" and in 1629 claimed he had been "careful to make up all breaches and rents in religion at home, so did we, by our proclamation and commandment, for the execution of laws against Priests and Popish recusants." In 1641 he reiterated that he did not seek "to alter the form of the Church government in England . . . I am constant for the doctrine and discipline of the Church of England," and as late as 1644 was writing to Commons to again assert his commitment to "the maintenance of the true reformed Protestant religion."[141]

Even as he sought to maintain absolutist powers, the king acknowledged his need for popular support and unity, forcing him to acclaim his own accordance with the popular faith to contain resentment or resistance. Charles understood, as he wrote in 1643, that "nothing on earth can be more dear unto us than the preservation of the affections of our people" and that such affection rested upon popular belief in his resistance to foreign influences and Catholicism.[142] But that affection had already been all but lost, with the citizenry and its representatives not only suspecting the king of Catholic sympathies but even coming to reject the monarchy itself as a foreign intrusion and "the English [as] a conquered people who had been deprived of their rights and liberties by the Norman conquest."[143]

By 1642, the conflict was moving out of the halls of the palaces and Westminster. With skirmishes in the streets beginning to bring casualties, the queen was sent by the king to the continent to pawn the crown jewels, raise funds, and buy arms on his behalf. Riots against enclosures, tithes, and rents exploded. By the end of the year, some 20,000 volunteers had begun to build an eighteen-mile-long rampart to defend London from "foreign" forces in service to their own King.[144] Clearly, the populace was now engaged. Indeed, the country was slipping toward civil war, amid accusations that "your Majesty hath, by the persuasion of evil counselors, withdrawn yourself from Parliament, raised an army against it . . . constraining us to take arms for the defense of our religion, laws, liberties, privileges of Parliament . . . which fears and dangers are continued and increased by the raising, drawing together, and arming of great numbers of Papists."[145]

Demands for exclusion of Catholicism remained central to the debates within Parliament as it moved toward greater assertion of its rights over the king, but it was the latter on which Parliament's army itself focused. Most notably, the army's "Heads of the Proposals" of 1647 argued for a much more limited monarchy, requiring that parliament meet biennially and have control over the militia.[146] The king, by then embattled, rejected such constraints upon his power as in "violation of his conscience and honour."[147] For the elite, the chief issue was the distribution of power: "Who was to be the boss?"[148]

But for the populace, the crucial issue remained the widespread fear of popery. Newspapers and pamphlets fanned this fear with images of "savage Irish Catholics" and of Rome seeking world domination. Sermons reaching the vast illiterate vilified Catholicism as "the debasement of Christ's teaching," as "blasphemous perversion," sinfully self-indulgent, as "idol-worship," and as "politically seditious, morally evil, and doctrinally damnable." To this was added Rome's connections with England's foreign enemies, notably Spain, and, in an updated version of John Foxe's widely available book, reminders of Catholic efforts to "depose or assassinate Elizabeth, the Armada and the Gunpowder Plot." The king's own ministers were keenly aware of the inciting power of this rhetoric of religious antagonism directed against the king. According to Secretary of State Sir Edward Nicholas, "ye Alarme of Popish plots amuse and Afright ye people here, more than anything, and therefore that is ye Drum that is soe frequently beaten upon all occasions." It did not help that in 1645 the king's papers captured at the battle of Nasely showed that he had indeed been negotiating with rebellious Irish Catholic nobles, increasingly seen as the most pressing papist threat.[149]

Passionate religious tensions, accusations of heresy and treachery, thrown on the tinder of the dispute over power between Parliament and crown, enflamed and engulfed the country's people. As John Milton would write in his Areopagitica of 1644, "methinks I see in my mind a noble and puissant nation rousing herself like a strong man after a sleep."[150] Clearly the nation was being so roused by the drumbeat of alarm, engaging many more than the one in ten who then had the franchise to vote for commons, though Parliament's own activism is further evidence of popular engagement.[151] The destabilizing effect of this engagement was profound, suggesting just how much that mass engagement had grown in the century since Reformation was imposed. According to Kishlansky, "the bonds that held society together were everywhere strained, and often broken."[152]

Once roused to civil war, the nation proceeded toward its fateful conclusion. While no more than one in ten Englishmen of fighting age were in combat from 1642 until 1646, Hobbes estimated that 100,000 died, the country's largest proportion of military casualties until the first World

War. Parliament's forces suffered major losses at first and then stalemated with the crown. But eventually the king's Cavalier forces were overcome, with their support drawn from the poorer north and west, while Parliament's Roundheads were drawn from the more advanced south and east. The Roundheads were perhaps further strengthened by crass motivations, for the seizure and redistribution of crown and royalist lands and rents were of comparable size and attraction as was the dissolution of the monasteries during Reformation.[153]

After the deadly war, the denouement then came more quickly. Charles, defeated by superior force, was charged with "wicked design to erect and uphold himself an unlimited and tyrannical power to rule according to his will, and to overthrow the rights and liberties of the people . . . against the public interest, common right, liberty, justice and peace of the people of this nation."[154] The religious issues that had so enflamed the country were not even mentioned in the charge sheet, as if to justify revolt on purely political and economic grounds and to distance the elite from the mass's fury. Having been found guilty, the king was beheaded on January 30, 1649. As the axe was swung, the large crowd reportedly "groaned," though whether in response to the king's final claim to martyrdom or in dismay at regicide remains unclear. At the time, the regicide was quickly blamed on the bad influence upon the king of his friends or his queen and later amazingly blamed on the Papists themselves. But for all the disputes and backtracking from the revolutionary act, that act in itself signaled that for England "absolute monarchy on the French model was never again possible."[155]

In the dawn of nationalism, or more accurately of popular engagement in and with the state, the masses were tentatively invited, or more forcefully invited themselves, onto the stage of power politics. Where they engaged most dramatically, they made their own entry on the basis of disputes over religion and with a binding violence enflamed by fear or animosity also inspired by faith. Seeking support and legitimacy, monarchs (or their opponents) learned to channel rising religious passion toward more secular and political issues, in particular by forging more unified allegiance on the basis of sectarianism and antagonism against heretics. Particular experiences varied, setting the course for future trajectories.

The Spanish Inquisition began as an expression of faith that then had more pragmatic consequences. As the only countrywide institutional authority, the Inquisition was the single mechanism for spreading state authority and was also a basis for gathering resources to pay for itself, to assist the crown, and to enrich officials thereby tied further to the center. As such, the Inquisition became a major tool for state-building, comparable to England's Reformation in bolstering royal authority and revenues, countering regional resistance, and curtailing papal power. But the Inquisition was also a tool for establishing a limited degree of national coherence, or early and somewhat more centralized allegiance. By building on long-standing xenophobia and anti-Semitism, and by attacking those of different faiths or "unpure" blood, the Inquisition effectively bolstered and channeled the Catholicism of the populace, bringing faith into the political arena as a basis for social order. The mechanisms for doing so remained largely institutional, in the form of trials, but also engaged the masses. The process reached crescendo with the final expulsion of Jews and Moriscos, leaving a country more unified and homogenous according to religious belief and ancestry. Non-Catholics accommodated by converting. Within the country, being Catholic and being Spanish were effectively merged, bolstering the coherence of the latter more secular category.

That this process had an early starting point and at least the semblance of an end point is notable. Having begun and even reached a climax already in the fifteenth century, Spain's Inquisition arguably came before the state was strong enough to take full advantage of the cohering effects. And those effects would then later be diluted by the state and crown's preoccupations with an also early gained empire. Officially, the Inquisition remained in force long thereafter, and Catholic unity was thereby maintained or reinforced. But the exclusionary process was largely completed by the time rising literacy and economic development might have further engaged the populace in this process. As a result, the opportunity to fully harness such popular engagement and channel religious passion toward nationalism was lost, or at least diminished by poor timing and happenstance.

The popularly cohering effect of the Inquisition was limited not only by timing and empire but also by the crown's hesitant invitation of the masses to observe more than join in its drama. Spain's attack on heresy not only served the interests of the crown but was directed and controlled from above, rather than more fully impelled by passions from below. As such, it had almost as limited an impact on popular loyalty as did England's Reformation. It remained more institutionalized than passionate, and its victims at any one time were relatively limited in number—killed by individual official processes rather than mass rampage. While some 150,000 cases were heard by all the tribunals of the Holy Office between 1550 and 1700, in that time fewer than 800 cases (or on average five per year) reported to the central tribunal resulted in execution, with a much larger number resulting in exile, imprisonment, punishment, or fines.[156] And as the Jews and other victims did not resist their persecution, there were no "religious wars."

Terrible to say, less blood proved less binding, for nothing is as powerful a basis of mass passion and cohesion than killings. And as the victims of Inquisition were seen as "foreigners," they could be expunged or expelled. With their final expulsion, the Inquisition then lost both its primary focus and much of its momentum, with few "others" left within the country against whom the majority could continue to cohere.

Still, the Inquisition's enforced unity through religious exclusion and violence provided a template for those countries that came later to similar experiences, or at least for understanding those experiences and their differences. France and England had earlier expelled their Jews, but unlike in Spain, Christianity was then split. In the absence of Jews, the binding effects of exclusion would instead be focused on Protestants or Catholics, whose continued presence provided a more permanent target and glue for the nation.

In France, centralized authority challenged by noble factions sought to bolster its uncertain hold over a culturally and linguistically diverse people. Sudden further weakness at the center after the accidental death of Henri II only further energized efforts both by the monarchy to retain power and by nobles to challenge it. And again unlike Spain, growing religious division among a populace "infected" with spreading Protestantism further exacerbated the potential for conflict, then aggravated it and reinforced the crown's imperative to contain it. A different basis than anti-Semitism would have to be found for binding the mobilized French nation.

The French populace forced its own entry onto the political stage, with that entry announced by bloody conflict. The monarchy was confronted by a new powerful force of mobilization from below, which it both feared and sought to benefit from by harnessing it. The passion of Catholic faith and antagonism against the Huguenots was inflamed further by the violence of war itself and by the venomous imagery of priests and pamphlets. Literacy thus spread both discord and cohesion, albeit taking a nasty turn. In a sense, the uncertainty and discord of domestic conflict opened the way and inspired more popular engagement to fill the vacuum of weakness at the center. Civil war brought the people into politics in a dramatic form. The crown and competing noble factions did not fully expect this level of mass engagement—or, at least, they feared its anarchical possibilities. But not being able to contain or control it, they came to appreciate that this rising social force could also be used to advantage. The passions of conflict could be and were directed toward a more passionate support of the crown and state as defenders of the faith against a present internal enemy. An initially more pragmatic monarchy tempted by compromise and coexistence, then joined in the religious passions of exclusion with a vengeance, for its own further empowerment.

In contrast with Spain, then, turmoil in France reflected and indicated a more popular form of engagement. Religious conflict was manipulated from above by competing elites, but it then exploded into civil war, drawing in and inflaming fanaticism from below. The Protestant enemy was not seen as foreign but instead as an even more dangerous domestic threat whose persistence within continued to bind the Catholic majority. And that cohering effect was exacerbated by the blood spilled in much greater amounts by civil wars than by Inquisition. Indeed, there were more victims of just the first day of the St. Bartholomew's massacre than from decades of Inquisition in Spain, and that massive violence only further enflamed the populace. Violence below spun out of control from above, with monarchs and elites scurrying to retain some control or at least to benefit from factional loyalties. But as much as it was uncontrolled, conflict did bind and engage the people of France, with the crown able to survive and eventually strengthen its hold over popular loyalty by siding with the anti-Huguenot fervor.

Like France, England suffered internal discord that the crown sought to mollify and contain, with religious passions ultimately serving as the basis for reinforcing and building popular unity. But England's monarchs were less challenged by civil violence and noble challenges than were their French counterparts. The Reformation had strengthened central power and changed religious authority with relatively little spiritual passions or conflict. Popular antagonism was directed against the pope, the Catholic monarchs of France and Spain, and the rebellious Irish Catholics more than against Catholics at home. Indeed, the domestic Catholic minority was allowed to remain, with the proviso that they remain loyal to the Protestant crown.

This stasis had ended when the head of both state and church became suspect, merging heresy and treason at the highest possible level. Charles I shifted the Church of England toward more Roman practices, or at least practices so perceived and resented. And at the same time he moved toward absolutism in more secular issues. The strength of the crown then itself became a subject of discord, with the Protestant populace and its representatives in Parliament increasingly resentful of absolutism and of the supposedly Catholic sympathies of its sovereign. Popular resentment rose, for instance as directed against the symbolism of Church rails setting the congregation off and below authority, much as absolutism subordinated the king's subjects and representatives. Thus antagonism against foreign Catholic authorities was redirected and focused on the crown itself, coinciding with political and economic resistance to absolutism and leading to exclusion at the highest level through regicide and revolution. The sovereign of the nation was turned into its adversary and victim, in turn bolstering a more representative national solidarity. Politics and religion again were merged, but against absolutism instead of for it.

Elite and popular motivations differed, but combined with revolutionary outcome. Parliament was largely focused on threats to its power, though it also used the rhetoric of anti-Catholicism directed against the crown to build popular support. The populace was seemingly more enflamed by the heresy of the crown, with that passion reinforced by texts and preachers. But popular resentment of popery infecting the head of the church was of course also resentment of the head of state, one and the same. Passions of power and of faith came together in a powerful mix, giving impetus to a revolutionary conflict in which the head of church and of state lost his head. But this outcome cannot be explained purely on the basis of liberal or rights-based motivations for revolution, contrary to most conventional accounts focused on Parliament's rhetoric or descriptions of early English nationalism as civic. Instead, the popular impetus against absolutism was aggravated by and channeled the passions of anti-Catholicism, with resulting bloodletting further binding the populace.

In all three cases the forging of early national unity then emerged in the intersection of efforts to consolidate (or challenge) power from above and popular engagement from below. But the mix of these processes looked very different in these three countries, with very different results. In Spain, where the impetus for unified authority came more fully from above and remained more controlled and institutionalized, less blood was spilled, popular passions were relatively less engaged, and the result was less binding. Like England's Reformation at the same time, Inquisition bolstered state-building more than nation-building. In the absence of any later Protestant-Catholic conflict, no later wave of mass passion would emerge to either strengthen or destroy royalism, which was left to float in the shallows. In France, pressures from above and below flowed together, with the crown maneuvering to survive and even benefit from greater mass violence. The weaker French crown embraced the anti-Protestant fervor and caught and rode the wave of mass engagement to strengthen its authority. The result was more binding of the populace, whose loyalty to the crown was reinforced by mutual anti-Protestantism. State-building and nation-building there were more fully merged, bolstering absolutism. In England, a seemingly stronger king resisted rising anti-Catholicism, which then turned against him; the wave of mass engagement then broke over his head. Religious passions exploded from below, spun out of control from above, and ultimately cohered the populace under parliament to impose an alternative basis of control no longer under the crown. Nationalism then consolidated against the crown leaving absolutism in tatters.

For all their dramatic differences, in all three cases conflict and popular mass intolerance was crucially tied to efforts at state- and nation-building. There was little about this process that was civic, individualistic, or unitary. To varying extents, the crowd had become politically engaged with strong collective sentiments, enflamed by sectarianism. The more the populace took the initiative in persecutions and violence, the more control from above was lost, though ultimately control was then reinforced by the resulting engagement and coherence of the people as loyal to its rulers or representatives. A new and stronger basis of control and state authority would ironically then be the result of a loss of control, which brought greater popular cohesion reinforcing state authority.

If nationalism is the sentiment binding the populace to the state, then it may only be possible—or emerge strongly—when that sentiment explodes beyond imposed limitations from above, even if it then later returns to solidify elite power in some form. If power ultimately is reinforced by popular engagement, then some loss of centralized power—even if fleetingly—is a part of that process. For power of the center to be reinforced by mass passion, the latter must be allowed or will force its expression on the street. To be effective for state-building, nation-building cannot be fully controlled from above, for it will not then bind.

INTERREGNUMS OF COEXISTENCE AND STATE-BUILDING
"Prudence to Make Mild"

The role of religious exclusions in bounding and binding early nationalism has been largely ignored or rejected. There remains among many scholars an established consensus that nationalism emerged in western Europe only at the end of the eighteenth century. Notably, with the French Revolution the masses demanded their integration into the polity, seeking to exert their will and determine the legitimacy of centralized government, so reformed. And the masses' entry then into the political realm under the banner of nationalism was seen generally as an "inclusive and liberating force" or for having "preserved pluralism . . . (and) political liberalism."[1] For instance, England's parliamentary rule is hailed for establishing "personal liberty with lessons learned about the need for religious toleration."[2] Inspired by such supposed respect for diversity, Yael Tamir has argued that nationalism and inclusive liberalism can and do go together, even at their start.[3]

The resulting image is of a consistently "civic" form of western European nationalism often distinguished from the more exclusive or "ethnic" nationalism that would emerge later in the east or elsewhere.[4] And this image of civic inclusiveness is consistent with arguments that such nationalism did not begin to emerge until the causal processes of spreading vernacular, literacy, and industrialization had also become more inclusive in the eighteenth century for Europe. Western nationalism has thus been associated with the rise of an industrializing and increasingly literate bourgeoisie coming to power, and not just with mass cohesion and loyalty to the state but with those masses actually exerting democratic control over the state. The implication is that European nationalism was from its start a liberal or inclusive sentiment associated with similarly liberal and inclusive forms of representation, as nobly envisioned by the Enlightenment thinkers.

This image of inclusive civic nationalism may indeed be relatively accurate for the period begun at the end of the eighteenth century, but in its particular historical focus it hides as much as it reveals. Demarcating the age of nationalism and examining it as an established social force when it had become so evident and relatively consolidated reinforces the image of European nationalism as civic. Indeed, because by then the populace within state boundaries was more homogenous, nationalism could be and was relatively inclusive and liberal. But this focus ignores the earlier processes that made this result possible. For instance, Rogers Brubaker's examination of the inclusive *jus soli* rules of citizenship in modern France is accurate but also rests upon a temporal focus that ignores France's earlier exclusions of Protestants.[5] This kind of analysis, focusing on established collective sentiment and boundaries of nationalism ignores the less static earlier and more uncertain processes by which such established nationalism emerged. It thereby reifies forms of nationalism, defining it as a secured collective sentiment of loyalty to a state and then directs explanation accordingly to those processes that fit the phenomenon as it had become established. But such a focus on consolidated practices should not be so constraining or determinant of explanation for the development of nationalism more generally.

To explain how nationalism emerged we must look behind the historical veil of when it had been consolidated to the period when its form, boundaries, or even existence were less sure. Indeed, nationalism was invented or envisioned in early forms well before it was consolidated as a liberal force under the Enlightenment or democracy. And exploration of the origins of western European nationalism has suggested a different form and set of explanations than the consensus on civic inclusiveness. Amid diversity and often violent internal discord, inclusion of all in what would become the nation was simply not possible. Nor had literacy, communication, or economic relations developed enough to either be so inclusive or to produce unity. Instead, collective solidarity was gradually and fitfully built or reinforced through exclusion, particularly of heretics, turning religious cleavages into a basis for selective solidarity. Homogeneity was established by such forceful and often violent exclusion, which was not voluntary. Where passions of faith had been fanned and so channeled, increased popular engagement and consolidated identity emerged as an early form of nationalism. In Spain, France, and England, religious antagonisms inherited from the past were deployed to bolster state authority (or resistance to it) and unity of a majority, consolidated to varying degrees on the basis of common faith.

Western nationalism then began not as fully civic but more ethnic, or at least on occasion exclusionary according to perceived differences. And it emerged not in the era of liberal democracy but instead in an era of absolutism and as an initially illiberal force, at a time when the very notion of toleration was widely seen more as vice than virtue. Indeed, exclusions and intolerance provided the early foundation and cohesion on which later more liberal and inclusive orders could be built, including parliamentary democracy. Such attempts at liberal nationalism and toleration as we understand it today were only possible after the earlier dirty work was largely completed and despite later denials.

But, like others I have criticized, we should not then fall into the trap of assuming a single pattern of nation-building based on analysis of one particular set of experiences or time period. Insisting that early Western nationalism was never and could not become civic would be no more accurate than insisting it was always civic. Indeed, building cohesion through religious fanaticism would not be consistently followed, even in the early modern era. In all three of the countries here considered, the seventeenth century saw dramatic breaks from the use of religious exclusion to consolidate popular support or central state authority. Monarchs put aside their own passions and enacted or allowed relative tolerance or coexistence, downplaying the binding effects of impassioned conflict. In a sense, they could afford to project tolerance because prior conflicts and exclusions had solidified authority or popular support that those monarchs at least thought they could take for granted and did. Exclusion had ratcheted up solidarity, which monarchs then sought to free from its basis in intolerance. They understood that where religious divisions remained, more complete cohesion would require compromise rather than enforced conformity that might reignite conflict. As Tennyson wrote, rulers then sought "by slow prudence to make mild a rugged people, and thro' soft degrees subdue them to the useful and the good."[6]

While we should not denigrate these efforts at pragmatic inclusion, the previous chapters have already demonstrated that tolerance was often disparaged and had earlier proved vulnerable. Passions and conflicts had exploded, pushing polities into the pattern of solidifying support through exclusion, and would again. Still, it remains notable that coexistence, if not tolerance in its modern sense of assuming equality, was attempted again in the aftermath of exclusion, albeit as interregnums between prior and then subsequent intolerance. The later return to exclusion would reaffirm the power of the more pervasive pattern of intolerance as a tool for managing discord; religious antagonism again reemerged as more cohering, overwhelming efforts at more "civic" nationalism. But in this period, early modern Europe itself wavered between ethnic or exclusionary efforts at nation-building and more civic or inclusionary efforts, the latter arguably more focused on state-building. Neither was a forgone conclusion, and that both were attempted suggests that the image of nations emerging from a single process consistently pursued is wrong, especially if we are looking at the formative period before more complete consolidation of national unity. And that greater toleration was even attempted in this period of religious antagonisms—even if later reversed—makes the attempts even more worthy of consideration.

In terms of nationalism theory, the implication of such variations in how political mass cohesion was built is that the "civic" and "ethnic" forms of nationalism have been falsely dichotomized as alternative paths. There remains an analytic and empirical distinction between more inclusion or exclusion, but nation-building did not consistently pursue one or the other. If the West itself varied between exclusion and inclusion, then we cannot definitively distinguish the East as "ethnic" and the West as consistently "civic," nor can we explain the development of nationalism in the West purely within either model. Instead, we must explain how and why the West varied in its forms of nation-building.

In charting such variations, we may find hints as to the conditions under which more exclusionary or inclusionary efforts at nation- or state-building are pursued. Earlier intolerance had forged greater national cohesion, which monarchs then took for granted, redirected, or put in abeyance so as to diminish conflict or the anarchic threats of mass mobilization and to build further state authority. Spain would follow this pattern only to a limited extent, for there nationalism remained relatively underdeveloped in the absence of any unifying antagonism against remaining heretics, and state-building was more focused on maintaining empire. France and England had no empire, and domestic religious conflicts had more passionately engaged and solidified elites and populace, which then wearied of ongoing conflict, allowing for a reassertion of control and renewed efforts at state-building from above amid efforts toward toleration.

The causal implication to be fleshed out here is that conflictual mass political engagement is curvilinear in itself and in its effects on the form of nation-building. As already suggested, such engagement emerges with religious conflict, bringing popular passions into play. Sharing such passions, elites then both aggravate those tensions and manipulate them, taking sides with formal and violent exclusions of a faction to cohere a core constituency of support. The result is "ethnic" nationalism. But such violence and engagement tends to become exhausted, the cost of ongoing conflict becomes too high, and pragmatic elites then seek to restore their control and to dampen conflict through inclusion. They settle for coexistence and prudence to keep the populace mild and governable. The result is "civic" nationalism, though not necessarily as an all-encompassing or permanent approach. Threats to the state or resurgent passions and potential conflict may then again bring a return to binding exclusions, as explored in the next chapter.

It is the intervening turn from earlier conflict and exclusions to imposed peace and some degree of toleration that is the focus of this chapter, and the focus of efforts by those monarchs who made this noble attempt. Of course, given past history, Henri IV in France and Charles II in England would remain mindful of again inflaming the nation and wary of a return to conflict. Henri was more pragmatic and successful, though he was eventually killed for his efforts. Charles was less sure, less successful at bringing toleration, and more provocative in his own religious leanings, though he did enjoy a peaceful death before antagonism engulfed his successor. Spain would pursue tolerance less fully and with less risk.

Spain: Exhausted Exclusions and Pragmatic Tolerance

As before, Spain emerges here as somewhat exceptional. The degree to which central state authority and popular allegiance to it had been consolidated together with the Inquisition remains arguable. But those efforts had reached a plateau in the sixteenth century, when Spain faced an array of domestic difficulties. By the end of that century, the economy had been weakened by foreign competition, Castile had lost roughly 10 percent of its population to the plague, and demand for food outstripped supply due to bad harvests and population increase.[7] To meet resulting challenges, state authority would have to be built further, while in France and England this project was more advanced.

Even in the aftermath of Ferdinand and Isabella's partnership of

Castile and Aragon, and the centralizing Inquisition, the Spanish state remained too weak to address its domestic difficulties. With local magnates still strong, Spain was more a loose confederation of provinces than a strongly unified state. "The areas in which the state had competence were limited, no proper bureaucracy existed, and the main business of the king was to raise a few taxes in order to keep the peace or wage war . . . Most provinces enjoyed their own laws, institutions and monetary system, and were subject to the political control of their local nobility."[8] Debt remained a pressing problem throughout the reigns of Ferdinand and Isabella's grandson Charles V and his son Philip II, with the tax burden shared unequally and particularly pressing upon Castile, which revolted in the 1520s. Aragon's protection of Antonio Perez against the king had to be defeated militarily in 1591, Catalonia revolted in 1640, and Andalusia nearly revolted in 1641.[9] Philip II summoned the general Cortes only twice, in 1563 and 1585, and otherwise continued to meet with provincial bodies as autonomous powers. And though he had established Madrid as the permanent capital of Spain in 1561, five years after the abdication of his father, bureaucratic centralism remained more a principle than a reality.[10]

Consistent with the lack of state consolidation was a comparable lack of national cohesion, reinforced by separate provincial institutions retaining loyalty that occasionally exploded into revolts. Indeed, the centralizing Inquisition itself had also provoked regional resistance, reaffirming the continued decentralization of loyalty. Charles himself was "conscious of the poverty of royal ritual in Spain" that might otherwise draw centralizing allegiance. Nor could or did printing of books or newspapers make much of an inroad into popular consciousness, as the level of literacy in the country remained low. Those who were literate continued to be the elite, with the most investment in their own local power, and even they read and conversed in their own dialects. The first Castillian translation of the Bible was not printed until 1569.[11] And the central state remained wary of using literacy or schooling to further cohere its population, fearing that it would instead bolster resistance and local loyalties. In 1558 Philip II imposed a penalty of death or confiscation for publication of books without official license, as compared to the 1502 penalty of fines or disqualification. Even by the early seventeenth century, grammar schools were being closed and the publication of books further limited.[12]

The state's faltering interest in national unity was evident in an increasing wariness to so utilize the most prominent instrument for achieving that goal, the Inquisition. Charles's written instructions to his son and heir urged him to "never allow heresies to enter your realm; support the Holy Inquisition . . . and on no account do anything to harm it." In 1558, with the discovery of some Protestant "cells" in Valladolid and Seville, Philip did fear the spread of such "creators of sedition, upheaval, riots and disturbance in the state," but the actual threat remained small. And he had already enacted statutes requiring "purity of blood" in four cathedrals in Granada. But Philip was also mindful of his father's 1548 decree calling for freedom of religion, and he executed only one-third as many heretics as did Mary Tudor, and half as many as Henri II. Indeed, the Inquisition seems to have been largely preoccupied with its own organization. In 1547 Philip approved paying salaries to Inquisition officials, replacing their prior dependence on confiscation, and from 1559 to 1566 the king was asserting the power of the Inquisition and disputing the power of the pope to try Cardinal Carranza.[13]

Clearly some of the previous passion had dissipated. Despite continued challenges from local powers, the central state had gained some confidence, bolstered by the revenues and power gained through inquisition and empire. As such, the state could afford to allow a relaxation of the Inquisition without loss of authority. But this apparent internal tolerance was probably more a result of the simple fact that the Inquisition had itself become exhausted and was reaching the end of its impetus. Jews had been expelled and Catholic unity reinforced. There was less left for the Inquisition to do, with apparent tolerance thus actually a reflection of consolidated intolerance.

The exception was in continued antagonism against the descendants of the Moors. Given that "Spain itself had been forged in the white heat of conflict with the Moors," it is not surprising that the legacy of this conflict was easily reignited by the rebellion of the Alpujarras in 1568–1570.[14] Immediately thereafter, 80,000 Moriscos were forcibly removed from Granada to elsewhere in the kingdom. In 1609 the king ordered the expulsion of the Moriscos, "the act of a weak government anxious for easy popularity at a time of widespread national discontent."[15] By the end of the expulsion in 1614, Valencia and Andalucia in particular had suffered a major loss in population and rural labor. The rising bourgeoisie had hoped that this expulsion of rural labor would weaken the landed aristocrats, but the nobility in turn reneged on its loans to the bourgeoisie, deepening the general economic difficulties further. With the prior fear of Protestants and then of Moriscos, the "chronic dread of heretics, even if few Spaniards ever saw one of those fearsome creatures, supplied the foe within the gates that Spain always had need of to distract attention from its real enemies, the rich."[16] But with few such internal heretics remaining as a threat, the passions and unifying effect of exclusion withered.

To a large extent, the Spanish crown's attention was more distinctly focused outside its gates, with the imperatives for holding its diverse empire cutting against any interest in further forging exclusionary cohesion. Philip was emperor of "the biggest accumulation of states ever known in European history," and in 1586 "with the absorption of Portugal, Philip's authority now reached also into India, Indonesia, and China. The empire, so extensive as to stagger the imagination, was the biggest ever known in history."[17] Such imperial reach brought great victories (over the Ottomans at Lepanto, 1571) and defeats (the Armada decimated by England in 1588 and later in the Thirty Years War), new sources of revenue (American silver), and great tax burdens (falling disproportionately on Castile). But empire also diluted homogenous cohesion and pulled against further exclusions, for instance with Philip accommodating Lutherans in his German holdings and considering marriage to Elizabeth of England after the death of her half sister and his former wife, Mary. Spain's army, brought together for particular campaigns, consisted mostly of foreign mercenaries who could be drawn from diverse imperial holdings only if the state downplayed further religious exclusions. Even top officials of the crown "focused their loyalty not on any single nation but on the emperor, a personage transcending nations."[18] The Count-Duke Olivares would ultimately conclude "I am not nacional; that is something for children."[19]

To consolidate governance both at home and abroad, Spain's rulers had concluded that their emphasis should be on building state authority more than on using religious passions to further cohere unity, which had always been more limited. Indeed, by the early seventeenth century, ruling elites had come to see the unifying effects of fanaticism as inconsistent with imperial state-building, abandoning any impetus for the former in favor of the latter. Relative domestic authority was taken for granted or accepted in its limited form, and sectarianism was downplayed to avoid resistance in the periphery. Continuing in the tradition of pursuing top-down interests, Spain proved again more interested in consolidating elite power and empire than in cohering internal loyalty from below, which might have been pursued through continued exclusions.

Instead, greater tolerance was seen as essential for effective governance of so vast a realm. Olivares, himself from a family including conversos, would argue in 1625 that exclusion from office or rights of those whose blood was not limpieza, deprived that state of many skilled men; "The law prohibiting honours is unjust and impious, against divine law, natural law and the law of nations . . . [Those so excluded] find themselves—even when they excel all others in virtue, sanctity and scholarship—condemned." Despite resistance from some elites, by 1627 the Count-Duke had arranged for "a temporary edict of grace" allowing "men of uncertain ancestry" to serve the crown. God was still prayed to, but faith was to some degree removed from the realm of political machinations, abandoning and diluting the binding effects of earlier exclusions.[20]

Instead, Spain's rulers focused more fully on retaining their imperial holdings, having the effect of building state authority. Olivares urged "your Majesty to make yourself King of Spain . . . work and secretly scheme to reduce these kingdoms of which Spain is composed to the style and laws of Castile." To fund increasingly centralized power, already in the 1560s and 1570s taxes in Castile had been tripled, and by 1624 Olivares had proposed a single consolidated tax and national banks.[21] Revenues were used to maintain the empire and to defeat external challenges, which had become more pressing than internal resistance. Notably, resistance in the Lowlands proved impossible to crush, though tremendous efforts and expense would be directed to this effort.

Two interconnected themes emerge. Spain's Inquisition remained in force, notably in its increasing prosecutions for witchcraft, but it had already reached a climax with expulsion of Jews and then Moriscos, leaving a domestic population more homogenous and somewhat more unified by Catholicism. The result had the appearance of tolerance but only the appearance, if that. Actually, there were few heretics or foreigners left to tolerate. And rather than produce a greater focus on domestic cohesion, Spain's official attention was then turned to the imperatives of state-building and of empire. To consolidate power over its diverse holdings, the cohering effects of religious exclusion were somewhat relaxed. The focus on state building brought the image of greater civicness or inclusion, foregoing the nation-building imperative bolstered by greater exclusion.

As we shall see in the next chapter, the imperatives of state would again inflame intolerance, though still more outwardly directed, leaving domestic cohesion oddly incomplete. Spain wavered between inclusive state-building at home and more exclusionary imperial consolidation, although attempts in both directions remained incompletely accomplished. Domestic unity of faith remained largely that, not as a bulwark for more secular cohesion. The project of empire distracted Spain's rulers from nation-building, with the crown's authority unchallenged by religious discord at home that might have impelled further efforts at building domestic loyalty. The risks of greater disorder that might come with further efforts to build such loyalty seemed hardly worthwhile. As a result, royal authority was maintained—but more as widespread institutional veneer and with relatively little deepening of mass engagement.

⫸ France: To Oppose the Storm

Spain's relative internal homogeneity and diverse empire contrast with France's experiences, with neither internal unity of faith nor then with empire. But as with Spain, internal challenges to central authority gradually diminished, even if they did not disappear. To consolidate rule, France would also relax its religious exclusions, turning its attention instead to less conflictual and more inclusive state-building.

But before this turn, internal conflict reemerged in France, as if as a reminder of the potential costs of a return to past civil wars. With the death in 1589 of Henri III shortly after that of his mother Catherine de' Medici, France again descended into the maelstrom of religious wars for four years, threatening the very existence of the state. The rightful royal heir was the most prominent Protestant survivor of the St. Bartholomew's Day massacre that had followed his later annulled wedding. But Henri de Navarre's ascension was resisted by the Catholic League, aghast that after all a one-time Protestant would gain the throne. Paris and most of the larger towns where anti-Protestant passions were most enflamed, also resisted the new king, refusing to recognize his legitimacy with either obedience or material support. Henri purportedly then described himself as "a king without a kingdom, a husband without a wife, and a warrior without money."[22]

Salvation was achieved, appropriately enough, by conversion. In 1593, Henri abjured the Protestant faith at the abbey of Saint-Denis. (Actually, he had done so once before, to save himself after the St. Bartholomew massacre, but that conversion was discredited for having been conducted privately and under duress.) Though ten years before Henri had disclaimed the idea of conversion, arguing that religion "is not something you discard like a shirt, for it dwells in the heart," (before and) after he apparently saw the necessity of a change of spiritual wardrobe.[23]

FAITH IN NATION

Catholic fanatics nonetheless decried this conversion as cynical, falsely ascribing to the king the famous quote that "Paris is worth a mass." But Henri "was a modern-thinking king who put reasons of state, order and politics ahead of religion as a priority."[24]

Here at last was a singularly pragmatic monarch, who had learned after 1572 to subordinate his own faith and even to swallow his pride, biding his time to gain power, serve his country, and preserve the state intact. When the opportunity presented itself, Henri concluded that if he were to stand on principle against conversion, "in a short time there would be neither king nor kingdom in France. I desire to give peace to my subjects and repose to my soul. Decide among you what is needed for your security; I shall always be ready to satisfy you."[25]

Conversion had the desired effect of appeasing the fanaticism of many and avoiding a return to conflict. Henri marched into Paris and Spain's troops marched out, with the King foregoing vengeance even against those Leaguers who had fought against him so long.[26] Weary of war, the people of France rallied to their new king. "In province after province the peasants banded together . . . and compelled the municipal authorities to come to terms with Henri IV. It was an extraordinary spontaneous movement, compounded of a hatred of anarchy and social oppression, and a mass rallying of the people of France to their anointed King."[27] The wealthy also rallied to the king, seeking to restore stability and to reaffirm social order based on the presumption of hereditary succession through the male line. The nation was drawn together, with those holdouts effectively bought by royal grants.[28] This popular and elite cohesion of support for the king was reinforced by its international implication, both ending Spanish royal claims to the contested French throne and effectively ending the power of the pope to interfere in France's royal succession. The pontiff's excommunication and royal exclusion of Henri from 1585 was overturned by Henri's conversion, with the pope's granting absolution in 1595.

At the same time, Henri remained cognizant of the need to retain some balance between the Catholic majority and the Protestant minority of which he had been the leading member, and also with international allies of both. According to Voltaire, Henri "was not so ungrateful as to wish to exterminate a sect, so long the enemy of kings, but to which he owed in part his crown . . . At that period the Huguenots in France comprised about a twelfth part of the nation. Among them were to be found many powerful lords and whole towns."[29] Keeping his ties to this group, Henri appointed Huguenots to his council and as marshal of France, while his personal entourage remained almost completely Protestant or converts therefrom. On the international front, Henri reluctantly made peace with Spain but also continued to support his old allies, the Protestant rebels in the Lowlands. And he repaid her long support for his ascension by also formalizing an alliance with Elizabeth of England.[30] Indeed, until her death in 1603, the briefly coterminous reigns of Elizabeth and Henri IV were a remarkable coincidence of relatively peaceful state-building in Europe's two greatest powers.

Seizing the opportunity of diminished internal conflict, Henri then made a dramatic move to consolidate peace among France's religious factions. In 1598, Henri's efforts to forge such cohabitation culminated in his Edict of Nantes, the single most important enactment for toleration of the age. The practical interest in establishing a lasting peace was made clear in the opening clauses, where the king thanked God for having been given "Power and Strength not to yield to the dreadful Troubles, Confusions, and Disorders, which were found at our coming to this Kingdom, divided into so many Parties and Factions . . . enabling us with Constancy in such manner to oppose the Storm, as in the end to surmount it, reducing this Estate to Peace." And the benefits of such peace, both for economic and political consolidation, were also clearly laid out: "all Hostility and Wars through the Kingdom being now ceased, and we hope he will also prosper us in our other affairs . . . as also that the fury of War was not compatible with the establishment of Laws."[31]

Looking back in 1666, Chatelet argued that the Huguenots gained the protections of the edict "by violent extortion, sword in hand."[32] And Louis XIV, in his 1685 revocation of the edict, argued that "our grandfather of glorious memory" had issued the edict originally "desirous that the peace which he had procured for his subjects after the grievous losses they had sustained in the course of domestic and foreign wars" not be undone. The edict, argued Louis, granted what was then "thought necessary for maintaining the tranquility of his kingdom and for diminishing mutual aversion between the members of the two religions."[33] While Chatelet and Louis thereby justified the revocation of the edict no longer needed to maintain peace, in doing so they acknowledged the prior necessity and logic of the edict to establish that peace and preserve the state. Until some future time when all Frenchmen shared a single religion as fellow Catholics, at least a temporary order of coexistence and relative tolerance was necessary to preserve peace, and the Edict of Nantes set the terms for this arrangement.

The particulars of the Edict of Nantes are not in themselves surprising, given the intention to establish peace through coexistence. Protestants were permitted "to live and dwell in all the Cities and places of this kingdom," observe religion in their houses or established places of worship, print and publish books "where the publick exercise of said Religion is permitted," and "be capable of holding and exercising all Estates, Dignities, Offices and publick charges whatsoever." And "any Prisoners who are yet kept . . . by reasons of the Troubles, or of the said Religion, they shall be released."[34] In a further set of secret articles and attached letters, the king further agreed to subsidize the salary of Protestant pastors, and even paid for fifty military garrisons to protect Huguenot strongholds.[35] Henri was prepared to offer any liberties, guarantees, or even bribes to ensure, if not buy, the loyalty of the Huguenots and thereby to ensure peace.

Consistent with but also reaching beyond the pragmatic interest in peace was the hope that this peace should and would provide a new basis for further social cohesion. According to Voltaire, the edict "brought the Calvinists together on equal footing with the rest of the nation. It was in truth bringing enemies together."[36] The first two clauses of the edict itself spoke directly to the point, "declaring and ordaining; 1. That the memory of all things passed . . . during the other precedent troubles . . . shall remain extinguished and suppressed, as things that had never been . . . 2. We prohibit to all our Subjects . . . to renew the memory thereof, to attaque, resent, injure, or provoke one the other by reproaches for what is past. . . . but to contain themselves, and live peaceably together as Brethren, Friends and fellow-Citizens."[37]

Henri's inclusive project was made all the more explicit by the king in speeches he gave demanding obedience to his edict. On January 5, 1599, an informally attired monarch summoned the parlement to the Louvre, "where I come to speak with you not in royal habiliments . . . but apparelled like a father to a family . . . to speak familiarly to his children . . . That which I have done is for the good of the peace . . . I will cut the root of all those factions . . . Those which will not have my Edict to pass seek wars . . . Necessity constrained me to make this Edict."[38] Henri concluded, "Simply do as I command you, or rather what I beg you. You will do it not only for me but also for yourselves and for the fair cause of peace."[39] In November that same year, he reiterated that the Edict should be "implemented throughout my kingdom. It is high time that all of us, drunk with war, sobered up."[40]

Though not everyone was happy with how it was accomplished, France did sober up from its binge of war. Protestants wanted more concessions while Catholics thought too many had been granted. Pope Clement VIII was appalled: "An edict that permits liberty of conscience, [is] the worst thing in the world."[41] But Henri retained his balance and his focus, temporarily expelling the Jesuits while also repudiating the Catholic League. His approach "signaled the triumph of political expediency over religion," reversing the prior approach of using religious antagonism for such expediency. Peace was achieved, both within and, from 1601 until 1610, on the borders as well.[42]

Henri then set out to use the opportunity of religious compromise and peace to build his centralizing state toward absolutism. In this project he was ably assisted by Sully, the son of a Huguenot who appropriately enough had had no compunctions about having compromised his faith to save himself, escaping the massacre of St. Bartholomew's by pretending to be a Catholic. Politique paid off for the state as well. Together, Sully and Henri doubled the state's revenues, largely by shifting to indirect taxes, rationalizing tax-farming, and establishing the sale of offices. An estimated debt of 296 million livres in 1599 was transformed into a reserve treasury and gold of more than 13 million livres by 1610. Industries were encouraged, Paris redesigned, armed forces reorganized, bridges and waterways improved, the currency stabilized. The power of intermediate bodies was curtailed. The Estates were simply never called.[43]

Henri even adjusted his personal life according to the imperatives of state building. In 1599 he requested the annulment of his marriage to Marguerite, who he had not seen since 1582, ten years after their eventful marriage that had set the stage for the St. Bartholomew's Day massacre. The next year he married Marie de Medici, simultaneously reaffirming his Catholicism and gaining him an astonishing dowry of 1.8 million livres, enough to cover half of France's debt to the grand duke of Tuscany.[44] And symbolizing his efforts to build more positively upon the foundations of past turmoil, Henri IV planned the construction of a beautiful square in Paris. The Place des Vosges was built on the former site of the Tournelles, where Henri II's accidental death had led to the religious wars, with that palace having been torn down by Catherine de' Medici in a fit of vengeance even against stone.

This impressive record of state-building coincided with a continued determination to retain a balance between religious factions, including in relation to international allies. In 1601, when the future Louis XIII was born, the pope agreed to serve as godfather. And in 1604, Henri's earlier alliance with Elizabeth of England was eclipsed by James I's treaty with Spain, leaving France more independent of foreign ties. On the other hand less favorable to Catholicism, Henri by 1609 had helped to win independence from Spain for the United Provinces. And perhaps more ominously for later relations within France, the Huguenots by the end of Henri's reign had been permitted to maintain eighty-four fortresses under their control within the country.[45]

Of course, not everyone in France appreciated such evenhandedness nor trusted the Catholic realm in the hands of a former heretic. Many resented the increased taxes used to build the state and the "revolutionary" way in which the king "undermined long-established customs, privileges, franchises and liberties." Indeed, the king survived sixteen attempts on his life and a total of twenty-three known plots against him. Finally, on 14 May 1610, Ravaillac was successful where so many had failed, mortally stabbing the king when the sovereign's carriage was stuck in Paris traffic. The assassin was an ardent Catholic and opponent of the Edict of Nantes, who believed that the king's conversion was insincere. But much as Henri merged his concern and efforts for religious tolerance with state-building, Ravaillac constrained his intolerance with similar concerns of state. The assassin claimed to have waited to kill the king until the day after the queen was crowned "to avoid precipitating outbreaks of civil strife in a country deprived of all legitimate authority."[46] In this amazing age, both kings and regicides were guided by shared imperative of state order.

The assassin killed the king but not his policies. Marie, acting as regent for then nine-year-old Louis XIII, reaffirmed the Edict of Nantes within eight days of the assassination, and that reaffirmation was repeated four times during the next five years. This ongoing toleration of the Huguenots was matched by a bolstered alliance with Catholic Spain, sanctified by the double marriages of French and Spanish heirs to their respective siblings, arranged in 1615. The overall result was a "secularization of identity," most notably with a centralizing state emerging "as an object of loyalty." Under the administration of Cardinal Richelieu, France "contained Huguenots and Jansenists; it received the fugitives of the Roman and Spanish Inquisitions; it published the works suppressed by the Roman censorship," all while remaining unquestionably Catholic.[47]

In effect, the French had embraced at least temporary or pragmatic coexistence, foregoing the cohering effects of further religious exclusion, with elites instead focusing on state-building. In part, France could afford this attempt given the coherence achieved by earlier exclusions. But those exclusions had also exploded out of control, threatening the unity of France and the very existence of the state, with the populace growing weary of ongoing conflict impinging upon stability and prosperity. And to continue with such purist exclusions would have left France without an heir to its throne, promising further conflict and instability. Instead, greater tolerance was enacted amid diminished conflict. The passions of exclusionary nationalism were put in abeyance, paving the way for the building of greater centralized state authority.

Henri's legacy was indeed, as Voltaire described it, in "bringing enemies together" to allow for state building, though his legacy of tolerance would not survive amid increasing internal discord. Without the "skill of that great King . . . in 1616 [adversaries] resorted to arms in certain places, and the boldness of the Huguenots combining with the dissensions of the court, hostility toward the favourites and the unrest of the nation, all was in a state of prolonged disturbance."[48] To contain this reemerging conflict, the prior pattern of exclusion would reassert itself. By the 1620s, intolerance was resurgent, in 1685 the Edict of Nantes was rescinded, and 1715 saw "the official fiction that there were no more Protestants in France."[49] Henri's interregnum of tolerance and inclusion proved to be just that, though no less notable for not lasting.

England: Burying Seeds of Discord

The pattern of coexistence established in the aftermath of turmoil and exclusion was also evident in England after the Civil War, if less fully than under France's Henri IV. Conflict had reached a crescendo, with intolerance and exclusion bringing national unity in opposition to the crown. Central power was then again consolidated amid attempts at greater religious tolerance, albeit with some ambivalence and only briefly. This attempted tolerance did allow for a restoration of monarchical authority, though constrained and reformulated, and for continued efforts at building state authority under crown and parliament. Restoration of stable authority, the popular desire for which would be enunciated by Thomas Hobbes, was achieved. But religious passions remained concentrated in a more independent Parliament than had yet emerged in France. Though Catholics by 1670 would represent only about 2 percent of the population and posed less of a threat, and Parliament would become more focused on divisions among Protestants, the rhetoric of anti-Catholicism remained.[50] Those passions would be exerted again against the crown, which compromised its toleration enough to retain the monarchy and ensure succession, avoiding a return to open internal conflict for a while.

At least in terms of policy, the Commonwealth and later Protectorate after Charles I's execution wavered between tolerance and exclusion. Under Oliver Cromwell, law-abiding Catholics were largely free from persecution. They were seen as too small in number to be a threat, and they had been more loyal than most Dissenters during the Civil War or Levellers thereafter. When criticized for his toleration of Catholics, Cromwell dissolved a more fanatical Parliament, complaining that "nothing will satisfy them unless they can put their finger upon their brethren's consciences, to pinch them there." The next year he even persuaded the Council of State to allow for the readmission of Jews into England. But Cromwell also argued that "no temporal government could have a sure support without a national church that adhered to it." In 1657 he was petitioned to exclude from Parliament any "who do or shall profess the Popish religion."[51]

But the Protectorate's somewhat ambiguous rhetoric and policy of toleration was to a great degree overshadowed by its suppression of Scottish Catholics and even more so by its strong-arm tactics applied against Irish Catholics. Following an established pattern, English anti-Catholic politics was played out in Ireland. In 1649, with crucial support from Scotland, Cromwell's army succeeded where prior ones had failed, conquering Ireland. Thereafter in Ireland, Catholic worship was outlawed, priests killed, and churches destroyed.[52] By 1652 the commonwealth had declared that all Irish "who have received orders from the Pope . . . be excepted from pardon for life and estate," and Catholics were deprived of land accordingly in three provinces.[53] At least as applied to the Irish, anti-Catholicism still moved the English nation. It certainly outlasted Cromwell's popularity, which fell amid a promonarchical movement, bringing a popular return of the monarchy after Cromwell's death in 1658.

Restoration then reaffirmed coexistence, amid a resurgent pragmatic interest in restoring tranquility under a monarch. In anticipation of his return to England, in April 1660 Charles II issued the stirring Declaration of Breda, comparable in intent to Henri's Edict of Nantes. Charles began by suggesting that "the general distraction and confusion which is spread over the whole kingdom doth . . . awaken all men to a desire and longing that those wounds which have so many years together been kept bleeding may be bound up." Charles granted a "free and general pardon . . . [for any] crime whatsoever committed against us or our royal father." To diminish "animosities" over religion "we do declare a liberty to tender consciences, and that no man shall be disquieted or called in question for differences of opinion in matter of religion which do not disturb the peace of the kingdom." With a flourish, the king proclaimed that "henceforward all notes of discord, separation and difference of parties be utterly abolished among all our subjects, whom we invite and conjure to a perfect union."[54]

And the first two years of Restoration did indeed see affirmation of the coexistence promised at Breda. In 1660, "to put an end to all suits and controversies" Charles issued an Act of Indemnity and Oblivion offering a blanket amnesty "to bury all seeds of future discords and remembrance of the former."[55] That same year, the king declared that "the peace of the State is concerned in the peace of the Church" so that it was impossible to "preserve order and government in civil [affairs,] whilst there is no order or government in ecclesiastical affairs."[56] Though the monarch himself remained somewhat discrete and aloof in terms of issues of religion—not surprising given the fate of his father—his initial instincts certainly led him to preserve peace in state and church through greater toleration. On a more strategic front, perhaps he envisioned an alliance of Catholics and Dissenters. If so, then the 1676 census would show the impossibility of this strategy, with the two groups together nowhere more than 5 percent of the population.[57]

Given the Protestantism of the vast majority of subjects and despite Charles II's predilections, pressure on the monarch to distance himself from popery was strong and quickly evident in royal statements. Cognizant of his father's fall having been connected to accusations of Catholic sympathy, already in 1661 Charles II made it illegal to "maliciously and advisedly publish or affirm the king to be an heretic or papist . . . to incite or stir up the people to hatred or dislike of the person of his Majesty or the established government."[58] Charles later felt compelled to reiterate his commitment "to the true Protestant religion," rejecting as an "injurious scandal . . . of our favour to papists; as it is but a repetition of the same detestable arts by which all the late calamities have been brought upon this kingdom in the time of our royal father of blessed memory."[59]

Following the prior established pattern, loyalty to centralized power was then consolidated again with religious exclusion. In a set of acts known together as the Clarendon Code, Catholicism was forcibly contained. No one was to hold office who had not sworn allegiance and taken sacrament from the Church of England. As of St. Bartholomew's

Day 1662, ninety years after France's massacre, Charles concluded "that nothing conduceth more to the settling of the peace of this nation (which is desired of all good men), nor to the honour of our religion and the propagation thereof, than an universal agreement in the public worship" thereby required by the Act of Uniformity. By 1665, to avoid the spreading of "the poisonous principles of schism and rebellion," only those swearing allegiance could assemble within five miles of any city or town. And in 1670, no assembly of more than five persons was allowed for purposes of religion that was not in accord with the Church of England.[60] Popular anti-Semitism also reemerged.[61]

This shift away from the king's preference for coexistence reflected popular pressures concentrated in Parliament. To head off accusations of tyranny that had explosively joined with religious aspersion against his father, Charles II ensured that Parliament would assemble at least once every three years. And Parliament used its more regular meetings to further constrain the King's toleration. For instance, in 1668 when Charles spoke for such coexistence, Parliament refused to vote their thanks and allocated a reduced amount of financial supply to the crown.[62] Even as the first monarch since the Middle Ages to have a standing army, the king could not resist such pressure, and was all the more vulnerable to cutbacks in funding for that army and bureaucracy.[63]

More informal popular antagonism against Catholicism also raged. The widespread belief that Catholics had started the great fire of London in 1666 was officially endorsed by inscription on the Fire Monument, attributing the disaster to "the treachery and malice of the popish faction."[64] In 1671 a papist Captain Blood was caught having attempted to steal the royal crown and globe, defeated by the alarm of a young man who "cried Treason, the crown was stole."[65] And the image of dangerous popery was continually reinforced. A popular pamphlet described the prospect of England under the Catholics as a place of destitution, "your wives prostituted . . . your daughters ravished by goatish monks, your smaller children tossed upon pikes, or torn limb from limb, whilst you have your own bowels ripped open . . . never more to see a Bible, nor hear again the joyful sounds of Liberty and Property. This gentlemen is Popery."[66] Fear of such a calamitous Catholic takeover was stoked further by the growing power of France, especially after its military victories in 1667 and 1672.

The strength of France had a different implication for Charles II, who was attracted to an alliance with this powerful and rich sometime adversary. Through his sister, married to the brother of France's king,

Charles negotiated a secret Treaty of Dover in 1670. The text of this astonishing document includes that "the King of England, being convinced of the truth of the Roman Catholic religion, is resolved to declare, and to reconcile himself with the Church of Rome as soon as the state of his country's affairs permit. . . . But as there are always unquiet spirits who mask their designs under the guise of religion, the King of England, for the peace of his kingdom, will avail himself of the assistance of the King of France." More specifically, France promised to pay England a sum that doubled Charles's ordinary revenues. And as if to confirm suspicions of a linkage between popery and tyranny, the two kings also agreed "to humble the pride of the States General, and to destroy the power of a people," in particular with English assistance to French efforts against the Dutch.[67]

The combination of English popular antagonism against Catholicism and an English monarch personally sympathetic to that faith and aligned with its leading foreign power made for an explosive combination of which Charles was wary. The year before the Dover treaty, the French ambassador had sought to dampen Charles's own religious zeal and to postpone his plans to convert, "warning him of the danger of kindling tumult; for religion is a 'fire of brimstone and nitre,' consuming everything in an instant."[68] By the next year, Charles was eager to keep the treaty secret, excluding even some of his closest advisors from seeing the clause attesting to his own Catholicism, and he later feared that Louis would publicly reveal the treaty's terms. The treaty itself had committed that "the King of France undertakes to provide, at his own expense, 6,000 troops for the execution of this design, if they should be required." This offer of French troops to quell English domestic resistance to the treaty acknowledged the prospect of public antagonism to such a deal with the Catholic devil, let alone to any revelation of the king's own Catholic leanings.[69]

But having made the alliance with France and therein at least secretly attested to his own Catholic faith, Charles was inclined to again test the waters of greater domestic tolerance toward the Roman Church. In 1672 he issued the first Indulgence, in which he declared the failure of "the many and frequent ways of coercion that we have used for reducing all erring or dissenting persons, and for composing the unhappy differences in matters of religion. . . . For quieting the minds of our good subjects" he first committed himself to preserve the Church of England but then went on to suspend all penal laws "against whatsoever sort of nonconformists or recusants."[70] In speeches justifying the Indulgence, the king argued that he "found good effect of it by securing peace at home . . . put out for ends so necessary to the quiet of his kingdom." While assuring the Commons that he would preserve the Protestant faith and was not offering papists the right to practice their religion in public but only at home, he also stressed that those papists had "been loyal and in the service of me and of the king my father."[71]

Contrary to royal intention, the Indulgence "united most of the political nation . . . against Charles and his ministers," who then faced significant protests if not violence. Commons declared itself "very sensible of the great dangers and mischiefs that may arise within this your Majesty's realm by the increase of popish recusants amongst us" and argued that "penal statutes in matters ecclesiastical cannot be suspended but by Act of Parliament" and not by royal declaration. The king objected that he had done nothing inconsistent with anything "done in the reigns of any of his ancestors" nor acted against "properties, rights or liberties . . . or discipline of the Church of England." But in light of his reliance on Commons for revenue, he relented; "as I daily expect from you a bill for my supply, so I assure you I shall [be] . . . giving you satisfaction in all your just grievances."[72]

In effect, the conflict that had cost Charles I his head was threatening to reemerge under his son. Charles II was focused on building his own and the state's authority through greater toleration and alliance with foreign Catholic powers. But to others, in the words of Andrew Marvell, this looked again like a "design . . . to change the lawful government of England into an absolute tyranny and to convert the established Protestant religion into downright Popery."[73] Inspired by such fears, Parliament resisted, seeking to ensure its own power and popular loyalty based on continued anti-Catholicism. Mindful of the vulnerabilities made evident by his father's fall, Charles II astutely maneuvered to maintain monarchical power and succession and to avoid conflict as best he could, backtracking on toleration. But nonetheless, the nation was again roused by sectarian zeal against a popishly infected and arbitrary sovereign. The king's efforts at "civicness" were compromised.

The withdrawal of Indulgence to Catholics again reversed the move toward co-existence and allowed for even further intolerance enflamed by the king's opposing efforts. Sensing royal weakness and seizing the advantage, Parliament passed its first Test Act "for preventing dangers which may happen from popish recusants, and quieting the minds of his Majesty's good subjects." The act barred from any office all refusing the oath of allegiance, the sacrament "according to the usage of the

Church of England," or the declaration "that there is not any transubstantiation in the sacrament of the Lord's Supper, or in the elements of bread and wine." Irish Catholics were also to be subject to such restrictions.[74]

Having won legal action against popery, Parliament then turned to attack the king's ministers, seen as preferring "arbitrary government" and popery, again indistinguishable. Antagonism grew against an informal cabinet composed of non-Anglicans whose initials gave rise to the term "cabal."[75] And that antagonism was finally focused on the Lord High Treasurer, Danby. Despite his 1675 order confiscating two-thirds of the estates of recusants, Danby was nonetheless accused of treason and popery for his support for the alliance with Catholic France in return for a much-needed subsidy.[76] In 1678 Danby was impeached for trying "to introduce an arbitrary and tyrannical way of government" and for being "popishly affected."[77] In that same year, Parliament enacted a requirement that Catholics be licensed for permission even to come into the presence of the king or queen, and twenty-four Catholics were executed.[78]

On the defensive, Charles sought to bolster his own and his family's anti-Catholic credentials with two fateful steps. In 1677 he agreed to the betrothal of James's eldest daughter Mary to William of Orange, reinforcing Stuart ties to Protestantism, though also bolstering an alternative to the Catholic James in line of succession. And the next year, Charles approved of the Second Test Act "for preventing the increase and danger of popery in this kingdom . . . and for the safety of his Majesty's royal person and government." According to this act, no adherent of the Church of Rome could sit in the House of Peers or Commons, and anyone who refused to swear against Catholicism or who attended mass would lose four-fifths of their property. There was only one notable exception to this Act: "nothing in this Act contained shall extend to his Royal Highness the duke of York." Thus Charles sought to isolate his brother and heir from the gathering storm, and indeed the king had explicitly argued that he would enact laws of religious conformity "provided the succession remained intact."[79]

Parliamentary action was reinforced by, and in turn reinforced, popular animosity, itself focused on a supposed plot by papists to kill the king, replace him with his Catholic brother, and impose absolutist rule. According to one pamphlet of the day, "4000 men, consisting all of Irish, Scots and French papists . . . were immediately to march to London to assist [in] the proclaiming [of] the duke of York, and under that pretense to fall upon and to massacre and slaughter the people under the notion of fanatics who had murdered the king."[80] Fears of Catholics, of foreigners, and of royal treachery and tyranny were all rolled together in an explosive mix. Titus Oates, the disreputable source about the rumored plot, swore out an oath to a prominent justice of the peace later found murdered, whereupon Oates and others accused the queen of that deed and of treason against her own husband. Charles knew such accusations and the supposed plot to be false, but he was wary to act against the tide of public opinion, while the lack of arrests for the murder only further discredited his government.[81] Indeed, the plot had also helped bring Danby's downfall, for he was accused of having "traitorously concealed, after he had notice, the late horrid plot and conspiracy contrived by the papists against his majesty's person and government . . . immediately tending to the destruction of the king's sacred person and the subversion of the Protestant religion."[82]

The plot was only the most dramatic of antipapist rumors and attacks, spread by pamphlets and at gatherings. As "the nation's curse" according to Dryden, passions spread like wildfire: "Not weighed or winnowed by the multitude,/But swallowed in by the mass, unchewed and crude."[83] An explosion of pamphlets that "appealed to the nation at large" spread rumors ranging from a French invasion to royal plans to take lands away from nobles and restore them to the church. Others described again a takeover by Papists "ravishing your wives and daughters, dashing your little children's brains out against the walls, plundering your houses and cutting your own throats . . . casting your eye toward Smithfield, imagine . . . your nearest and dearest relations, tied to the stake in the midst of flames . . . which was a frequent spectacle the last time Popery reigned amongst us."[84] More level heads suggested that "where they cannot find Popery they will make it . . . It is no new thing for a popular outcry in the matter of religion to have a state faction in the belly of it."[85] But such attempts at analysis were pushed aside by the popular fever. Even Oxford University, concerned about "the machinations of traitorous heretics and schismatics" declared as "false, seditious and impious" a set of historical facts, and condemned books by Hobbes, Milton, and others "to be publicly burnt by the hand."[86] Burnings of the pope in effigy became a regular event in London, drawing large crowds that at least on one occasion numbered 200,000.[87]

As so often in the past, English anti-Catholic fervor was further stoked by fears and antagonism against Irish Catholics. "There had been recurrent reports in the 1660s and 1670s that the Catholic powers of

Europe, and especially the French, were preparing to make an attempt on Britain through the back door of Ireland ... In early January 1681, the Lords declared that they were 'fully satisfied' that 'for diverse years. . . . There hath been a horrible and treasonable Plot and Conspiracy, contrived and carried on by the Popish Religion in Ireland, for massacring the English, and subverting the Protestant Religion, and the ancient established Government."[88] The Catholic "Old English" of Ireland had reinforced such fears and antagonism by supporting the suspect monarchs, Charles I and later James II. Even when protestant nonconformists allegedly conspired against the crown in the Rye House Plot of 1683, the state moved to instead crush Irish Catholics seen as an aligned threat.[89]

But popular fanaticism came to focus more domestically on the duke of York, James, the royal heir who was a publicly declared Catholic and thus made papist tyranny a real threat. Like his Holiness the Pope, his royal highness was also burned in effigy and was the subject of defamation. According to one pamphlet in 1679, "without a miracle, our apparent ruin is at hand, the sword already hangs over our heads, and seems to be supported by no stronger force than that of a single hair, his Majesty's life." This pamphlet went on to suggest a solution: shifting the line of succession to Charles's bastard son, the duke of Monmouth, a Protestant. Indeed, his bastardy was described as a further advantage in making him beholden to Commons for his ascension and thus diminishing the prospects of tyranny so often linked to popery: "He who hath the worst title, ever makes the best king, as being constrained by gracious government to supply what he wants in title, [so] instead of 'God and my right,' his motto may be, 'God and my people.' "[90]

Parliament took up the cause of changing royal heirs, which the king resisted, producing a crisis over the exclusion of James II. As recently widowed duke of York, James had exacerbated the issue, publicly acknowledging his own Catholicism in 1673 when he resigned as lord high admiral to conform with the first Test Act and then married a Catholic princess, Mary of Modena. That was enough, without parliament even knowing that he was also hosting meetings with Jesuits in his own apartments. Parliament moved to insist on its own right to approve of royal marriages, an astonishing affront to the personal and power prerogatives of the crown. And on his side, despite his dislike of James and love for Monmouth, Charles refused to acknowledge the latter as his legitimate son so as to clear the way for the exclusion of James.[91] Instead, the king sought to allay popular fears by enforcing penal laws against Catholics and by delaying debate on exclusion until after the passions generated by rumors of a papist plot had cooled.[92]

But while a return to civil war was averted, the crisis over succession could not be avoided. Parliament drew up a bill of exclusion, citing that James "is notoriously known to have been perverted from the Protestant to the popish religion, whereby not only great encouragement hath been given to . . . horrid plots and conspiracies for the destruction of his Majesty's sacred person and government . . . if the said duke should succeed to the imperial crown . . . a total change of religion within these kingdoms would ensue." At the crucial moment, Shaftesbury reportedly offered to Charles to "make laws which will give legality to a measure so necessary for the quiet of the nation," altering the succession. The king refused: "I will not yield, nor will I be bullied."[93] Parliament was dissolved. Rather than reconvene at some tennis court and risk revolutionary conflict, as would their counterpart in France a century later, Commons dispersed to bide its time.

Though not yet revolutionary, the debate over exclusion had profound political effects within the bounds of formal institutions. Arguably this is when the two-party system came into existence in England, with Charles's supporters as founders of the Tories, opposed by supporters of parliamentary sovereignty, the Whigs. With the rather notable exception of protecting dissent by enacting habeus corpus in 1679, the Whigs focused their efforts on the exclusion of James. And though by no means a modern mass party, they did engage the populace in their cause to an unprecedented degree, for instance organizing petitions for the calling of Parliament, again pitting nation against crown. As we have seen, Charles had even earlier felt sufficiently threatened to make an alliance with France in return for funds, preferring "to become the client of France rather than the dependent of his own subjects," whose resistance the treaty anticipated. In 1683, when he did briefly recall Parliament, he did so to Oxford, thereby hoping to avoid the "influence of the London mob."[94]

Partisan efforts to skip over James's succession to the crown were eclipsed by the death of Charles II, who had blocked exclusion long enough to assure his brother's rise. Though there was little love lost between the brothers, Charles was committed to the uninterrupted line of succession, having seen that broken with his own father's execution. The king believed that such succession was essential for peaceful preservation of the state, or at least its monarchy.

But Charles's death raised another explanation of his defense of James, apparently not maintained despite James's Catholicism but at least plausibly also because of it. For on his deathbed, Charles himself finally kept his promise at Dover and converted. According to the dramatic report of the French Ambassador, the king summoned the one English-speaking priest still at court, John Huddleston, "a Scotsman who saved the king of England after the battle of Worcester, and who by Act of Parliament had been excepted from all laws made against the Catholics and against the priests." Huddleston entered the dying king's bedchamber with "a wig and gown on him to disguise him . . . The duke of York in presenting him said, 'Sire here is a man who saved your life, and is now come to save your soul.' "[95] Though derided as "fire insurance," this last-minute conversion likely reflected the monarch's true faith, placing him finally in that awkward line of Catholic-inclined monarchs of a Protestant people. The linkage between popery and absolutism was again confirmed.

Charles's conversion would again exacerbate anti-Catholicism directed against the crown, though politicians still held back from the revolutionary implications of this development. As Sir Henry Capel had earlier told the Commons in 1680, "in the descent of four kings, still the parliaments have been troubled with Popery; laws have been made against it, and all failed."[96] Not only did Catholics remain in the country and among foreign allies or enemies, but at least three of the four monarchs referred to by Capel had some Catholic links or inclinations themselves. Elizabeth's Protestantism, by political instinct and heritage, was unimpeachable. But James I, the son of Mary Queen of Scots, had made some attempts toward toleration. Charles I was married to a French Catholic and seen as overly sympathetic. Charles II most notably attempted toleration but was then forced to enact anti-Catholic legislation yet still ensured the succession of his Catholic brother and had himself converted at the last minute.

Of course, royal efforts at coexistence and leanings toward Catholicism paled in contrast to what would come next. The death of Charles II brought an actual Catholic to the throne, bringing to dramatic climax the rift between a popishly infected crown and an anti-Catholic nation represented in Parliament. With this distinction now again clear, the monarchical state would prove less powerful than the nation so inflamed. James II's own exclusion and that of his faith would ultimately be achieved in a "glorious revolution" reflecting the consolidation of a Protestant nation. Again, efforts at coexistence, more short lived than those of Henri in France, proved to be interregnum.

Despite their limitations and reversal, the attempts at toleration under Charles II are still worth consideration. As in France, the populace of England had already been relatively united by religious exclusions that they could now relax; they gradually tired of conflict and sought stability. Charles II took advantage of this opportunity to dampen popular passions and to attempt greater tolerance, providing for a period of renewed state-building or, more precisely, restoration of the monarchy. But whereas in France earlier religious conflict and exclusion had bolstered royal power, in England it had bolstered popular unity in opposition to the crown and had already cost one king his head. When Charles II went further toward toleration in opposition to Parliament, Commons reasserted itself in demanding limits on the rights of Catholics and of the crown itself. Exclusionary nationalism was reemerging as a popular force against the king's more inclusionary state-building, decried as popish tyranny.

That early modern Europe experienced periods of relative toleration and inclusion reminds us that historical developments do not follow a mechanical or unitary pattern. Popular cohesion previously built on the basis of religious fanaticism then gave way to a more civic ideal, though only after the former approach had provided a base of support on which to build and diminished conflict. But the relatively limited periods of such attempted inclusion—they stand out as exceptions in an age of intolerance—also reaffirm the more powerful impetus for exclusion. Monarchs assuming they could afford coexistence found that they were not as absolute in popular allegiance as they believed. As such, central state power remained weak and subject to challenge, which would force those monarchs and their successors or opponents to fall back again on the crutch of enflaming exclusive faithfulness. Indeed, the return to intolerance would be aggravated by those very efforts at toleration, apparently premature and therefore provocative of renewed animosity, discord, and renewed pressure to use religious shortcuts to restore a semblance of unity.

Given pressures against tolerance and the ultimate reversal of such efforts, why then was tolerance attempted in the interregnums? At least in part, the answer lies in a temporary convergence of pragmatism from below and above. After the upheaval of the French religious wars and England's revolution, the populace and elites of both countries were exhausted and fearful of the anarchic possibilities of continued conflict. Popular engagement having been unleashed against authority was contained to restore some version of authority and peace. Finding some semblance of unity clearly required compromise and coexistence with remaining minority religious factions and elites. And both Henri and Charles had learned from the painful experiences of prior war or regicide that a new form of pragmatism was necessary to ensure their hold on power and to strengthen their states. That both monarchs had been or remained themselves believers in the minority faith in their own countries surely reinforced their interest in a more tolerant form of cohesion, allowing them to hold and build power. And in Spain, elites, who had long been more focused on state power than volatile popular coherence and had never seen or fully enflamed popular religious passions, kept the Inquisition under tight control and then relaxed it to allow for more orderly state-building.

Pragmatic interests in building or restoring peaceful order impelled efforts not only to implement policies of relative tolerance but also to forget or put behind images of the past conflict that could still enflame domestic animosity and reignite conflict. Spain's rulers distanced themselves from the Inquisition. And cognizant that remembrances of past conflict tend to keep such conflict alive and cut against efforts at appeasement, both Henri and Charles issued official edicts mandating that memories of prior animosity be abolished.

But memory proved impervious to royal command. The wounds of the prior conflicts were still too fresh to be forgotten, popular loyalty to the crown remained constrained by faith, and state authority remained subject to challenge enflamed by memory. The resurgence of antagonistic memories took concrete form, with the dagger plunged into Henri and with the partisan daggers out in Charles's parliament.

Kings may hope that memory is subject to their command, but in its collective form it remains an element of popular engagement that had grown beyond and was uncertain in its loyalty to central control. In contrast to Spain, France's religious wars and England's Revolution had brought the masses more dramatically onto the stage of state politics, bringing with them their memories and prejudices. Earlier monarchs had sought instead to direct popular passions into exclusionary forms of loyalty, which Henri and Charles sought to convert to a more inclusive form of state-building. But under circumstances of recent conflict and remaining state weaknesses, those passions could not be dispelled by edict. The genie could not be so easily put back in the bottle. Conflict reemerged and popular engagement turned from support of royal tolerance to resistance against royal tolerance.

Moves toward tolerance, inclusion, and state-building had emerged in the eye of the storm, after the initial winds of spiraling intolerance had wiped away previous regimes and passed. But that eye would itself pass, with the return of the winds of passion and discord. After the interregnum of order and tolerance, Henri and Charles's royal successors would again attempt to bolster their popularity and power on the basis of the passions of religious fanaticism and exclusion.

In a sense, what connects the interceding attempts at coexistence is that the cohering passions of religious exclusion were taken for granted and put in abeyance during discrete periods of greater focus on state-building. Earlier fanaticism had either run its course or reached a level that threatened state authority more than it bolstered it—and in the case of England, actually brought down a monarch. Commoners and elites feared the anarchy posed by further conflict and backed down for a period to restore order and to allow for further consolidation of state power pursued more inclusively. Eventually, resulting tolerance again enflamed passions and conflict, bringing a revived focus on exclusionary nationalism.

The implication is that although nation- and state-building emerged together, they took different forms that were pursued more *ad seriutum* than together at one time. National unity was forged in response to conflictual passions resolved through exclusions akin to "ethnic nationalism," while-state building required more peaceful order and inclusion akin to "civic nationalism." The two processes did complement each other, with unity allowing for further state-building, but they also remained in tension. That tension would reemerge and bring a return to exclusion and intolerance in the aftermath of more inclusive state-building. Later heralded and consolidated civic inclusion proved premature in its earlier attempts, suggesting that the logic of "ethnic" exclusion was more applicable to emergent nation-building, even in Europe.

COHESION BY EXCLUSION, REDUX FROM ABOVE

"Dole Unequal Laws upon a Savage Race"

5

Fanatical exclusion was not the only course open to or attempted by nation and state builders. In the aftermath of earlier exclusions and some achieved popular coherence, Spain, France, and England to varying degrees had all turned to an inclusive approach to state-building. Earlier fanaticism was put in abeyance to restore order within which central state authority could be built further toward absolutism. Imperatives from above eclipsed and held in check the passions, at least for a time.

But the circumstances of popular exhaustion and elite pragmatism allowing for these inclusive efforts at state-building passed. Consolidation of institutional power and of popular allegiance remained incomplete, confronted anew by challengers and factions, themselves enflamed by both tolerance and greater central state power. To shore up authority and cohesion and to dampen potential discord, elites reengaged in the project of national consolidation during the seventeenth and eighteenth centuries, the more conventional focus of analysis of such efforts. But this reengagement revived the pattern of using exclusion to bolster unity that had proven effective a century or more earlier. Thus, nation- and state-building in the eighteenth century was neither as inclusive as much analysis has suggested nor explicable without reference to the earlier experiences as foundational. At its climax, the processes of consolidation forging central power and unity built upon the past, both in terms of inherited animosities channeled accordingly and in terms of the prior exclusionary techniques for achieving these goals revived and refined.

Attempted tolerance had again enflamed the populace, or at least threatened renewed conflict and challenges to established authority. As Tennyson wrote, rulers then sought to "mete and dole unequal laws upon a savage race," so they subdued by acceding to and encoding their prejudices.[1] To cohere popular support, elites had to again channel passions and avoid conflict that threatened to return after the previous interregnum, with a vengeance of the familiar.

But what appears familiar was not simply a repeat of the past. At least in France and England, earlier "founding" exclusions had emerged in response to more spontaneous religious conflict and engagement from below, which similarly impassioned elites themselves aggravated but also sought to get out in front of and ride rather than be thrown off. Resurgent exclusions emerged instead in the face of somewhat more limited mass conflict and engagement, with elites instead more purposefully manipulating images of intolerance for their own ends. Those powerful elites— imperial rulers in Spain, the French absolutist crown, and England's Parliament—were stronger than they had been but sought to reinforce their popular support by themselves reinvigorating intolerance. They had painfully learned what would work to bind their core constituency, and they now used that lesson. Nationalism was pursued more explicitly, with the crutch of religious exclusion cynically orchestrated from above more than it was forced from below. The memory of past passions and conflicts was reinvigorated and applied as a tool for nation-building, even if the actual level of conflict and violence from below was not equally resurgent.

Nationalism is always constructed as a bridge between elites and masses, requiring some convergence of forces and efforts from above and below. But the impetus for such efforts can vary. Whereas elites had briefly sought to control or harness mass passions that had exploded from below, after the interregnum of tolerance and state building elites now manipulated further religious exclusions from above to cohere loyalty and head off a return to full-scale civil war. In effect, the earlier possibilities and moves toward exclusionary nationalism were now embraced anew by elites more surely from above, reinforcing their efforts at statebuilding. This second wave of exclusionary nationalism suggests that this goal and technique for achieving it had become more sure, conscious, and planned by elites reaching down to their populace. Such nationalism was being consolidated, still before the late-eighteenth-century adoption of a more "liberal" political order.

Spain: Fitful Resistance to Imperial Decline

By the seventeenth century, Spain's central state authority built from above had proven insufficient to rule its expansive holdings. "The word [state] itself seemed peculiarly inapplicable to the Spanish Monarchy, composed as it was of such a multitude of territories." Even the leading official of that state, Olivares, concluded that "the present state of these kingdoms is, for our sins, quite possibly the worst that has ever been known." His efforts to build the king's power, unify the territories, and ensure economic revival, remained unaccomplished.[2] "The administrative system was becoming fossilized; the vitality of Castille had been sapped." Indeed, the economy overall was weakened by debt, foreign competition, and population growth, if not also by the more subjective justifications of a relative Catholic disinclination toward capitalism, "a general indifference towards prosperity," or an assumption that such a rich land would provide without needing to work.[3] Certainly the costs of empire weighed heavily; there were "too many enemies to fight, too many fronts to defend" in 140 years of ongoing wars. The "military revolution" of the age, eclipsing cavalry, raised costs, forcing expenditures consistently "two or three times more than the ordinary revenues provided."[4]

To meet these challenges, the authorities embraced varying solutions with mixed and often unforeseen results. With the state crucially lacking in revenues, it tried to reform the tax system, then avoided via contraband or resisted by locals in the tradition of the ancien régime tax revolts. By 1641, Catalonia went so far as to declare itself an independent republic. Even the importation of American silver could no longer be relied on to make up the shortfall, with shipments of silver lost in storms or to pirating enemies, and then with production decreasing by 1615.[5]

Nor had the Spanish crown effectively consolidated national unity or loyalty from below, never as much a priority as more orderly state-building from above. The Inquisition had lost some of its momentum and largely failed to bind the populace. The Spanish had rid themselves of heretics found within, reinforcing Catholic unity, with state authority piggybacking on this process to also reinforce and pay for increasingly centralized power. But the Inquisition had remained more institutional and controlled from above, foregoing its potential to enflame passions and loyalty from below, and with that potential largely lost with the expulsion of "others" against whom further coherence might have been encouraged. Catholicism remained more a common faith than a basis of secular cohesion. Olivares regretfully acknowledged failure also on this front, seeing that continued "diverse humours" were "a profound source of weakness." His proposals to increase cohesion through integrating others into Castile, negotiating from strength or with royal visits, all proved unviable. Given the continued "separation of hearts between the various kingdoms of the monarchy," effective rule was impossible.[6] State-building was constrained by the lack of comparable nation-building.

Spain's empire, then at its height, arguably distracted from internal efforts at centralization and diluted popular cohesion at home within a larger and more diverse unit. As an empire rather than emergent nation-state, Spain's authority was overly stretched and enjoyed little popular engagement even at home. And the empire beyond the Spanish homeland itself suffered from the same failings of authority and cohesion. State efforts to bolster central authority based on a mutually beneficial and self-preserving "Union of Arms" within the empire faltered amid resistance and distrust of Madrid. Olivares's alleged interest in imposing the rule of "one crown, one law, one coinage" remained an illusive goal.[7] Resources proved insufficient for imposing rule over the far-flung holdings, particularly given the complex challenges to central authority. For instance, a multifront effort to crush rebellion in the Lowlands and resist French incursions in Italy stretched those resources too thin.

The prospects of building popular cohesion proved even more difficult on the imperial scale, multiplying the challenges of domestic diversity. According to one analyst already in 1589, such "a scattered empire is weaker than a compact one because the distance between its parts is always a source of weakness."[8] The Spanish empire's efforts to then address this problem, or at least to crush discord and heresy, mimicked elements of the earlier internal inquisition. But on the wider scale of empire, nothing approaching national solidarity could be achieved, with nationalism per se simply inapplicable to empire.

The strains of empire were nowhere more evident than in the Lowlands. There, religious persecution of the Protestants enflamed resistance to Spanish taxes and military billeting, producing a revolt that "lasted from the 1560s until 1648, with only a brief intermission."[9] Though Spain did not export the Inquisition to the Low Countries—the Inquisition was officially limited to policing the faith of Catholics and not those outside the Catholic Church—it did use direct state force to try to defeat heresy. Philip was particularly intolerant, sacrificing his alliance with England by sending Alba to suppress the revolt, with Alba declaring that the rebels "must be made to live in constant fear." The duke went so far as to state his preference for waging a war that left the kingdom "impoverished and even ruined" rather than avoid war and "benefit . . . the devil and the heretics, his disciples." Silver imports were then still sufficient to pay for a vicious campaign, with Alba's "council of Blood" executing over a thousand and later Spanish soldiers running amok.[10]

Forging allegiance on the basis of exclusion was inapplicable to imperial holdings where there was no loyal core constituency that could be so cohered. Exclusion was therefore attempted more as stark repression. But instead of achieving submission or loyalty, imperial force succeeded largely at provoking further Dutch antagonism against Spain and attacks in which some 400 churches were sacked. With the Sea Beggars controlling the coast, Alba lost military advantage and then the support of the king.[11] Unable to defeat the Dutch, by 1576 Philip was ready to concede to all demands from the Dutch, "saving above all religion and my obedience," but those too were lost.[12] By 1581 the seven northern provinces of the Netherlands had declared independence, while much of the south remained within the Spanish Empire. By the turn of the century, the Netherlands had effectively gained independence, which it defended amid renewed conflict with Spain after 1621.[13]

Loss of the Netherlands and in 1655 of Portugal, defeat of the armada, "the anticipated exhaustion of the American mines . . . all these suggest that the sun was slowly setting on the splendour of Spain."[14] Economic travails, particularly in the heartland of Castille, the Catholic Church's resistance to reforms, and imperial overreach all significantly contributed to this decline. A Spanish diplomat accurately predicted that "I doubt whether we can sustain an empire as scattered as ours."[15] According to Wallerstein, with perhaps some overstatement, "political extremities are a financial burden . . . especially perhaps in this early stage of capitalism. Spain was an empire when what was needed in the sixteenth century was a medium-size state. The bureaucracy was inadequate because imperial Spain required a larger one than it could construct given its resources, human and financial."[16] Another explanation focuses on the heterogeneity of such an empire. According to a Spanish priest: "Never has a republic been well governed or peaceful where division and diversity of faith prevail . . . And where there is such rancor and inner fire, there cannot be good fellowship or lasting peace."[17] State and church had failed to put out this fire, arguably instead fanning resistance outside of Spain.

Imperial overreach came together with diversity and lack of cohesion, with dire results for Spain. "After a short glorious period of world leadership, Spain ceased to be of Europe. . . . Although she had been, after France, the first state in Europe to lay the foundations of nationhood and national unification, she was unable to enter modern nationhood. . . . For the wave of national pride . . . had nothing in common with modern nationalism. It did not transform the Spanish people; it did not awaken new energies in them. . . . The seventeenth century no longer belonged to Spain," but rather to France, and then later England, neither of which then were paying the costs of a comparable empire.[18]

Spain found itself united by faith but diverted from a primary focus on internal cohesion by the imperatives of state-building within and imperial control without, neither of which were fully achieved. Domestic intolerance had achieved the goal of relative homogeneity but then been faced with the difficulties and distractions of heterogeneity without, in lands over which it claimed control. Exclusion or repression of non-Catholics failed to subdue the populace in the imperial holdings and failed to further cohere the populace within Spain against distant enemies rather than domestic threats. Under these circumstances, neither internal nor imperial unity as such could be achieved, for the unit of political control was simply too vast and diverse. Spain could not isolate itself from this challenge without forgoing the empire it was unwilling to abandon, though the empire was lost nonetheless. As such, Spain could not find itself or forge itself as a contained and cohesive unit. It remained weak as both state and nation, with and even after empire.

France: Faithful Absolutism

Unlike Spain, early modern France inherited no empire, enjoyed somewhat more robust economic growth, and had earlier built a stronger centralized state. But France had faced its own difficulties, notably with internal conflicts exploding into large-scale civil war. That conflict had been turned to advantage by the crown, which joined the popular anti-Huguenot fanaticism, further cohering loyalty among the Catholic majority directed then toward the state. With greater national unity thereby achieved through passionate exclusion, the crown then embraced coexistence as a pragmatic basis of peace, allowing for a shift of focus back to state-building. But neither nation- nor state-building was yet complete, with conflicts reemerging not only between faiths but increasingly between classes and estates, including peasant uprisings.

Henri IV had gained the French throne by abandoning his own faith and then sought to build unified popular support and to end the prior conflict through compromise and greater tolerance. Under his Edict of Nantes, France had enjoyed a golden age of inclusion and of state-building toward absolutism. But anti-Huguenot antagonism had remained and focused on the convert king, who was assassinated by a resentful Catholic. Henri's widowed queen had then sought to maintain his policies. But as internal challenges gained strength, albeit short of the same scale of civil war, the crown again embraced the temptation to contain those potential challenges by endorsing and channeling religious animosities. The use of religious exclusion as a bulwark of national support for absolutism and for domestic solidarity would emerge again in the seventeenth century, following and refining the pattern of the sixteenth. Memories of past conflict and exclusionary cohesion, consistently stronger than those had been in Spain, further inspired a more explicit return to fanatical and exclusionary nation-building imposed this time more from above.

By 1616 France saw a return to civil conflict, more limited than before but sufficient to bring a renewed focus on nation-building via forceful exclusion. Huguenots "threatening the national unity of France" gained support from various grandees arguing for toleration of the Protestants as a way to resist growing absolutist power of the crown. Those grandees even protected the garrisoned "states within a state" of the Huguenots as a form of resistance to increasing royal authority, preferring disunity and discord to a loss of their relative power.[19] King Louis XIII in response laid siege against the Protestant stronghold of La Rochelle and offered to compensate Huguenot nobles who would side with him and return church lands. With the king's victory, the peace of Alais in 1629 ended the political rights of the Huguenots and forced the demolition of their fortifications. By the 1640s, letters of naturalization routinely equated Catholicism with the possibility of citizenship in the French nation.[20] These attacks and exclusions of Protestants provided the basis for the consolidation of absolutist rule, as both a defensive response to end the resurgent civil wars and class conflicts, and to reinforce the monarchy with religious bulwarks. Not coincidentally the ancien régime relied on the leadership of Cardinals, notably Richelieu and Mazarin.[21]

The preeminent absolutist of the age, Louis XIV, then further engaged in exclusionary nation- and state-building, as with his predecessors in response to challenges coming in new forms. At its very start, the Sun King's rule was shaken and seriously threatened. With the king still underage, depression and famine raged in France during the late 1640s, and officials in the Paris parlement protested their loss of power. When the people "wished to take affairs into their own hands," violence erupted in the Fronde uprising, joined later by restive princes of the blood, most notably Condé.[22] Cognizant of the travails of Charles I in England, in January 1649 the queen mother, king, and family were forced to flee from the Paris mobs to save themselves. According to Voltaire, in flight they "slept on straw . . . obliged to pawn the crown jewels. The king was often in want of the necessities of life." Mazarin was forced into exile, arguably appeasing the crowds enough to save the crown.[23] But in 1651, those crowds forced their way into the very bedchamber of the king, contributing to his later decision to move the court to the safer location of Versailles. These experiences, so contrary to the image of absolutism, "made an indelible impression on the young king," not yet fourteen.[24] Thereafter, Huguenot, noble, and peasant demands for rights would come to be lumped together by the crown as religious and republican sedition to be crushed.

But Louis XIV and his successors would also face another challenge seen as related to Protestantism, though it came from within the Catholic Church and gradually replaced the Huguenot conflict with an intra-Catholic dispute. Jansenism went "to unprecedented lengths in its stress on the radical separation of God from a corrupt, concupiscent humanity," including the ruler of men, the king. The crown in turn perceived Jansenism and its advocacy of limits on the divine right of kings as another incarnation of Calvinism to be contained.[25] Thus religious discord and the imperative to head it off with exclusion or suppression would be turned from its initial anti-Huguenot focus to also include an anti-Jansenist front. Even within Catholicism, neither of the opposing extremes of greater loyalty to Rome or sectarian limits on the king's divinity would be permitted to interfere with the linkage between Catholic unity and absolutist rule.

The experiences of revolt and growing religious discord focused the king's later attention on building a more solid popular base of support for his rule. Louis had painfully learned that even under absolutism, holding central state power required a modicum of mass loyalty, or at least avoidance of further open revolt. And commoners came to a similar conclusion, eager to avoid violent conflict and preserve the state and their well being. "The Fronde compelled all Frenchmen who placed much value on stability and prosperity to be ardent royalists," including the traditionally rebellious Huguenots, who were rewarded with some relative tolerance.[26] With rebellion so discredited, the king did indeed enhance his hold over the realm, for instance with tax revenues nearly doubling during his reign. Authority coalesced around the Sun King, so much so that "loyalty to the king was piety."[27] With the Gallican Declaration in 1682, the King affirmed his primacy not only in temporal affairs but also in spiritual, placing the crown above the pope and reinforcing the nationalist particularism of religion even within Catholicism. In doing so, Louis set himself off against not only Protestantism per se but also against Catholic universalism or Jesuit loyalty to the pope and above intra-Catholic disputes.[28]

Louis XIV's success at shoring up the weaknesses made evident by the Fronde and then the rising challenge of Jansenism makes his later intolerance against the then much weakened Huguenots perhaps all the more surprising. But as in the past, royal authority was reinforced and built amid religious exclusions, even if against a less threatening "other." And this time such exclusion was purposefully and even more cynically used to heal or divert class conflict and intra-Catholic discord. Limitations on the rights of Huguenots were gradually increased from the 1660s on. The final and decisive act of exclusion was straightforward. On October 22, 1685 the king revoked the Edict of Nantes, which had provided for considerable religious tolerance. The order went on to "forbid our subjects . . . to meet anymore for the exercise of the said religion . . . We enjoin all ministers . . . who do not choose to become converts . . . to leave our kingdom. . . . We forbid private schools for the instruction of children of the said Protestant Reformed Religion . . . henceforth they be baptized by the parish priests . . . and thereafter the children shall be brought up in the Catholic, Apostolic, and Roman religion."[29] Some 200,000 of the remaining Huguenots fled to avoid the implications of this forceful implementation of "un roi, une loi, une foi," while others engaged in extended resistance as Camisards and were eventually pacified. The king himself celebrated this final service to his faith as a spiritual vindication, and he had struck a commemorative medal proclaiming "Haeresis extincta, religio victrix."[30]

For all the supposed religious justification, the revocation of the Edict of Nantes and suppression of the Huguenots were explicitly defended on political grounds. The king's own order stated that "we have determined that we can do nothing better in order wholly to obliterate the memory of the troubles, the confusion and the evils which the progress of this false religion has caused in this kingdom . . . than entirely to revoke the said Edict of Nantes."[31] A more complete explanation of the king's motives was suggested well in advance by Châtelet in 1666, here quoted at length: "A King can have no object more worthy of his care and attention than to maintain in his realm the religion which he received from his ancestors. For diversity of belief, cult and ceremony divides his subjects and causes them reciprocally to hate and despise one another, which in turn gives rise to conflicts, war and general catastrophe. On the other hand, unity of beliefs binds men together . . . to fight [only] in the same armies and under the same flag . . . There can be no doubt that, by the principles of Christianity and by the maxims of politics, it is necessary to reduce the King's subjects to a single faith . . . If these Huguenots were to create a disturbance, the King would be preoccupied in quelling the revolt; and the King, being thus distracted, the [Spanish] Emperor could seize the occasion to extend his domain."[32] In addition, the church itself rewarded Louis for his expulsion of the Protestants, providing additional offices to the nobility thereby further tied to the crown.[33]

These explanations suggest a reemergence of the seventeenth-century logic of nation-building piggybacking on religious exclusion, albeit with a difference in the lack of comparable religious conflict or passions. The Huguenots were not actually a threat to the unity or security of the state and had not been so to any significant extent since the end of the previous century. Indeed, they had been largely appeased by earlier tolerance and come to accept state authority. But their exclusion from rights and effective expulsion provided a clear signal from the crown of religious unity among those French left behind; "the alienation of the Huguenots was of momentous significance in the development of the French national ideal . . . The state was redefined as the people, and the good of the state came to mean, the public good," with that public excluding the Huguenots. As Sahlins argues, France had become officially a Catholic country and would remain so until just before the Revolution. Or, as Fauchet asserted at the start of the Revolution, "The catholic Faith is national in France; this is not a question, it is a fact."[34]

Absolutism was not possible without a minimum of popular allegiance and unity, across class or estate, and sufficient to reduce internal challenges, revolt, and discord. The prior impressive attempt to forge such authority on the basis of coexistence had worked for a time but then come undone amid threatening division. To restore and enforce unity, absolutist monarchs returned to the earlier pattern of religious exclusion, channeling remaining popular antagonism into secular legitimacy based on Catholic fanaticism. But unlike in the past, Louis XIV in particular, who was not as threatened by the Huguenots, embraced sectarianism not so much to avoid being toppled by religious passions but instead to cynically direct those passions toward loyalty and thereby avoid further civil war or religious discord. The result was no less powerful; the Sun King's wily diversion from class and intra-Catholic discord with anti-Protestant unity paid off handsomely. The French were cohered under absolutism ostensibly against the Huguenots but in reality to forge unity as French Catholics whose own divisions challenged the crown.

Where Spain had faltered at both state- and nation-building, France succeeded at both, for a time. Intolerance was used as a basis for further cohering of popular loyalty without another explosion of internal conflict comparable to the Fronde. And enjoying relative support and stability, the state proceeded to build further its power. The sometimes competing imperatives of exclusionary nation-building from below and inclusionary state-building from above were artfully merged under Catholic absolutism, with the Protestants still victims. Such was the glory of France.

 England: Delivering the Kingdom from Popery

As in France, if less in Spain, the English would also seek to combine exclusionary nation-building with state-building but, unlike France, not under absolutism. Instead, exclusionary fanaticism would again remove a monarch who merged tyranny and popery. But now popular passions were more purposefully engaged, aggravated, and manipulated by Parliament for its own purposes. The result would be an even more consolidated nation under the rule of monarchs constrained by Parliament, and selected precisely for their Protestantism.

Like Henri IV in France, Charles II in England had turned popular exhaustion and pragmatic interest in restoring order to an effort at coexistence and inclusive state-building. But, again like Henri, Charles saw a resurgence of popular religious antagonism and pressure for a return to exclusion—in Charles's case, even before his death. In acceding to this pressure and enacting forms of exclusion against Catholics, Charles had retained the throne lost by his father and was able to ensure the succession of his brother. But James II's own Catholicism again provoked sectarian passions merged with anti-absolutism, with antagonistic engagement again focusing against the king rather than allowing for consolidation of royal power as in France.

The events in France and England were connected, with resurgent intolerance against Huguenots in France enflaming an opposing but similar resurgence of anti-Catholicism in England. Exclusionary efforts to bolster absolutism in France would help to undermine any such consolidation of restored monarchical power in England. In 1685 Louis XIV reinforced his rule by revoking the Edict of Nantes, sending a flood of Huguenot exiles into England thereafter. The French king's intolerance reinforced popular English views as to the cruelty of Catholic absolutism, enflamed by sermons on the matter. Guy Fawkes Day that year was so tumultuous that thereafter fireworks were only allowed with official license.[35] And this popular antiabsolutism and anti-Catholicism was then turned against the monarchs closer to home. It did not help matters that Charles II had negotiated an alliance with France and that his brother and heir, James, had publicly declared his own Catholicism. Before the year was out Charles himself would make a deathbed conversion.

The pattern of a generation earlier, of a monarch vilified for his Catholicism and distrusted for his absolutist tendencies, was about to be eerily replayed. The sins of the father were visited on the second son, who unlike his father would, but barely, escape with his head. That less bloody conclusion to England's second revolution reflected, in part, that this time exclusion was more orchestrated from above rather than more fully exploding below as civil war and passions demanding a head.

Explanations for the travails of James II have varied widely. As a would-be Catholic tyrant, James was described by Halifax in 1687 as being influenced by "the Church of Rome (which) doth not only dislike the allowing liberty, but by its principles it cannot do it," and neither could the king.[36] Alternatively, James II simply favored religious tolerance for his fellow Catholics, much as did Henri IV so successfully encode coexistence for the Huguenots earlier in the century in France. But more than for Henri, who had converted to the popular faith, James's intransigence and tolerance was seen as both heretical and treasonous, his absolutism no less than Henri's but rejected. Perhaps, as Christopher Hill suggests, it was just James's "stupid obstinacy" that explains rising resistance to him.[37] Or perhaps James was ill advised. The result was that James sought to force his tolerance upon an unwilling populace and a

Parliament already engaged on the issue by recent tumult, and he lost all.

James's political motivations, connected as they were to religious issues, are just as disputed. The king described himself as "a man for arbitrary power," and indeed he was rash in this regard. During the crisis in the years before his ascension when Danby sought to bolster the strength of the crown by acceding to some anti-Catholic moves, James demurred—either because he valued his faith as much as power or, more likely, because he knew he could not hide the former to gain the latter. Once on the throne, James apparently came to believe that he could build an alternative base to bolster both his power and his faith. He eventually supported repealing penal laws against dissenters (and not just Catholics) so as to divide Protestants, and by 1687 he entertained the fantastic notion of forging a new majority of supporters among Catholics and Dissenters.[38] But such unrealistic strategic calculations were generally overwhelmed by the king's own passion.

James made clear his preference for tolerance of Catholicism from the very start of his reign, although, given his own controversial public profession of that faith, this was no surprise. Within three weeks of his accession, James "issued instructions that no proceedings were to be taken against Catholics"; he later sought to prevent sermons attacking Catholics and even appeared to favor the Irish Catholics. Meanwhile, Louis in France, though distracted by the impending death of Charles of Spain, was being urged to "join with James in extirpating heresy in England."[39] And the new king would appear to be sympathetic to such a treasonous proposal. Astonishingly, even as Charles II lay dying, James, yet to ascend to the crown, took aside the French ambassador to say that "I desire you to assure your master that he shall always have in me a faithful and grateful servant."[40]

James's leanings toward a French alliance and for Catholicism have fed a debate about his primary motivation and the subject of popular dismay. Pincus has argued that popular antagonism against the king was due to royal dependence on French support seen as inconsistent with English national interests, and a royal inclination toward the French model of absolutism seen as consistent with Catholic rule. The implication is that resistance to James II was more the result of a "glorious," popular defense of liberty, rather than an ignoble intolerance for Catholicism; "his policies—not his beliefs" were the problem. But even Pincus admits that Protestantism was at minimum "constituent [of] . . . English national identity" turning against James.[41] Or, as Lawrence Stone asked rhetorically, "Was British nationalism fueled by fear of France or hatred of popery, or were the two indistinguishable?"[42] Still, it was James's actual policies at home, in favor of Catholicism, that would become the particular focus of popular engagement orchestrated by Parliament, solidifying national identity.

The most concrete action consistently pursued by James was to replace Protestant officials with Catholics, which was seen as a revolutionary attack on the established elite. In 1685, the king requested that Catholics be permitted to remain as army officers, arguing simply that "most of them [are] well known to me, and having formerly served with me in several occasions, and always approved the loyalty of their principles by their practice." Commons objected "that those officers cannot by law be capable of their employments," but the chief justice ruled the following year that the king retained the right "to dispense with penal laws in particular cases."[43]

James proceeded to replace Protestants with officials drawn from the Catholic minority, even if that meant promoting incompetents, putting power to service of faith. Catholics were named lord lieutenant of Ireland, admiral of the navy, privy councilor, lord privy seal, and chief minister. Parliamentary boroughs were remodeled so as to reduce opposition, with Parliament prorogued in the meantime.[44] Asserting his legal control over education as well, the king insisted that a monk be admitted at Cambridge and dismissed all the fellows in order to impose a Catholic master onto Magdalen College at Oxford, then the "symbol of Anglican educational monopoly." Among those at Cambridge forced to listen to an official tirade asserting royal authority over academic freedom was a promising young physicist, Isaac Newton.[45]

By 1687 James was impetuously ready to further assert his absolute authority over religion, acknowledging his preference for Catholicism while pressing for unity through coexistence. Astonishingly, in his Declaration of Indulgence of that year the king admitted "we cannot but heartily wish . . . that all the people of our dominions were members of the Catholic Church." But the king recognized that this was unlikely, to say the least, and indeed that no unity of religion was possible. Efforts to "exact conformity in religion" had failed; "it is visible the success has not answered the design, and that the difficulty is invincible." Abandoning this preferred outcome, he instead fell back to demanding accommodation of Catholics. His declaration asserted that "there is nothing

FAITH IN NATION

now that we so earnestly desire as to establish our government on such a foundation as may make our subjects happy, and unite them to us by inclination as well as duty; which we think can be done by no means so effectually as by granting to them their free exercise of religion. . . . Conscience ought not to be constrained, nor people forced in matters of mere religion." Accordingly, the king suspended all "penal laws in matters ecclesiastical," and the following year the reiterated his indulgence to "secure to all people the free exercise of their religion for ever."[46]

Opposition to the Indulgences brought matters to a head. The king ordered that his declaration be read in all "churches and chapels throughout this kingdom," thereby utilizing his primary method of communication. Seven Bishops, including the Archbishop of Canterbury, petitioned that "because that declaration is founded upon such a dispensing power as hath often been declared illegal in Parliament," they would refuse to publicize it. In the court case that followed, the justices argued that a guilty verdict was required against the bishops if their petition was judged "anything that shall disturb the government, or make mischief and a stir among the people," or an "ill intention of sedition."[47] But the jury found the bishops not guilty, pitting Parliament, the majority Anglican Church, and now also the law courts against the crown.

As if to reiterate that the crown still had longevity, just before the verdict a son was born to James. The legitimacy of the child was contested amid rumor that someone else's healthy baby had been hidden in a warming pan and smuggled into the actually barren queen's chamber. But the mere existence of a male heir promised a Catholic dynasty standing against Commons, church and courts, thereby further provoked to dramatic action.

On the very day of the bishops' acquittal, seven leading Protestant nobles wrote to invite William of Orange to invade and take the throne, in effect proposing a revolution from above to retain the social order threatened by the king. They chose William because he was the husband of the Protestant daughter of James's own earlier marriage and because of William's interest in protecting the Netherlands against an alliance between James and Louis XIV of France.[48] Their letter to William argued that "the people are so generally dissatisfied with the present conduct of the government in relation to their religion, liberties and properties (all of which have been greatly invaded), and they are in such expectation of the prospects being daily worse, that your Highness may be assured there are nineteen parts of twenty of the people throughout the kingdom who are desirous of change and who, we believe, would willingly contribute to it." The letter also noted that regarding the recently born heir, "not one in a thousand here believes [it] to be the Queen's."[49]

The "revolution" that followed was a distinctly inglorious affair. James tried to backtrack on recent appointments and intrusions onto university freedoms. Meanwhile, William and his troops landed on Guy Fawkes Day 1688, having faced no resistance from the British fleet. James, with a standing army of matching size but questionable loyalty to a Catholic monarch, refused to engage while suffering from an extended nosebleed, "about the only blood shed." The King fled, at first unsuccessfully, and then arriving in France on Christmas Day.[50]

James's own predilections were displayed in the process of flight and his later exile, confirming the suspicions of those who had deposed him. Reaffirming both his own autocratic tendencies and his misunderstanding of the role of the King and his baubles as still central to government, James "damned [the Stuart monarchy] for ever by an apparent appeal to anarchy. He departed without handing authority over to any government. He destroyed the writs summoning Parliament and threw the Great seal into the Thames in the vain hope of preventing one being called." And once in exile, he proved that he was not truly "pro-tolerant" but more simply "pro-Catholic," with not a single Protestant official within his exiled court.[51] It was reported at the time of James's death in exile in 1701 that he had "first fell ill" amid the singing of an anthem in chapel, at the verse "Our inheritance is turned to strangers, our houses to aliens."[52] But it was the king himself who had been ejected from his inheritance and houses as the stranger. Even his descendants would remain forever as aliens, with the remains of the next three in line for his lost throne buried in the heart of hated Catholicism, St. Peter's in Rome.[53]

James had been expelled by an upper-class coup, but he was also effectively "rejected by the nation" supporting that coup.[54] The king's actual removal was the result of an invasion organized from above by Parliament, rather than a full-scale revolution or civil war comparable to what had removed Charles I. Popular engagement was more fanned from above than exploding from below, although it was no less powerful as such. There had been widespread disturbances at the arrest and trial of the seven bishops, and rioting had helped to convince peers to support William, who found upon his landing in England "his ranks were swelled by a multitude of common people."[55] When James fled London, Catholic chapels and embassies were sacked by the mob. The king's first attempted flight was blocked by fishermen at Faversham, who held the disguised monarch.[56] Only the king's later escape to France prevented the possible repeat of regicide, though perhaps he was allowed to flee to avoid the disquieting spectacle of spilling more royal blood. By then, not only had the monarch been rejected by the nation but his rejection had itself helped to further forge and engage that nation.

With what was formally called the "desertion" from the throne of James and his replacement by his eldest daughter and her Protestant Dutch husband, a pattern was firmly and finally established of national unity represented by limited monarchy and bound by anti-Catholicism. The symbols were clear. At the April 11, 1689 coronation of William and Mary in Westminster Abbey, for the first time the English Bible of the Reformation was carried in the procession. The coronation oath also now included two new planks. The monarchs had to swear to abide by "the statutes in parliament agreed upon" rather than the earlier oaths obligating allegiance only to the laws of royal predecessors. The new monarchs were effectively no longer sole law givers but instead part of the legislative body. And the monarchs had to swear to uphold "the Protestant Reformed Religion established by law."[57] Constitutional monarchy and antipopery would remain the twin pillars of state- and nation-building.

The supremacy of Parliament was established by its decisive replacement of one monarch with others but was also codified in a Bill of Rights to which William and Mary had to accede in order to succeed. That bill of 1689 attacked James for his efforts to "subvert and extirpate the Protestant religion . . . the execution of laws without consent of parliament . . . levying money . . . keeping a standing army . . . without consent of parliament." James's abdication by flight, "delivering this kingdom from popery and arbitrary power," was celebrated as "glorious." And his successors were foresworn from suspending or executing laws, erecting courts or commissions, levying money, or raising an army without Parliamentary consent.[58]

The Bill of Rights also encoded anti-Catholicism, mandating an oath of allegiance to the king and against papal authority. Despite deep splits between Whigs and Tories on other issues, the 1689 convention framing the bill of rights was united in anti-Catholicism, quickly and unanimously adopting that "it hath been found by experience that it is inconsistent with the safety and welfare of this Protestant kingdom to be governed by a popish prince." Accordingly, anyone who "profess the popish religion, or shall marry a papist, shall be excluded [from] . . . the crown and government of this realm."[59] According to Ogg, "this link with the

Puritan Revolution was evidenced by the passing . . . of a resolution that a Popish prince was inconsistent with a Protestant state." Indeed, this requirement would be reiterated in the Act of Settlement of 1701 and would lead to more than fifty relations of Queen Anne being passed over before the throne was given in 1714 to George of Hanover, who spoke no English but at least was not Catholic.[60] According to one preacher at the time: "He that can bear to think of a Popish Pretender, and an arbitary French Government, deserveth not to tread on English Earth, or breathe in English Air."[61]

Already under William and Mary, limited religious tolerance was offered only to Quakers and other Protestant dissenters, and not Catholics. In order "to unite their Majesties' Protestant subjects in interest and affection," the cruelly misnamed Toleration Act of 1689, required an oath renouncing as impious, heretical, and damnable "that princes excommunicated or deprived by the Pope . . . may be deposed or murthered." That act, if there was any doubt, did allow for dissent within Protestantism but should not "be construed to extend or give any ease, benefit or advantage to any papist."[62] Eleven years later, Parliament again committed itself to "preventing the further growth of popery and of such treasonable and execrable designs and conspiracies." Anyone apprehending someone saying Mass, or a priest, would be rewarded with £100, and those so found sent "to perpetual imprisonment."[63] Only in the context of such intolerance could George I in 1722 claim as a signal of his generosity that he had seized only one-third of the land he was entitled to seize from Papists.[64]

The notion of uniting subjects as Protestants by attacking or excluding Catholics applied immediately after the Glorious Revolution, not only within England but also beyond its borders. Within a week of William and Mary's coronation, Commons was calling for war with France—declared a month later.[65] Anti-Catholicism was also again extended to Ireland and Scotland, ostensibly serving as a basis for drawing together what would become Great Britain but also to block James's efforts to regain the throne. In Ireland the Catholic majority that had supported James was defeated by William in 1690, much like Cromwell in 1649, and then placed under the rule of a Protestant and often absentee minority ruling elite.[66] Ability to sit in Ireland's parliament was restricted to those swearing against Catholic beliefs, and later anyone "professing the popish religion" was made "incapable" to buy or purchase any manor or land, much of which was transferred to Protestants. Indeed, penal legislation against Irish Catholics would remain for four decades.[67] Similarly, the

Act of Union joining England and Scotland in 1707 stipulates "establishing the Protestant religion and Presbyterian Church government within the kingdom of Scotland."[68]

Unifying against Catholics did appear to provide a sure basis for social order, at least as indicated by allowing for substantial advances in state-building. Officials reporting to Parliament within the admiralty, the war office, and especially the treasury exploded in numbers by 1720, dwarfing the previously larger court. The number of tax collectors in particular grew dramatically, while "royal income rapidly doubled after 1688." In 1694 "salaries replaced fees and prerequisites," thereby regularizing the bureaucracy. In that same year, the Bank of England was founded, stabilizing finances and currency.[69] This building of state power and national unity continued together amid continued exclusion of Catholics. Even if such exclusion was not a necessity for such state-building, anti-Catholicism certainly brought internal stability and popular allegiance, making state-building easier.

The populace participated in this juxtaposition, celebrating its own unity as English subjects with anti-Catholic imagery. The execution of Charles I was commemorated every year on January 30, and every May 29 the 1660 restoration was celebrated. "The first day of August marked the accession in 1714 of the first Hanoverian king, the securing of the Protestant Succession. And November 5 was doubly sacred, not just the anniversary of the landing in England in 1688 of William of Orange to do battle with the Catholic James II but also the day when in 1605 Parliament and James I had been rescued from the gunpowder plotting of Guido Fawkes, yet another Roman Catholic."[70] With newspapers sold in England rising to almost ten million in 1760, it was easy enough to spread further anti-Catholic images and messages. This mass media would help spread polemics, such as "that it was the expulsion of those Stuart princes who had inclined toward Catholicism, and the uniting of the island under a Protestant dynasty that had transformed Britain's position in the world. Now this second Israel had the rulers it deserved and God required, was it to be wondered at that it reaped victory and dominion?"[71]

The culmination of state authority in the Atlantic seaboard great powers of western Europe thus emerged amid a return to religious intolerance and exclusion. Any semblance or efforts at coexistence were overcome by the imperatives from above for bolstering allegiance and unity, which apparently could not be achieved on purely secular or inclusive grounds. And greater unity provided a basis for further state-building, at least in

France and England in different forms, though less so on both counts for Spain.

As an early comer in state consolidation, religious exclusion, and empire, Spain was the least willing or able to attempt tolerance, and its efforts at building state, nation, and empire ultimately also failed early. Within Spain itself, the Inquisition had reinforced both unity and central state power but then been largely exhausted with the final expulsion of its victims. Spain was left more homogenous, and the fervor of religious intolerance dissipated somewhat, though neither state nor national consolidation had yet been fully consolidated. And then any suggestion that decline of the Inquisition implied tolerance was overwhelmed by attacks on the Protestants of the Lowlands as heretics. Intolerance was again orchestrated from above, though now increasingly directed against foreigners elsewhere rather than foreigners found within but now gone. As a result of this foreign focus and relative lack of mass engagement, such exclusion proved less binding of the domestic population. Indeed, the focus of the Spanish state was shifting to empire, diluting the efforts at building cohesion at home more than it reinforced those efforts. Gradually, with domestic cohesion left undeveloped and state efforts diluted into expansive holdings that proved expensive to hold and then were lost, Spain settled into decline.

Coexistence was more truly attempted and state-building more fully achieved under Henri IV, with France's efforts to build internal cohesion also not diluted by empire. But as if to reaffirm the imperative of religious passion being harnessed into more secular loyalty, this pattern was repeated in a different form in the next century. When the Huguenots again rose up, with support of again restive nobles, Louis XIII defeated them. But rebellion emerged again against the young Louis XIV, though the Fronde was not a religiously motivated movement and less pervasive or popularly engaging than earlier civil wars. Having regained control thereafter, the Sun King still sought means to contain discord and further bolster his popular support; he found that means in the religious antagonism of the earlier century and manipulated it accordingly. By finally expelling the Huguenots in 1685, Louis XIV reinforced the unity of his Catholic subjects against the heretical but now less-threatening minority, piggybacking national cohesion on the religious.

Over the course of a century, to be French was merged with being Catholic. "L'état, c'est moi" for the King, but the nation was faith. In an overarching sense, the crown pursued exclusion of the Huguenots to bolster Catholic unity and support. Popular engagement enflamed by religious ardency was aggravated from above and harnessed further into nationalism, still centered on a monarchy that could and did represent that nation in terms of both power and common faith.

In England, royal efforts at coexistence were eclipsed by antiroyal intolerance. Forty years later, the pattern of the Puritan Revolution was replayed in the Glorious Revolution, though this time more as a farce of elite competition than as popular tragedy, belying the imagined glory. Even more than his father, James II impetuously risked resentment with further absolutism and his more explicit Catholicism, ignoring the threat suggested by his father's fate. Again antiabsolutism and anti-Catholicism were combined in animosity against the crown indulging in both, although which was more engaging of the populace remains subject to debate. And as compared to the first English Revolution, that mass engagement was more an effort directed by Parliament against the crown and less a spontaneous expression from below. The official invitation to William and Mary to replace James combined these elements, merging noble interests in constraining the power of the monarchy with the promise of popular support of subjects demanding Protestantism on the throne. Constitutional monarchy was put in place to more truly represent a nation united, both in terms of political representation and faith.

In the aftermath of revolution, exclusion and discrimination against Catholics continued to be used as a tool for consolidating the nation. To reinforce their hold on the throne and popular support, William and Mary worked with Parliament, which had enacted further anti-Papist legislation, including a Bill of Rights that denied rights to Catholics. Irish Catholics were further constrained. And later another monarch was chosen for succession, apparently with his Protestantism seen as more important than his foreignness as a German who could not even speak English, suggesting that popular anti-Catholicism outweighed xenophobia. The populace remained committed to ensuring that Catholics would remain excluded from nation and crown. In the end, state-building proceeded with popular support ensured by such exclusion.

The English revolutions of the seventeenth century thus forged and symbolized the consolidation and power of a nation led by Parliament and united by religion against absolutism. To be English meant to be Protestant, not least at the head of both state and church. The exclusion of Catholics, most evidently from the throne, was the demand that unified the nation and served as a crutch for that unity, contrary to the more liberal and inclusive basis of unity suggested by Greenfeld and others.[72] The populace had been engaged through religious passions unleashed in civil war and revolution, thereby forging the basis of national unity cohered through violence and then further manipulated by Parliament against the crown. Emerging economic interests represented in Parliament were thereby served, though not justified solely in that regard. Literacy and other forms of communication did spread unity but as forged against popery.

For all the difference in outcomes in these three countries, the powerful imperative for intolerance and exclusion to build authority and cohesion was reaffirmed by and after attempts at alternatives. Monarchs and their opponents had learned that popular support could not be ensured directly through civic inclusion. Religious passions and intolerance remained more salient among the populace than more secular attachments, for the latter had not been consolidated enough to be freestanding. Absolutism had proven incomplete and unstable without popular support. And so, monarchs (or their opponents) returned to the previous pattern of basing their legitimacy on religious passions and animosity, reinforcing exclusion and attacks on heresy at home or abroad. Empire in Spain was thus defended for a time, absolutism in France thus built further, and constitutional monarchy forged in England.

Antagonisms from the past could not be forgotten and instead were again channeled into current politics, though in this second wave more orchestrated from above. The nation-state or empire could not be freed from religious passions; faith still impinged on the secular and the secular on faith. Instead, the legacies of the past were turned to meet pressing demands. Particularly for France and England, the nation could not be more fully consolidated without the crutch of faith, for this was the basis on which the populace's allegiances could still be engaged. An intolerant past had to be embraced and manipulated by state authorities seeking allegiance before that past could be officially forgotten in assertions of more purely secular allegiance.

SUPERIMPOSING DEMOCRATIC INCLUSION ON FORGOTTEN EXCLUSIONS

"A Wardrobe of Excuses"

6

The end of the eighteenth century would see greater national cohesion in support of more democratic state authority in France and England. And as historians have long argued, such popular solidarity was indeed expressed in terms of inclusion and greater religious tolerance, and for France even in the rejection of all official connections to faith. Amid consolidated images of the nation's civicness, elites and followers purposefully dismissed and forgot past sectarian foundations, finally asserting secular authority supposedly free of a prior religious crutch. And as religious fanaticism had forged cohesive identity then indirectly bolstering allegiance to the state, the denials of a direct connection were plausible. Representative state power was then reinforced by popular cohesion, projected and legitimated as inclusive, and the earlier attempted tolerance in state-building was revived, this time with more persistence.

But even these assertions of civicness were not so freestanding. Projections of inclusion would be possible only because past religious antagonisms and exclusions had built sufficient solidarity and unity; intolerance had provided the foundation for civicness. Secular allegiance had been forged on the basis of religious sectarianism. Liberal inclusiveness was consolidated on the basis of prior illiberalism. But by then, the work of building national cohesion had been more fully completed or at least provided a strong enough foundation on which to build further, with state strength and reach consolidated in its varying forms.

And at least in France and England that form was increasingly democratic.

The consolidation of national cohesion and democracy were connected. According to Dunkwart Rustow, democratization requires "a single background condition—national unity . . . the vast majority of citizens in a democracy-to-be must have no doubt or mental reservations as to which political community they belong . . . the people cannot decide [for democracy] until somebody decides who are the people." Or according to Robert Dahl, "the democratic process presupposes a unit," clarifying who is part of the political community so represented.[1] In other words, democracy requires the prior process of deciding who will be a member of the nation. Democratic processes in themselves cannot predetermine to whom democracy applies, and the establishment of such boundaries is necessary for democracy to function.

Democratization depends upon first specifying national boundaries, however such cohesion emerges. According to Rustow, "no minimal level of economic development . . . is necessary as a prerequisite" for such bounded cohesion, suggesting that national unity may indeed emerge before industrialization, contrary to Ernest Gellner's argument. Similarly, popular unity could not be the result of schooling or literacy, with the former still undeveloped and the latter spreading discord as much as cohesion. Beyond that, Rustow is agnostic as to how national cohesion was achieved, though all his examples imply an inclusive "consensus." He does argue that the "background condition, however, is best fulfilled when national unity is accepted unthinkingly."[2] And such unthinking acceptance of national unity is most likely when it accords with established prejudice as to who is part of the nation and, by implication, who is not. Of course, such a consensus is unlikely to initially include the victims of prejudice or exclusion.

National unity might emerge out of conflict and purposeful exclusion, as unintentionally suggested by Rostow's own analysis of the preconditions of democracy. The process "is set off by a prolonged and inconclusive political struggle . . . [in which] the issues must have profound meaning . . . The fight among religious . . . groups . . . has proved most tenacious . . . [and such] conflict in themselves constitute creative processes of integration." Indeed, that such conflicts in which "there is no middle position" are hard to resolve also makes them all the more binding as a potential basis of national unity, though not inclusive. "The marshalling of additional human resources" and support required cohering popular political engagement and diminished conflict, which could be achieved selectively through religious exclusion.[3] Thus, while democracy impressively has included lower classes, that cross-class inclusion may have been based on forms of exclusion aimed at diminishing other internal conflicts.

National unity may require and then emerge out of such conflict resolution. Rustow disagrees, arguing that national unity proceeds conflict, that these processes must be "assembled one at a time" and cannot be "imposed."[4] But in France it was an elite reinforced resolution of religious conflict through exclusion that brought national unity, setting the stage for later democracy. And in England these processes were merged. The English civil war was a crucial "contribution of early violence to later gradualism," with selective national unity emerging in conflict as a salve for it.[5] Rustow argues that democratization rests upon "a deliberate decision on the part of political leaders to accept the existence of diversity in unity."[6] But history suggests to the contrary that such unity was forged precisely by a violent rejection of diversity.

With the transition from the early modern to the modern age, much of this past conflict and exclusion could seemingly be put behind and demarcated from democratization, allowing for projections of nationalism that seemingly cut across remaining diversity. Liberal nationalism and democracy were projected as inclusive, denying that the issue of who to so include had been hotly contested and that resolution of this issue was crucial to the founding of democracy. National unity was falsely conflated with inclusion and democracy. Even former victims of exclusion cooperated, having learned to bury their differences and resemble insiders so as to enjoy the benefits of inclusion. The result was a greater popular focus on secular authority less distracted or cognizant of the earlier antagonisms and fanaticism of religious exclusions, which had both bound the nation and fanned continued instability.

But modern inclusion was not so fully disconnected from that early modern intolerance on which it was founded; the fiction of distinct time periods or processes should not blind us to hidden inheritances and trajectories from the past. Earlier exclusions and sectarianism still seeped through the facade of inclusion, less tolerant than it appeared. What Auden described as "the wardrobe of excuses" did not fully hide the ugly reality underneath.[7]

Still, we must account for why and how the illiberal underpinnings of nationalism and democracy have been ignored or forgotten. The answer is not just that these prior processes had taken hold and were no longer needed for national unity, for such functionalist logic ignores agency. Instead, we shall see how forgetting was a crucial innovation forged under duress. National unity, once gained through ignoble means, could be and was justified by elites with the ahistoric image of inclusion. Membership in the community was made more binding for its appearance of unthinking and unquestioned cohesion. Nationalism is then a form of self-congratulation, often denigrating "others" and eclipsing the memory of past internal conflict or discrimination in a celebration of unity, so as to reinforce that unity. Any image of mass solidarity is so bolstered or reinforced by purposeful forgetting of prior discord. Indeed, the history of nationalism is replete with such selective forgetting. As Renan wrote, nationalism is about "getting history wrong."[8] Forged on the basis of exclusion, it is then solidified by the false image of past inclusion and later practices of such inclusion.

My focus here is on France and England, both of which would come to combine more inclusive national unity and democracy. In France, this merger came indirectly, with mass cohesion based on earlier exclusion forged under and in support of absolutism, sufficient for the state to survive its religious wars intact.[9] Resulting popular engagement then later forced inclusive democracy through revolution against the crown. In England, the merger came more directly, with religious exclusion cohering nationalism at the same time it brought greater engagement and participation through Parliament against the crown. Exclusions remained in place in both cases to varying degrees, though they were also denied in both. I leave Spain aside at first. Simply put, Spain, mired in imperial decline and decay, had fallen away from the modernizing processes of further state- and nation-building. National cohesion remained at least as undeveloped as elsewhere, with cohesion evident in terms of Catholic unity but less in secular forms. Neither liberalism nor democracy emerged, and no image of tolerant inclusion was projected. The implications of this distinct trajectory will be taken up afterward, reversing the prior order of my analysis.

France: Civic Nationalism and Instability

The rhetoric of religious coexistence returned to France before its Revolution, when both the ancien régime and its adversaries seemed to agree on this point amid diminished sectarian conflict. With the defeat of the Camisards, fear of the "peril protestant" seems to have all but disappeared, even if aspects of religious discord remained. Elite and popular activism then shifted its focus increasingly to a more secular conflict over the form of state now itself strong enough to again shift toward inclusion and away from the earlier fanaticism that had bound the nation. In 1787, the Edict of Toleration restored the legality of Calvinist marriages, "uncoupling of religion and citizenship" despite a wave of pamphlets proclaiming Catholicism as a "national religion." Louis XVI believed that the relative absence of Catholic-Protestant tensions in France during the emerging upheaval compared with those faced in the English Civil War by Charles I meant "there won't be the same bitterness."[10] He was right in terms of religion but wrong in every other respect of the coming explosion of bitterness.

Rising challenges to absolutism emerged within France's representative bodies. The Estates had not been called to meet between 1615 and 1789 until the need to raise revenues to pay the debt from war forced the king to call it again. Still, the Estates remained divided by social class or category of nobles, clergy, and bourgeoisie, which Catholic fervor had previously and might again have cut against to unify. But with few Huguenots left in France, religious fanaticism did not fill the Estates' "all too heterogeneous sails," which were instead filled by the fervor of revolution.[11] In the absence of the Estates being convened, the parlement of Paris and other regional parlements sought to unify themselves as a national body, but this effort resisted by the King. By 1789, the third Estate was pressing toward the creation of an antiabsolutist national assembly despite ongoing tensions with the first two Estates.[12]

The Revolution that then engulfed France represents an exceptional historical moment in terms of the relatively secular basis of national unity. Representation in the new order was formally based on individuals rather than religious categories.[13] Given the past, it is striking that the emergence of such nationally unifying citizenship and representation in France did not build that unity officially on the basis of Catholicism and a return to Protestant exclusion. Beyond the simple defeat and then relative absence of Huguenots, resulting in greater homogeneity, a variety of possible and interconnected reasons might explain this outcome.

First, religious exclusion had long been tied to and used by the crown for its own purposes, going back at least to the age of the religious wars and then reiterated by Louis XIV with his revocation of the Edict of Nantes. The crown had repeatedly used this crutch and indeed wrapped itself in the cloth of Catholic divinity. The notable exceptions of toleration, particularly under Henri IV and then briefly under Louis XVI, appear as just that, exceptions. When the revolution turned national unity into an attack on absolutism, it was consistent that this attack would also be turned against the royally controlled institutions of the Catholic Church. Popular national unity emerging in opposition to the crown resisted its own association with Catholicism more generally, rejecting such a religious justification and the King's own claims to divinity and authority. Instead, the emerging revolutionary cult of reason drew no distinction between Catholic and Protestant and retained its distance from either church. In this regard, the Revolution was deeply informed by the secular liberalism of the Enlightenment, and in particular the anticlericalism and anti-Catholicism of its French form, despite some claims that the Revolution "represented the fulfillment of Catholic prayers."[14] Indeed, counter-revolutionary movements proclaimed the revolution to be heretical, a view reiterated by Pope Pius VI in 1793.[15]

Second, religious fervor so long used as the basis of forging unity under the crown had become discredited, not only by its royal association but also by its potential to reignite divisions threatening the state. Louis XVI had himself acknowledged the need for religious coexistence to end "continual troubles within families" and to achieve "prosperity and tranquility of our kingdom" with his Edict of Toleration two years before the revolution. According to that edict, "while waiting for divine Providence to bless our efforts and effect this happy revolution [of the conversion of all non-Catholics], justice and the interest of our kingdom do not permit us to exclude any longer from the rights of civil status those of our subjects or resident foreigners in our empire who do not profess the Catholic religion."[16] The decrease of violent religious conflict may also have fed confidence that national unity had advanced, allowing for relaxed religious fanaticism and less focus on exclusion.

Third, discord within French Catholicism had generally undermined unity based thereon. As discussed by Dale van Kley, Jansenism had already divided Catholics and helped inspire the antiabsolutist Enlightenment in France. To defend itself, the monarchy had increasingly aligned itself with the papacy against Jansenism, "alienating itself increasingly from the Gallican tradition." Jansenists and allied parlements could and did then "deploy the Gallican tradition against the monarch and its absolutism." The result was a revolutionary nationalism that "defined itself against both the monarchy and Catholicism, and a Catholicism that defined itself against the revolution," with the latter thereby popularly discredited.[17]

Fourth, the possible merger of revolutionary and Catholic fervor was unlikely, given the leading role in the Revolution of both Catholics and non-Catholics. The Jansenists had implicitly questioned the divine right of kings and allegedly had joined in the Fronde against the crown. In this regard, they moved toward the Calvinist position, rejecting any temporal authority over the Church standing between believers and Jesus.[18] Some Jansenists and Protestants, both of whom had been attacked by the crown until 1787, then joined forces within the Estates General two years later. In doing so, they were inspired by Rousseau, who had himself once been a Jansenist. Already in 1787, the Protestant leader Rabaut Saint Étienne had called for civil rights for Protestants "like those of other non-Catholic subjects."[19] And like others less prominent, the revolutionary martyr Marat was himself a Protestant.

The spirit of unifying toleration or, more accurately, intolerance for divisive religious symbolism, was then carried forward into the Revolution. Catholic universalism was reformulated by the revolutionaries who advocated a secular alternative, a universalism of rights. The Declaration of the Rights of Man and Citizen itself proclaimed that "no one should be disturbed for his opinions, even in religion, provided that their manifestation does not trouble public order as established by law."[20] While not everyone within the assembly agreed on whether this vague phrasing ensured equal rights for the few remaining Protestants, the implication was there amid debates. And such implied equality was in any case reinforced by the revolutionary attack on all forms of religion, not just against the Catholic Church.

The Revolution of 1789 would go so far as to replace toleration of religion with a more complete rejection of religion as royalist or divisive superstition diluting antiabsolutism. "Revolutionaries imprisoned or massacred many clergy, hounded many more into hiding or exile, 'persuaded' still others to renounce their 'superstitious' profession, rewrote the Christian calendar and changed Christian place-names, destroyed or defaced Christian iconography, cut down church towers and melted down church bells, and rechristened—or dechristened—churches themselves as 'temples of reason' or of some 'Supreme Being.' "[21] National unity once forged on the basis of religious sectarianism was reversed and unified against. As Van Kley concludes, "if, as seems plausible, there exists some kind of law of the conservation of the sacred, then the price paid for the desacralization of the remaining symbols of transcendence was an ideological resacralization of a 'regenerated' body of the politic—the nation, the patrie, the people."[22]

We might conclude that the revolution could afford to turn against the religious crutch for national unity because that crutch had apparently already done much work. Catholic France was more united and the populace had been engaged, with that unity and engagement now turned to democracy. This is not to suggest that no disunity or diversity remained. In 1794 the Jacobins began a campaign against patois and for the greater use of French to unify, reiterating that linguistic and other differences still and long remained within France.[23] But absolutism had used religion to forge greater national unity that antiabsolutists and revolutionary authority then pursued further under secularism.

Some Protestant and Catholic sectarianism remained and would even play a role in the Revolution, amid ongoing debates as to selective allocations of citizenship rights. But two centuries of discrimination, attack, and expulsion of non-Catholics had unified the French, if not in all respects then at least enough to end religious civil war and allow for the consolidation of central state power. For the revolutionaries to return to religious exclusions risked again dividing or destroying the prize of state power, now being fought over. In terms of curtailing the religious element of violent domestic discord, national unity had been more fully achieved, and the revolutionaries believed they were now free to turn that unity against the crown, cutting the nation off from its religious anchor.

In a sense, the revolutionaries were right, at least for a time. They could unify much of the populace against the crown, ending absolutism, without using religion as a basis for resistance, and instead also attacking that religion associated with the crown. Still, exclusion more generally played a role in cohering and mobilizing the nation, though during and after revolution such exclusion was instead directed against royalists or outward. In 1792, émigré nobles were decried as traitors, and the following year all foreign-born citizens were deprived of their rights by the Committee on Public Safety. In the postrevolutionary era of wars with other European powers, xenophobia helped to keep French unity intact.[24] But such exclusion and antagonism was directed against foreigners and political adversaries rather than heretics found within. Indeed, by 1808 Napoleon asserted that he valued Protestants "as my best subjects" and decried that their expulsion "drove industries and arts into foreign lands . . . This is the fruit of prosecutions."[25] And this pattern of purported domestic inclusion, forged by revolution, would itself become entrenched in modern France, even as Catholicism reasserted itself in popular beliefs. Even today, the French state rejects any group claims or any racial or religious categories of distinction or exclusion.[26]

But a purely secular basis of national unity would prove insufficient to legitimate or solidify the French state in the aftermath of the Revolution.

While there was no significant challenge to the unity of France (other than in Corsica), regional differences and loyalties would remain to be subordinated by later state efforts despite the general commonality of Catholicism.[27] And after the Revolution, it would take France at least another century of violent vacillations between competing forms of secular authority before national unity would come to rest and be represented by a stable democratic order. "Since 1789 there have been five republics, two monarchies, two empires and about fifteen constitutions ... an indication of the numerous changes which took place."[28] In other words, while there was no threat of France breaking apart, there were major disputes about how and by whom it would be ruled. It is perhaps too much to blame this instability on the attempt to build secular authority without religious backing. But the ongoing fervent Catholicism of the populace by itself did not bind the nation within a stable institutional form. It would seem that without official endorsement of the passion of religious unity, national unity and relative homogeneity in themselves would not or could not consolidate the secular order.

In rejecting absolutist rule built upon religious exclusion and Catholic passion, France's revolutionaries had assumed that they could have unity and democracy without that glue. To a degree, they were right, though arguably at the cost of the discord over the form of rule that followed. Secular loyalty proved powerful, even as faith reemerged among the populace. That degree of national unity earlier achieved through religious exclusion did persist, notably with France's unity remaining unchallenged, and was then reinforced by extensions of the suffrage. But such unity also proved insufficient to allow for consolidation of democratic authority. France could then project itself as inclusive, with citizenship based on *jus soli*, though in doing so it forgot its earlier exclusionary basis and foreclosed the further use of exclusions to manage diversity or instability.[29]

An irony is at work here. The edicts attempting to end the religious civil wars of the sixteenth century, culminating in the Edict of Nantes, had proclaimed that the memory of that exclusion, discord and basis of unity be forgotten. In a sense, the French revolutionaries had themselves later abided by these earlier absolutist orders to expunge memory, in particular of the religious basis of unity so achieved. They had effectively acceded to the royal edicts to forget the past, or at least had rejected that past as inconsistent with more secularized national unity.

But the Revolution's heirs would find later that the imperatives of the past could not be forgotten without cost. Cut off from its memory of unity forged upon religion, the French nation varied dramatically and violently in its institutional expressions, intact but unsure of its state form. Unlike the situation in England, the defeat of absolutism was not based on religious passions, for the French king had still represented the nation's and his own Catholic faith, with all rejected together. Then Catholicism reemerged but without the same political content or impact. Without a merger of representative secularism and popular religious fanaticism, the former was left less sure. The nation remained consolidated but less able to find stable form. Religious belief and secular nationalism both remained, but in being officially kept apart they no longer reinforced each other.

And such relative national unity did come with another price—or perhaps benefit. Amid relative popular cohesion, and with no faction officially excluded or discriminated against, France's working class was also relatively united and therefore capable of more powerful assertions of its interests. They actively resisted property limits on suffrage begun in 1791 and reinforced even more than in England after 1830, and they then challenged property itself. The country was torn by strikes in 1833, an uprising in Paris in 1839, and strikes the next year, followed by a mass movement calling for socialism in 1848. Compared with Britain, "throughout the nineteenth century, the French working class had the (deserved) reputation of being particularly rebellious."[30] Indeed, the comparison is striking with Britain, where except for the Chartist riots there was no comparable mass worker unrest during the nineteenth century. France in the late 1890s, though it had only 4.6 million workers in manufacturing (compared with 6 million in the United Kingdom), suffered 3.5 million days of work lost to industrial disputes in 1899, a particularly conflict-ridden year (compared with 2.5 million in the U.K. that year).[31] Worker activism in France brought dramatic instability, with both arguably in part the result of the lack of religious exclusions that might otherwise have divided and constrained the lower class, as it would in England. This counterfactual is impossible to prove, but France's ongoing instability and conflict were apparent.

Post-Revolution France was explicitly secular but also relatively united as a Catholic nation, with the process by which unity was forged and reinforced by earlier religious exclusions then put aside, or at least assumed as completed. Even its working class was so united, not divided by religion, and as a result more assertive. National unity could be more fully taken for granted as a basis for democracy, with the focus of politics shifting to issues of state authority and economic structure. While this focus did not formally divide the French nation, it did produce dramatic instability. Perhaps a greater retained focus on the need to preserve and build national unity through further religious exclusion would have produced a more stable political and economic order, though with its own costs. But the historical disjuncture of secular revolution made this impossible, with all the divisive energies of the country instead focused on the secular realm. France came to take its religious unity for granted, with popular energies shifting to other issues over which the country would long tear itself apart. But its civicness would remain a source of national pride, disconnected from the earlier intolerance on which national unity had been built.

England: Liberal Nationalism Built on Illiberalism

England's trajectory toward unity and democracy followed a path in some ways similar but in other respects very different—and with different outcomes. To explore this comparison, we need to focus again on England's comparable moment of antiroyal revolution, when the English nation like the French cut itself off from any prospect of absolutism, albeit with a more selective reformulation of authority and forgetting. A brief examination of the leading ideas of the time will set the stage.

The often underplayed role of religious passion against the crown in England, as contrasted with the rejection of religion that had bolstered the legitimacy of the crown in France, is evident in the seminal documents of each revolution. In France, the Declaration of the Rights of Man and Citizen promised tolerance of all faiths, with revolutionary authority then distancing itself from all such faith under secular humanism. In England, the leading statement on religion by John Locke became comparably seminal, though not officially so. And while that English statement appeared to provide a stirring call for tolerance akin to that of France, it was actually less definitive in its inclusion and more selectively forgetful of exclusion. As such, it reflected that resistance to the Catholic crown and religious intolerance more generally remained central to how national unity and democracy were forged together.

On its face, John Locke's "Letter Concerning Toleration" appears to take a similar stance to that enacted by the French National Assembly a century later. Locke upheld "the mutual toleration of Christians in their different professions of religion," and this principal is all the more inspiring in its rejection of then still strong religious fanaticism.[32] In Locke's view, not only should the state not force a particular religion but it should not engage in any legislation regarding faith. In his words, "the whole jurisdiction of the magistrate reaches only to these civil concernments; and that all civil power, right and dominion is bounded and confined to the only care of promoting these things; and that it neither can nor ought in any manner to be extended to the salvation of souls . . . For no man can, if he would, conform his faith to the dictates of another." He reiterated that "all the power of civil government relates only to men's interests, is confined to the care of the things of this world, and hath nothing to do with the world to come . . . All the rights and franchises that belong to (a person) as a man or as a denizen are inviolably to be preserved to him. They are not the business of religion."[33] Locke even cited biblical authority (1 Corinthians 5:12, 13), instructing that followers "judgeth not those that are without."[34]

Locke thus made a pivotal move in advocating tolerance as a virtue and a corresponding separation of church and state. In his words, the "church itself is a thing absolutely separate and distinct from the commonwealth."[35] This stirring call for secular politics was a central component of the Enlightenment in which Locke was a leading figure, and it inspired that later adoption of secular democracy in France and the United States. The import of this move should not be underestimated, and it has been rightfully hailed as a hallmark of liberalism.

But Locke added an important though veiled caveat to his defense of secularism and toleration. In what appears as almost an afterthought toward the end of the letter, Locke wrote "that [a] church can have no right to be tolerated by the magistrate which is constituted upon such a bottom that all those who enter into it thereby ipso facto deliver themselves up to the protection and service of another prince." For instance, a religion that claims the right to excommunicate and thereby threaten a sovereign is beyond the pale, as Locke stated explicitly earlier in 1667. In such an instance, where a religion is "seditiously and contrary to the public peace," tolerance should not be extended.[36] The example Locke gives is of a "Mohometan . . . himself bound to yield blind obedience to the Mufti of Constantinople."[37] But of course there were few if any Muslims in England to be tolerated or not.

Locke's contemporaries well understood his exception to tolerance to be a veiled reference instead to Catholics, owing allegiance to the pope, and thereby not deserving of tolerance. Locke explicitly claimed to be open to tolerating Catholics presumably as long as they do not give primary allegiance to the "foreign prince" in Rome. As this was an impossibility, his implicit intolerance to Catholics remained, camouflaged as an attack on loyalty to the pope rather than Catholicism per se.[38] His tolerance was more directed at differences within the dominant religion, which had emerged more forcefully in England than in France. Locke's selective tolerance envisioned or assumed a bounded political community already integrated, albeit cohered by anti-Catholicism as the basis for popular engagement and democracy.[39]

Locke's proclamation of tolerance thus implicitly excluded the one group arguably most needing tolerance. Acceding to anti-Catholicism was no idle or insignificant exception to the principle of toleration. Locke argued that "the business of laws is not to provide for the truth of opinions, but for the safety and security of the commonwealth, and of every particular man's goods and person." Indeed, when weighed against "liberty of conscience," Locke "attached greater importance in all of his writings to the peace and stability of the social order."[40] In Locke's view, "only limited toleration was consistent with life in society . . . excluding papists and atheists, he always gave the magistrate a right to interfere in religious matter, where peace and public order necessitated it."[41] In the midst of a Protestant revolution against a Catholic monarch, Locke apparently justified an exception to the separation of church and state when it came to excluding Papists, from the highest to the more common, in order to protect the state, preserve national unity and the social order, and make liberal democracy possible.

But this implicit exclusion of Catholics undermines the central logic of Locke's own position. His argument for a separation of church and state and for tolerance rested on the assumption that "churches have neither any jurisdiction in worldly matters, nor are fire and sword any proper instruments wherewith to convince men's minds of error, and inform them of truth."[42] However, it was not true that the coercive force of the state had no bearing on belief, nor that beliefs had no bearing on the uses of state force. Certainly this neat distinction did not hold in the particular period of religious passions when issues of state power and faith were so merged, and amid conflicts over the religious role of kings or the secular power of the pope. Locke may have wished to create such a distinction between secular and religious authority, but his veiled justification for exclusion of Catholics from tolerance or succession undermines his attempt. By excluding Catholics for owing primary allegiance to the pope, he acknowledged that religious beliefs and secular power intersect.

Locke's intolerance toward Catholics cannot be understood in terms of philosophical consistency but is instead connected to his own biography. Born into a Puritan household and having lived through the 1660s when "15,000 Quakers—the most uncompromising of the nonconformists—suffered fines, imprisonment, transportation and 450 gave their lives," Locke clearly valued toleration among Protestants.[43] But Locke was also influenced by news from France in 1685, where "Protestants who refused to convert, under orders of Louis XIV, were beaten, pillaged, dragooned, their children taken from them; men were sent to the galleys or driven into exile . . . we can hardly doubt that those events did much to undermine the allegiance of the English people [and of Locke] to James II, and smoothed the way for the Revolution of 1688." Indeed, Locke advocated that England provide refuge to Huguenot exiles.[44]

Anti-Catholicism was evident in Locke's own engagement as a political activist, even more explicitly than in his later writings. Locke aligned himself and worked for the Earl of Shaftesbury, whose own advocacy of limited religious tolerance was combined with antagonism against France. Shaftesbury broke with Charles II in leading Parliament's efforts to exclude the Catholic successor, fleeing to exile in Holland in 1682. "Locke remained to become involved with Algernon Sydney in the plot to assassinate the king in September 1683. Sydney was hanged [while] Locke managed to escape to Holland and became involved in the organization of the ill-fated Monmouth Rebellion of 1685," the same year in which he drafted the Letter on Toleration.[45]

It would seem consistent that having risked his life in plots to exclude a Catholic from the English throne and to replace James II with Protestant monarchs unsympathetic to Catholic rights, Locke's tolerance did not extend to Papists. The resulting exception to his principle of toleration is, then, consistent with his primary concern for "peace and stability of the social order." In his view, that order and national unity were threatened by a Catholic monarch and could only be ensured by intolerance toward James II and his fellow Catholics. Again, this is not a surprising conclusion for someone whose life experience spanned the Puritan Revolution, protectorate, restoration, exclusion crisis and Glorious Revolution. In his own words: "After declaring that 'there is no one can have greater respect and veneration for authority than I,' he remarks that from earliest childhood he has found himself 'in a storm, which has lasted almost hitherto,' so that 'he cannot but entertain the approaches of a calm with the greatest joy and satisfaction.' "[46] Like many revolutionaries, Locke thus claimed to actually be a conservative defender of order, to be restored by excepting Catholics from toleration and from the royal succession. But he cloaked this position within his call for liberal toleration.

Contrasted with the French rejection of intolerance and of memories of past exclusion, Locke proposed and helped to ensure a more selective version of tolerance and forgetting. Unlike France, England engaged in revolution in the same period as its greatest religious strife, when the passions of fanaticism were still enflamed and not yet spent but instead seeped into that supposedly civic liberalism that Locke proclaimed. Anti-Catholicism would not and could not be denied, even if it was hidden in theory. Instead selective intolerance helped to drive the revolution forward, harnessing Protestantism against Catholic kings executed or exiled as heretical foreigners. The only discord to be ended, covered over with tolerance and forgotten, was among Protestant factions unified at least against Catholicism as a nation. That this selective form of toleration would be hailed as purely liberal principle is incredible enough. That this sleight of hand would be celebrated on face value attests to England's own willingness to forget and suggests that Locke's successors were less conscious of the limits of liberalism than was he.

Indeed, Locke's subtle argument helped to consolidate the outcome of the revolutionary period in England. By proposing a distinction between faith and power, while excluding one faith from power, he justified the Glorious Revolution and the retaining of more limited monarchy transferred to William and Mary and their successors. The result was that the religious passions that had enflamed England to revolution, and were thus very much alive at the time, were not forgotten or dismissed and were retained as the glue that held together the nation as it made its dramatic transition toward constitutional monarchy. To appear liberal and consistent with the Enlightenment, Locke veiled his intolerance for Catholics, knowing that he could take for granted such popular intolerance and national unity based thereon. By contrast, France did more firmly distance itself from its past religious intolerance than did England, despite the latter's denials. Unlike England, France retained neither its monarchy in the long term nor the religious glue officially holding together the nation through a more troubled transition to democracy.

England's more direct path to constitutional democracy was paved, even made possible, by past and ongoing religious intolerance and exclusion. The more standard interpretation is that "Parliament won out over the crown because of the enmeshment of ideas about personal liberty with lessons learned about the need for religious toleration." Others have suggested that England's early democratization was due to its relative geographic isolation, protecting it from constant military challenges that were met by "military-bureaucratic absolutism" on the continent.[47] But my argument here suggests an alternative explanation. If democracy requires prior national unity, in England that unity was achieved through religious exclusion and intolerance, in which Parliament played a leading role, for instance in curtailing the rule of two Catholic leaning monarchs. Thus, even England's much-celebrated constitutional democracy was founded on the basis of illiberal intolerance.

England was indeed then fortunate in being "God's firstborn,"[48] but not as a shining example of a civic founding or tolerant nationalism. Instead, England successfully converted religious fanaticism into a passion for secular but still exclusive nationalism. And such exclusion was then encoded further after the Glorious Revolution through democratic processes so delineated. In 1691 Catholics were barred from Parliament; in 1692 they were excluded from the army and prevented from possessing firearms; in 1695 Catholic children were not allowed to be sent abroad for education; in 1697 Catholic bishops and missionaries were barred from England; and in 1703 Catholics were excluded from all public offices. Nor were they permitted to buy or inherit land, leading to a decline in their land holdings in Ireland from 59 percent in 1641 to 5 percent by 1778. The result was "a state in which one official confession of faith, Anglicanism, was established by statute and enforced through law." By 1792 Burke would argue that "in a Christian Commonwealth the church and the state are one and the same thing."[49]

That the English had not forgotten or rejected the religious basis of their cohesion was evident in continued exclusions. Perhaps the single most dramatic moment of continued mass engagement against Catholics came with the Gordon Riots of 1780. In that year, his Majesty's government was in need of more troops for fighting in the American colonies and agreed to repeal laws against Catholics in order to attract them into military service. But pragmatic elite tolerance for Catholics enraged popular intolerance.[50] The reform proposals again enflamed anti-Catholic sentiment, led by Lord Gordon, which produced massive rioting in London. The popularity of anti-Catholic fanaticism was evident in that troops called in to quell the riots were often seen as instead sympathetic to those rioters. Parliamentarians feared that mob rule was overtaking the rule of law, but they did largely backtrack on the proposed reforms, and the riots ended. Gordon himself was later acquitted of charges, though he did leave politics and later converted to orthodox Judaism.[51]

Popular resistance to any reform of Catholic exclusion would remain evident, even as such reforms took hold. Under Daniel O'Connell, the Catholic Association pushed for such reforms, but there was also considerable counter-pressure, for instance with 20,000 people joining an anti-Catholic meeting in 1828. The Welsh had also joined in such anti-Catholic mobilization. Earlier, in 1801 George III had sided with the anti-Catholics, vetoing a "proposal to integrate Catholics (Irish or otherwise) into the new realm's public life." But pressure from the Catholics, together with the ideology of purportedly inclusive liberalism and the state's pragmatic interest in recruiting Catholics into the army to defend illiberal imperial extension, finally forced reform over popular opposition. The 1829 Catholic Emancipation (Relief) Act "rendered Catholics eligible for all offices of state," albeit with the notable exceptions of lord-lieutenant, lord chancellor, regent, and monarch. Even after 1832 Catholics remained subject to discrimination, deprivation, and unequal rights, enforced by antipopish politicians eager to "defend the faith" and win popularity on this basis.[52]

Indeed, anti-Catholicism remained a relatively stable, if not defining, feature of Britain. "Until 1829, British Catholics were not allowed to vote and were excluded from all state offices and from both houses of Parliament. For much of the eighteenth century they were subject to punitive taxation, forbidden to possess weapons, and discriminated against in terms of access to education, property rights, and freedom of worship. In other words, in law—if not always in fact—they were treated as potential traitors, as un-British."[53] And the ongoing antagonism against Irish Catholics long provided constant reminders of Protestant unity, with England's vulnerability to that conflict or to invasion through Ireland keeping the "Papist threat" alive. It is difficult to fully agree then with Hastings that while "English nationalism had been determinedly Protestant . . . British nationalism was essentially secular."[54]

Consistent with remaining tensions within Britain, arguably England's experiences were still shaped by continued exclusion of Irish Catholics, bolstering selective national unity. While France's working class was not divided by ongoing religious conflict and proved itself instead united and assertive throughout the nineteenth century, England's working class looked and acted very differently. There was a continued influx of Irish Catholics taking jobs in England, and they came to be resented as "foreign" competitors, reviving prejudice and producing conflict among workers who might otherwise have unified.[55] For instance, while French workers were uniting to demand socialism in 1848, in England workers were divided in their support of Chartism and less powerful per se. Most Protestant workers kept themselves separate from Catholics and even supported the Tory party for its anti-immigrant policies.[56] In return, the Tories could and would allow for lowering of property requirement for the suffrage, which empowered more Protestant workers but still left many Irish excluded.

England's path to industrialization was thus eased by continued sectarianism. Protestant workers enjoyed relative privilege compared to Irish Catholics, while business benefited from a working class so divided, unable to unify, mobilize, act, or vote uniformly against more conservative governments. "The making of the English working class" as a unified social movement was constrained to a significant extent by ongoing antagonism against Catholics. Protestants were so unified across class lines, thereby providing for greater stability, while the working class remained divided and weakened by religious division. Rather than industrialization requiring and encouraging homogenization, conflict between emerging classes was diminished by continued diversity.

Continued anti-Catholicism not only helps to account for England's relative lack of class conflict but was widely perceived to be a basis for her prosperity more generally and as influencing the construction of an empire which fed that prosperity. As with consolidation of political authority, economic expansion also requires a relative lack of internal conflict, made possible for England by that national unity forged by exclusion of Catholics. Already by the 1750's, Hogarth's engravings of France "reflected the view that popery and poverty went inevitably together," and by contrast England's prosperity was associated with Protestantism and democracy.[57] By the following century, justifications for England's profitable imperial rule over others included the image of spreading Protestant prosperity and of "scientific racism" evocative of earlier anti-Catholicism kept alive by antagonism against the Irish. Thus the legacies of intolerance were carried forward.

The import of anti-Catholicism as a central component of Englishness for close to three centuries cannot then be overstated. From the Reformation "onwards only their common hatred of Catholicism could bring English Protestants together . . . [even after] the threat of popery had diminished the fragile Protestant unity of 1688 crumbled."[58] Indeed, "hatred of [the Catholic] Church is after all the only foundation of the Church of England," much as it was arguably the foundation for national unity and democracy.[59]

But that anti-Catholicism remained so salient on the law books as a source of mass hysteria, and as providing the ongoing glue to Protestant England, is often overlooked. Christopher Hill concludes that "if the age of faith ever existed, it was over by 1714." Similarly, according to J. P. Kenyon, "the last priest was executed in 1680, and nothing more is heard of popish plots except during the brief hysteria of the Gordon Riots of 1780. The Catholic problem was no longer a political issue."[60] But if this "problem" largely disappeared from public view, it was less due to tolerance than to continued intolerance and legal discrimination retaining unity based on Protestantism.

Yet it remains striking that England retained its Catholic exclusions at the same time that it embraced an image of liberal inclusion and pretended that religion was no longer a political issue. But what appears contradictory was not. Simply put, anti-Catholicism continued to provide the glue for national cohesion, democracy, prosperity, and imperialism, which increasingly solidified on this basis could and did pretend to be other than it was. Religious fanaticism had been transformed into sectarian unity, though no less exclusionary or binding.

Having consolidated exclusively Protestant nationalism, the exclusionary element of this process was largely forgotten, with Locke himself having played a role in this forgetting both in his time and in later interpretations. That his letter, published in 1689 after the Glorious Revolution, made only veiled reference to anti-Catholicism and appeared instead to tolerate Papists contributed to a false sense of more complete toleration, consistent with the general tenor of liberalism. A cynical interpretation is that Locke felt he could afford to downplay anti-Catholicism after the successful exclusion of Catholics from the throne and from civil rights. English culture as a whole appears to have followed this path. According to Walzer, "Lockeian liberals found it possible to dispense with religious . . . controls . . . But this was only because the controls had already been implanted in men . . . Zeal [was] no longer a worldly necessity."

Certainly as a founder of liberalism and an Enlightenment advocate of the separation of church and state, Locke was impressively tolerant, as were those he inspired. They put explicit religious exclusions behind them, for "indeed, there was much to be forgotten." But also as an anti-Catholic activist and revolutionary, Locke would appear to have been capable of cynically veiled selective intolerance to ensure continued national unity as the basis of "discipline and order" within a consolidated liberal democracy.[61] In this, liberals also followed.

Nor has the purposeful forgetting of the limits of English liberal tolerance ended or been insignificant. As one modern analyst would proclaim, "the battle for toleration was already almost won when [Locke's] Letter was published."[62] But what had been won in the Glorious Revolution was just the opposite, an intolerance toward the most salient other religious group headed by the crown. The forgetting has clearly not ended yet. Even in this century, England has continued to wrestle with the contradictions between supposed liberal inclusion and a willingness to encode racial or ethnic categories of distinction and informal exclusion.

Spain: Faith without Nation

Spain, by contrast, followed an altogether different trajectory, though one which further confirms the general argument here as a negative case. It had been first to attempt to harness religion to bolster efforts at both state and national consolidation, with its Inquisition begun already in the fifteenth century when Aragon and Castile were linked to create Spain. But in a Catholic country with little Protestantism, the Inquisition was instead turned against those seen more as foreigners: Jews, Moors and converts rather than domestic "Spanish" heretics. Perhaps this attack on supposed foreigners was less binding of Spaniards than were attacks on "others" found within, elsewhere forcing more clear demarcations of who was to be included in the nation. Arguably it was also less binding to the degree that it remained institutionalized and controlled from above rather than engaging mass passions in violence. And certainly the glue of such exclusion and attack lost its hold as those heretics largely disappeared under attack. Their removal was accomplished long before Spain or other European countries had gathered force for more fully consolidating the state and nation. This left Spain with the fervor of Catholicism but no "other" within against which to refine secular authority and direct and maintain that fervor toward national unity.

Without the same religious conflict and passion for nationalism, Spain long lagged in building such solidarity. Catholicism did not engage secular loyalty to the same extent it would in France or that Protestantism would in England. Without comparable ongoing internal religious schisms, Catholic unity was not as constantly reengaged in the secular political realm. Relative homogenization had its costs. According to Juan Linz, "the identification of the state and even the nation with Catholicism . . . would be an obstacle to secular state- and nation-building."[63] Catholicism remained largely a religious force, relatively unharnessed by power to consolidate that power, as it would in postrevolutionary France. But Spain's Catholic exclusions were then neither fully nor as selectively forgotten as in France, retaining their hold on Spain, trapped in otherworldliness and its own orbit. But this religious glue proved insufficient on its own to cohere secular politics, which then failed to progress amid concealed deep divisions.

Catholicism did bolster the authority of the crown that shared the religion of the populace, and it did so all the more after the French Revolution when those secular forces to the north were rejected as heretical "others." But in focusing on top-down authority, "the Spanish state never achieved what French kings and ultimately the Revolution did: to create the fully unified state and nation-state with its linguistic-cultural and emotional integration." Or, according to Sanchez-Albornoz, "it is the enormous responsibility of Charles V and Philip II to have neglected to unite Spain. Spain can claim against them a great debt."[64] If those kings believed, with absolutist hubris, that Spain could progress just as well without popular engagement or internal cohesion, they were wrong.

As if relative homogeneity and early exclusion ironically were not enough to disadvantage Spain in its nation-building, Spain was further cursed by its windfall of empire. Also much earlier than France or England, Spain inherited through royal lineage and bribery a European-based empire more vast than any other country would gain even later. This inheritance sapped resources from the state and diluted loyalty to its crown, held by at least one monarch who could not initially even speak proper Spanish. The monarchs enjoyed legitimacy as fellow Catholics, but that also brought difficulties. Charles and Philip as Holy Roman Emperors ruled over large Protestant followings, and though they attacked heresy, they could not and did not expel all heretics from the fold. Under such circumstances of extended authority, building a nation proved difficult, to say the least. The center proved "singularly ineffective in promoting either institutional or emotional unity among its Spanish kingdoms" and holdings.[65]

The result was long stagnation and political and economic backwardness, reinforced then by the loss of empire and its revenues. Nationalism not having been consolidated by religious fervor and mass exclusion neither unified or engaged the populace in its secular authority nor inflamed revolutionary or liberal efforts to cut itself loose from absolutism. Instead, popular identification with regions remained often stronger than loyalty to the whole, with large-scale nationalism challenged by "a veritable craze for disintegration" or "particularism." The nineteenth century later saw explosions of such localism, notably among the Basques and Catalans, for instance, with the latter questioning whether they should "continue participating in a [centralized] system that is decaying, that is out of tune with the times, and whose inefficacy is patent."[66] The efforts of Spanish historians to instead assert "national sentiment . . . as splendid as those traditionally claimed by the French and the English" could not hide its relative absence.[67]

Largely cut off from Europe's Enlightenment by the unchallenged Catholic Church, attempts at reform faltered, civil wars continued to divide the nation as late as the 1930s, and consolidated democracy was not finally achieved until late in the twentieth century. Without more cohering nationalism elsewhere forged by religious conflict, the populace was not engaged or united enough either to support absolutism or later to demand and achieve democracy. As Linz concludes, "Spain, born in the era of state-building, could not undergo the deep emotional process of democratic nation-building."[68] Even if its later failings cannot be fully ascribed to earlier failings, the consistent result was that Spain long remained un-national, illiberal, and undemocratic.

Focusing again on the comparison of France and England suggests some unusual implications. Their ultimate divergence in retaining or rejecting the legacies of religious exclusion set the trajectories of continued nation-building off in different directions.

England's pivotal period of revolution against its crown came more than a century earlier than did the comparable events for France. For England, resistance to the king was ushered in earlier by a vibrant tradition of localized authority dating back at least to Magna Carta. Certainly decentralization did consolidate alternative loci of power that could be and were turned against the crown. But France also had a tradition of localized power, pursued by nobles and then instituted in the parlements and representation in the Estates—even though the latter was infrequently called and more subject to royal control than was England's Parliament. And the Reformation did long tie England's thereby enriched nobility to the crown. We should then be careful not to fully ascribe the earlier and more effective assertion of antiabsolutism in England to the path dependence of a historical legacy of decentralization. More may be at work in explaining the timing and outcomes of the divergent histories than the relative strength of such localized alternatives to royal authority, which have so often been the focus of explanations of difference.

What is much less the focus of earlier analysis is the pivotal role of religion, or, more precisely, the difference in how religion and royal authority were connected. England's revolutions in the seventeenth century were directed by the nation's representatives not only against the crown but also against the religious directions of that crown as unrepresentative. The Puritan revolution was energized not only as opposition to increasing absolutism but it was also enflamed by the Catholic sympathies of Charles I and his French queen. The Glorious Revolution was even more directly an effort to prevent an acknowledged Catholic King James II from remaining on the throne. The English rejected their sovereigns both as absolutist and for being far from God. The religious passions of the age were merged with secular efforts against absolutism in a combustible mix of national unity and engagement that left one king without his head and another without his realm. By contrast, the French King Louis XVI a century later was not pursuing an alternative faith to that of the majority of his subjects but rather had inherited a Gallican tradition of representing, leading, and being legitimized by the Catholic faith. The French Revolution did not turn faith against the crown, for the two were merged, provoking the anti-absolutist movement there to abandon religious faith and turn against it.

This difference is striking, particularly in an age when religious fanaticism was arguably the strongest force of popular engagement. While England had merged nationally unifying religious exclusion with popular resistance to the crown in the same revolutionary moment, in France these processes were separated. The English Parliament's resistance to the crown was reinforced by simultaneous popular resentment against two kings seen as heretics, or at least as sympathizers or followers of a foreign and earlier rejected faith. By contrast, religious passions had first unified the nation of France as loyal to the crown, and later both that crown and the church were rejected, though this double move may have delayed democratization. But this disjunction did allow the French Revolution to turn its back on religious passion, taking national unity more for granted and then directing that unity against the crown on a more secular, humanistic, and rights-related basis. With religious faith having been closely tied to the monarch, both were rejected together, at least at the moment of crisis. In England, where popular faith was increasingly divergent from the monarch, faith was harnessed as a popular basis for revolution and then encoded in further exclusions. Religious images of having been "chosen" as a people could be used to bolster antimonarchical claims to political power, while the French rose against a king himself so "chosen."

This contrast of France and England suggests that not only does the path to democracy vary but as part of that variation its "ingredients" may come together or be "assembled at one time." Rustow is then wrong that these ingredients of modernization must emerge separately.[69] They did come in stages in France, where the resolution of religious conflict cohered the nation through exclusion, predating efforts by a thus more unified nation to then throw off absolutism and move toward democracy. Ironically, the unity forged and in part imposed from above by the crown was later turned against it. In England, these two "ingredients" were merged, bringing a more direct and earlier transition to democracy.

There remains a further, more profound and troubling implication for the liberal tradition symbolized by England's revolution against absolutism and by the writings of John Locke: that revolution and liberal tradition wrapped itself in the banner of tolerance but was based on intolerance. Liberalism was founded on, indeed was made possible only, by illiberalism. Selective forgetting of essential exclusion, and the celebration of false toleration, later made this contradiction possible and flower. But liberalism, like nationalism, was possible only by being bounded to a particular community, demarcated at its start by faith. That boundedness was seen as necessary for forging the solidarity of the nation to which liberal rights would be ascribed and in which democracy could be consolidated, for democracy requires such unity. And then that boundedness was forgotten, creating a false impression of a liberalism and democracy more true to its supposed inclusive values than was the case.

In this sense, the French Revolution was perhaps more true to liberalism and tolerance, though with some cost: that Revolution did more fully enact toleration, rejecting the glue of exclusionary religious passion. Perhaps the French revolutionaries felt confident in so discarding religion because faith had already longer been used as the basis for forging national unity that could then be turned against the crown without retaining the religious crutch. Two hundred years after the St. Bartholomew's Day massacre and religious civil wars, religious passions had consolidated national unity to a large extent, and in doing so they had been spent as a political force. After all, by the time of the French Revolution most Huguenots had become obedient or been converted, exiled, or killed, so that they no longer served as the basis of Catholic unity. Perhaps the revolutionaries discarded religion because it was supportive of the monarch rather than a basis for resistance to a monarch of another faith, as contrasted with England. Or perhaps it was all such factors together. In any case, the crutch of religion for national unity was officially thrown away by the state, leaving the still strongly Catholic French nation in the long term to limp more fitfully toward its revolutionary goals and democracy.

What emerges then is the benefits of hypocrisy. Post-Revolution France remained more consistently and officially liberal in its rejection of religious exclusion and other forms of official categorical discrimination. But it paid a price for abandoning the official glue of religiously enflamed nationalism, with internal discord continuing over how best to represent and govern the nation. The nation was united as Catholic, but in officially distancing itself from this basis of unity it allowed for the reemergence of internal conflict, such as over issues of class. By contrast, England's projection of liberal inclusion was maintained amid contradictory exclusions, with anti-Catholicism remaining on the books and still unifying the nation selectively despite denials of its import. England then enjoyed greater unity, at least among the Protestant majority, was able to more peacefully consolidate democratic governance, and avoided more explosive class conflict with a working class still divided by religion. Liberalism paid off in its ultimate aim of preserving social order by retaining its hidden legacy of excluding some from the benefits of that order.

ANGEL OF HISTORY AND
PATRON SAINT OF NATIONALISM

7

As nationalism did not preexist, it had to be built. Causal accounts for the emergence of nationalism have suggested the timing of this development coinciding with those social processes that purportedly encouraged popular cohesion. If nationalism was the outgrowth of spreading vernacular and printing, generating a sense of simultaneous experience, then it could take hold only once "print capitalism" had become pervasive, as with the explosion of book or newspaper distribution or schooling. If such collective solidarity was the result of shared economic interests and interaction, it could emerge only with the spreading of capitalism, or even industrialization, undermining peasant isolation. And if it was the result of state allocated rights, then it could emerge only with the blossoming of democratic regimes allocating such rights. All of these arguments thereby coincide with the consensus that Western nationalism was built during and after the era of the French Revolution, when literacy, industrialization, and citizenship became pervasive in Europe.

Most current theories also agree on the inclusive tendency or internal homogeneity of nationalism within specified boundaries. The common assumption is that states seeking or benefiting from popular unity, whether for warfare, revenue, or development, come to encourage or enjoy the common allegiance of their population, excluding only foreigners. According to Benedict Anderson, this "imagined community" emerges out of language, suggesting that no one is purposefully or even accidentally excluded from the emerging cohesion. As he says, "language is not an instrument of exclusion . . . it is fundamentally inclusive."[1] For Ernest Gellner, such homogeneity is "imposed by objective . . . imperative" of the economy, with "industrial society allergic to counter-entropic institutions" or traits.[2] For state theorists, pervasive loyalty or devotion to the polity is purposefully encouraged through the allocation of services and privileges, with the state adjudicating disputes to bolster unity. According to T. H. Marshall or Bendix, the granting of distinct citizenship rights may vary and its extension to particular groups may lag, but the tendency is toward universal extension, again with exclusions as anomalous.[3] All of these arguments thus accord not only on timing but also with the tendency toward civic inclusion symbolized by the "liberty, equality and fraternity" of the French Revolution era.

In contrast with this consensus, I have here argued that nationalism at least began to emerge much earlier. Building on even earlier roots, the absolutist rulers of early modern Europe's great state powers shared a growing interest in building the coherence and loyalty of their subjects in order to bolster their authority. Their opponents also sought popular support. Crown and commoners both faced this imperative for popular cohesion before relevant social processes had spread enough to be so used or effective. Literacy and economic development were limited, and the idea of citizenship rights had not yet fully emerged or been enacted. If we look then for the early foundations of nationalism before it was consolidated, we cannot explain it on the basis of such processes, which were also not yet consolidated.

Nor could early nationalism emerge as inclusively as suggested, for the social processes that supposedly forged such unity were still not only weak but also often divisive in their earlier effects. Language could be exclusive and divisive. And as we have seen, as literacy was beginning to spread, the messages so communicated often enflamed conflict. Sermons and printed tracts or pamphlets exacerbated internal discord. Emerging economic interests also often provoked conflict, as between lords and crowns, regions, or nascent classes. And the initial provision of rights or privileges was similarly selective and discordant, as between, again, lords and crowns, parliaments, or estates.

If we look for the early roots of nationalism before modernizing social processes had taken hold or become inclusive, then explanations that rest on such later processes are less compelling. Instead, we should focus on how early efforts to build national solidarity built upon those social processes and sentiments that were then salient. In effect, what is needed is a more explicitly political account for the rise of nationalism, which incorporates the pivotal role of conflict and exclusion.

Nationalism in the core countries of western Europe was built, more or less purposefully or successfully, not only in the context of but also on the back of fanatical religious passion and conflict. Though this contradicts images of Western "civic" nationalism, this conclusion is not in itself surprising. In the early modern era, religion was *the* popular passion often shared by elites. State rulers, needing popular support to wage war, gain obedience, and solicit revenues, sought a comparable passionate loyalty to their own authority. With literacy, capitalism, and state mechanisms of coercion or education still undeveloped, the most obvious—perhaps the only—alternative was to redirect the rising passion of religion to secular passion for the state, in other words for nationalism itself. And commoners increasingly shared with elites a strategic interest in such greater unity to avoid the costs of further conflict.

As state rulers learned, while serving their own interests the surest way to enflame religious passion and redirect it was to attack heretics within as evident and present threats to religious homogeneity. Opponents of the crown learned the same lesson, also seeking to harness religious passions to their movements, thereby taking advantage of pressing conflict while seeking to resolve it. The "imagined community" of the nation, otherwise vague and uncertain, was so bounded and reinforced. Building greater popular cohesion was necessary precisely because of conflict, prominently over religion, and could be built in the context and on the basis of such conflict. To assume otherwise is not only naïve but inaccurate.

The evidence for this process is to be found in how conflict fed rising popular sentiment, identity, and engagement with issues of state governance, the central component of our definition of nationalism. In particular, the French religious wars and English civil wars saw an unprecedented level of mass political mobilization directed at upholding or reconfiguring state power, which cannot be fully accounted for by patriotic efforts to protect against foreigners. The sheer numbers of combatants and deaths in these processes suggest the degree of popular engagement and thereby suggest the initial emergence of what would become nationalism.

But this mass engagement did not directly bolster national unity. Rising religious passions solidified divisive cultural identities, while state rulers or their opponents sought such a form of identity that might be turned into more secular forms of unity and support. These two processes converged on the middle ground of identity, consolidated from below and harnessed from above. What began as religious fanaticism aggravated by elite conflicts was gradually transformed into more explicitly political identities reflecting the interconnection between issues of faith and power. These identities still rested on religion as a crutch for long periods, before they were sufficiently consolidated to become more or less secular, or at least with religious foundations forgotten. And despite later denials, the reliance on religious identities to bolster secular solidarity was exclusionary, reflecting sectarian passions with nationalism forged by such exclusion.

Such a schematic argument implies an orderly process, but national unity built on the basis of fanatical religious exclusion was instead disorderly and a disordering process, impossible to fully control. Indeed, it cohered the populace only to the degree that blood was spilled in conflict, and less so when orchestrated or institutionalized from above. The more the populace below became engaged, the more control from above was lost. As such, emergent nationalism often cut against efforts to impose stronger centralized state authority and order, even as the state sought greater national unity and cohesion.

Nation- and state-building were thus both complementary and in tension, with this conundrum resolved in varying fitful attempts. Where order was maintained from above, as in Spain, cohesion was limited and ultimately state authority remained underdeveloped. Too much order brought gradual disorder. Where authority was more fully and early challenged, as in England, cohesion emerged against that authority and then reinforced a new form of order under democracy. And where disorder was ridden by the crown to bolster both unity and authority, as in France, eventually disorder ran free in a more complete revolution and its aftermath. In no case did the mutuality of nation- and state-building proceed in a smooth straight course.

The path to nation-building or its attempt varied according to circumstance in ways not anticipated but also on notable occasions ultimately contrary to the interests of those rulers who sought to benefit from it. Exclusion of others found within did indeed prove to be a powerful force of mass mobilization, often too powerful to fully control from above. It gained its ultimate power to the degree it was turned against the crown as such an "other." Put differently, the closer to the bone of established political power religious exclusion cut, the more it forged nationalism set lose from or then defined against the crown. Religious antagonism to the crown was then merged with popular demands for secular representation, setting the stage for democracy. Such variations in how religion was so turned into greater national unity, either in support of or against rulers, had tremendous consequences for the political and social orders that would emerge.

This pattern emerges from comparison. Where the king remained representative of homogenous faith, secular nationalism was not enflamed against the King, as in Spain, where absolutism then remained more intact. Where the king had been seen as the chosen head of the church and successors then rejected as spurious or infected by other faiths, as in England, the passion of religiously inspired nationalism was set loose into revolution. "Chosen-ness" was then transferred from crown to the nation itself, against the crown. In this regard France suggests a more varied process, with the king's authority buttressed by faith, so that when the king was finally cut loose, so was faith—at least officially. Postrevolution France remained relatively united by Catholicism but rejected official cohesion on that basis in favor of a more secular official form. Recapitulating from our three cases let me make the argument more clear.

Spain early on directed religious institutions to exclude foreigners (or those so perceived despite long integration, conversion, and mixing), thereby directing its venom against those farthest from power. Such exclusion was less cohering than it was where directed closer to the core of power. Cohesion through exclusion there remained top-down, institutionalized, and less engaging of the populace, reflecting limits on mass communication and elite fears of greater mass participation or violence. And as such cohesion is generally based on a combination of fear and love, with the Spanish Inquisition generally resting only on fear, it was less binding. Finally, once exclusion had culminated with expulsion, within Spain this left no ongoing religious tension that could be harnessed to further consolidate nationalism. Combined with the diluting effects of empire, Spain was barely consolidated as a nation, and religion remained intact in the spiritual realm without being as transformed into secular cohesion. The result was a somewhat weaker and apparently less autonomous form of popular nationalism, which inspired neither effective challenges to absolutism nor its replacement with a more liberal or democratic order. Thus, Spain emerges as a negative case consistent with the more general pattern. Her early efforts at exclusionary nation-building perhaps provided a template for others later but proved premature for Spain herself, and it failed to take hold.

In England, by contrast, religious passion more unified after Reformation ultimately was turned into a force against kings sympathetic to or of another faith, combining religious antagonism with antiabsolutism. Whereas in 1671 an attempt to steal the crown was decried as treason, by 1688 (as a generation before) the crown itself was decried as treasonous. The result was an increasingly politicized religious fanaticism and unity transformed into nationalism represented by Parliament and newly imported Protestant monarchs. The anti-Catholic component of this transition was then purposefully downplayed to appear more liberal and tolerant, consistent with the emergence of a constitutional monarchy and rising democracy. Nationalism then continued to develop, albeit fitfully as the national unit expanded to further include Great Britain.

France might have followed a path similar to England had the Protestant Henri IV retained his faith and had Catholics united against him. But as a Protestant, Henri likely would never have been able to consolidate his hold on the crown and instead he converted, with his heirs serving as Catholics and the earlier religious conflicts diminished over time and officially forgotten by edict. Having been forged with earlier anti-Protestantism, emergent nationalism then grew more secular and ultimately turned against all forms of royalism without a religious basis. That engagement inspired revolution, ending the monarchy and more fitfully ushering in democracy and ongoing consolidation of national unity.

Religion was then the basis for building early and exclusionary nationalism, albeit in very different ways. By itself, as homogenous within a remaining population as in Spain, it largely remained just that, religious faith, less transformed into the secular passion of nationalism. When merged with secular passions, as with England's Protestant fervor contributing to the opposition to Catholic monarchs, religion filled the sails of nationalism and set it loose from its anchor in absolutism. And once set loose, it could then become increasingly secular, denying but also retaining its religious basis. In France, religious fanaticism was harnessed to build national unity under absolutism but was then spent and purposefully forgotten as the nation outgrew and threw off its monarchy. The result then was the more purely secular nationalism of the French Revolution, though a less stable form for having earlier moved beyond its religious base.

Only by thus excavating the role of religion in nation-building can we account for the manner and differences in how this process was played out in Western Europe. To deny the role of religion would leave us with little understanding of the foundations of this process before it reached its climax or how it developed thereafter. Religious fanaticism was the basis for popular engagement with—for or against—centralizing state authority and, as such, the basis of emerging nationalism. And it was so engaged through violent conflict, cohering through exclusion, for without conflict it remained otherworldly and when compromised as relative toleration it did not stick. Nationalism emerged when the masses were invited onto the political stage or invited themselves in. But that invitation did not come inclusively from books, enrichment, or schooling but rather from sectarian conflicts, enraging sermons, and callings. The passions of faith were the stuff of which the passions for the state were built.

And differences in how the emerging passions of faith and power were directed also then help to account for the form of those states as they entered the modern era. Democracy required prior national unity, built most effectively on the basis of religious exclusion. Ironically, then, the later liberal allocation of rights rested upon the earlier illiberal exclusion of some from those rights, bounding the community to which rights would be allocated. The exclusionary origins of nationalism were also the basis for later democracy built upon such bounded unity. Put most forcefully, the extension of democratic rights was a result of prior exclusions; rights were allocated as a reward for participation in such exclusion. If democracy provided selective rights and benefits reflecting earlier exclusions, aggravating later disputes about allocation, then these results may be tied to original exclusions as a founding flaw of democracy itself.

Perhaps, then, the most important conclusion is that the processes and outcomes of the modern era of nationalism cannot be understood without connecting these to the premodern. Earlier religious conflict and intolerance were not mere relics, irrelevant to the supposedly civic or tolerant orders that would be built thereafter. Where intolerance forged national unity, it was on that basis that liberalism and democracy were built, with ongoing exclusions reflected therein. And where intolerance did not forge comparable national unity, liberalism and democracy did not emerge, posing its own difficulties. That the modern era would prefer to forget these connections, ignoring the illiberal basis of liberalism, does not make them any less significant. Indeed, that earlier basis proved essential in what would come later, setting countries off on distinct paths. Without cognizance of the premodern, we cannot account for the modern or understand our inheritances.

Ironically, while accounting for the modern requires remembering the premodern, the actual process of becoming modern seemingly required or at least encouraged purposeful forgetting. For national unity and then democracy to be further consolidated, past conflict and founding exclusions used to resolve that conflict were dismissed as irrelevant. Illiberal origins were repudiated by leading thinkers so as to reinforce the liberal image and reality of national unity. Earlier exclusions were played down by elites to foster an inclusive "imagined community." And that sense of community was consolidated among the populace by forgetting the selective and violent means by which membership in it had been determined. Standard accounts for the emergence of nationalism as inclusive reinforced its consolidation. The modernizing effects of rising literacy, communication, and industrial development did indeed play a central role in later consolidating nationalism, but they also helped to spread and inspire efforts to forget its earlier basis.

And yet the legacy of past exclusions would not be fully forgotten; they would at least remain as pentimento, their shadow reemerging and their effects replayed in different forms later. Forgotten earlier processes of exclusion would still resonate and shape what would come later. Despite denials and formal commitments to liberal secularism, the glue of religious exclusion as a basis for domestic national unity has still not been fully abandoned. "God and Caesar, church and state, spiritual and temporal authority, have been a prevailing dualism of Western culture," and yet this separation continues to be violated. Five of the fifteen members of the European Union, plus Norway, retain an established church. Only one member of the European Union (Portugal) has a constitutional "prohibition against political parties using religious affiliation or symbols . . . The only constitution of a member state . . . that explicitly calls its democracy 'secular' is France. . . . But by 1959, in the most secular country in western Europe, the Debre Bill allowed for state support for teachers in Catholic schools. Indeed, by 1961, 20 percent of the total education budget in France was for Catholic private schools. France in the 1990s still had a separation of church and state; but, in political terms it had become a 'friendly' separation."[4] More generally, France, England, and much of Europe also remain uneasy about inclusion of immigrant Muslims or racial minorities.

Not only would the exclusionary basis of unity continue to be evident at home in Europe but it would also be reflected on a larger scale in Europe's international relations. By the nineteenth century, the image of unity, cohesion, and legitimacy of colonizing countries was reinforced by "the systemic and sustained political exclusion of various groups and 'types' of people." Recapitulating earlier internal processes, imperial subjects were later excluded or denigrated, thereby further solidifying cohesion within the empire's core. According to Lord Curzon in 1898, "imperialism is becoming everyday . . . more and more the faith of a nation." Racial denigrating of colonial subjects, for instance with disparaging images of "orientalism" or anti-Semitism, implied both unity and superiority of the colonizing nation.[5] Colonizing nations in themselves and as a group were so unified in their projected superiority over subaltern "others," reaffirming the image of internal European "civic" nationalism. This later application of derogatory exclusion to international relations further reinforced the ahistorical image of an inclusive core.

The cohering effect of exclusion and intolerance is still reflected in the West's views of the rest of the world. Denigrating "others" as a basis of cohering "us" was not only central to the origins of Western nationalism and then justifications of colonialism. It is also recapitulated in our current denigration of latecomers to nationalism. Ironically, as western Europe now begins to move beyond national solidarities, its own coherence as a developed block is again solidified by distinguishing itself as more consistently civic than those others still fitfully forging national unity. Thus, "the West" is itself distinguished and thereby given coherence by denigrating "the rest" and by pretending that our own past was somehow different, mimicking the pattern by which our own earlier national-level solidarities were forged and then forgotten.

The West's idealization of its past has indeed gone hand in hand with denigration of those who were encouraged, attempted, and failed to live up to that noble standard. Western "civic" nationalism has been contrasted with the "ethnic" or exclusionary forms later adopted by the East or South. Seeking their place in the modern world of nation-states, much of Africa has been disparaged for its "tribalism," while much of eastern Europe has been chided for its descent into ethnoreligious Balkanization. Even in the West's own core, violent ethnonationalist movements have sprung up or continued among the Basques and Irish, while even Welsh and Scots pursue some degree of separatism. These current nation builders have been criticized for distorting the supposedly noble invention of their priors and betters. "They" perverted and sullied what "we" inherited or designed and had offered as a positive model. The idea of nationalism was fine; others have distorted it.

But I hope to have suggested here that the ethnic conflicts and exclusions imbedded in recent nation-building are not fundamentally different from the processes of Western nation-building. The purposeful and cohering victimization of "others" today resembles on the global scale the domestic victimization of "others" in the West's own past. Muslims in India, Tutsis in Rwanda, or Muslims in much of southeastern or Balkan Europe are the Jews, Moors, Huguenots, or Papists of our day. These and so many other groups have been sacrificed on the altar of collective solidarity, with their victimization central to the process of forging cohesion.

The early modern construction of nations apparently remains a template for its currently emerging successors, with countries today going through conflictual and exclusionary processes of nation-building resembling those western Europe experienced earlier. We should therefore resist comparing currently exclusive efforts at nation-building with the West's modern, solidified, and inclusive nations. We should instead compare these recent efforts with the corresponding earlier and intolerant origins of Western nations. The faults imbedded in the West's own nation-building would then appear as more comparable to the flaws of later processes.

If we are then wrong in thinking that nationalism in the West began more inclusively than it would develop later or elsewhere, there is a powerful implication. At the very heart of liberalism is an ugly secret: Supposedly inclusive nationalism was founded on the basis of violent exclusion, used to bound and forge the nation to whom rights would then be selectively granted. Democracy itself was so founded also on exclusions in demarcating the unit to which rights of citizenship would be granted. Founded on this basis, liberal democracy would then eventually serve as cover, with gradual enfranchisement hiding past exclusions and obfuscating that at the heart of liberalism is an illiberal determination of who is a member of the incorporated community and who is not.

Forgetting the ignoble foundations of Western nationalism and liberalism would then not only be inaccurate but also dangerous in having enticed latecomers to try to follow a path that was not and perhaps could not be so pursued. Despite later denials, the scars of past processes of conflict and exclusions have indeed remained and seeped through into the present, plaguing those who naively later sought and seek to embrace liberalism and nationalism without cognizance of its illiberal foundations and exclusions. As I have argued, Western nationalism began as nastily as elsewhere later, as a form of "tribalistic" coherence amid conflict. Such illiberal nation-building is comparable to the process by which recent efforts at nation-building have also all too often proceeded. The history of the emergence of nationalism during the last half millenium thus appears as less consistently positive across time and space. Our "models" of the past have not been distorted by others or latecomers whom we denigrate as much as they have been accurately recapitulated, with flaws in the original design of nationalism allowed to remain unquestioned. Having forgotten those flaws in our own past may be self-satisfying but has dangerously provided no warnings for successors, who still pay a great cost.

By misremembering our own history, we have been condemned to expect repetition of what did not happen in the first place. We look for an idealized image of the past to be confirmed by recurrence. And when others do not follow that path assumed to have previously proven effective and ennobling, we are shocked and disapproving. We hold our disappointment against those who fall below a false standard, which we smugly believe our predecessors had met, though they had not. But as the mythic image of the past retains its hold, others still attempt to follow, drawn into unforeseen dangers, and are denigrated for their failure to repeat what did not happen and may not be possible. The result is an ongoing tragedy of huge proportions.

If we instead recognize our own earlier discord and exclusions, we will perhaps not be so quick to self-righteously condemn those who now similarly seek to build nations. Violence and exclusion are part of the inheritance we have provided. In the millennium we have just begun, if we have any hope of moving beyond the bloody past of the last half millennium of nation-building, then we must acknowledge the path from which we have come and from which we hope to learn and divert.

So arguing that nation-building exclusions and conflicts today resemble those of yesterday is in no way intended to minimize or excuse current (or past) tragedies. I am not suggesting that we should be more forgiving of such currently violent processes but rather that we should be more understanding that such discord is etched in the very nature of nation- and state-building. We should remember that "we" of the West were not unsullied by such self-imposed tragedy. This should help us understand but not excuse recent travails as the stuff of which national-level solidarities have long been built, with important implications for current efforts to build nations or move beyond nationalism. If we can be more honest and accurate in our appraisals of our own past and others' present, then I hope we will be better positioned for dealing with both that past and that present. Failing to do so has already produced much tragic misunderstanding and recriminations.

If anything, the terrible processes by which large-scale solidarities have been and are built now threaten a tragedy of even greater proportions, already apparent in current global politics and conflict. In forgetting that our own domestic liberalism and democracy were forged on the basis of exclusion and illiberalism, we are intolerant toward the faults of others that may be more similar to our own faults than we care to admit. This may help to define and bind the West as such, but in disparaging others to consolidate ourselves we also encourage their sense of exclusion and aggravate conflict accordingly. The result has been dramatic resentment and terrible efforts by some in the non-West to in turn consolidate themselves and gain support in antagonism against the West. In other words, the West's own earlier logic of using exclusion and denigration as a basis for mass engagement and solidarity is being turned against the West on a larger scale. And as the world now searches for alternatives to the nation-state, with peoples elsewhere increasingly demanding an expansion of the unit to which democratic processes might be applied and social benefits distributed, this process is proving as violent as its earlier version. Cohering conflict has been globalized, bringing a level of violent threats comparably expanded.

What has been recently described as a current global "clash of civilizations,"[6] resembles on a larger scale the earlier clashes of culture and religion within the West that was the basis for our own founding as nations. As we have seen in the core of early modern Europe, perceptions of difference were aggravated and exploded into conflict that forged identities and solidarity. As religious linkages and perceptions of inequality have become less localized and more global, the terrible process of asserting engagement and consolidating solidarity on the basis of antagonism has similarly been globalized. The result has exploded most dramatically not in the streets of Paris or London but in the towers of the new global capital, New York. Of course, the images of difference and antagonism that have come home to us are simplifications, much as they were in early modern Europe, though no less conflictual or inspiring of binding enmity. Indeed such false simplifications and dichotomies are always tempting in being all the more binding and are subject to manipulation rather than being truly primordial, as was true in the past.

Fanaticized images of a clash of civilizations were and remain binding and engaging, nonetheless so if we understand that such images are themselves constructions. But perhaps greater historical understanding can also weaken our assumption that such terrible processes and outcomes are unavoidable. As we have seen, early modern Europe itself wavered between such antagonism and attempts at greater tolerance. This earlier variation should remind us that simplifying antagonisms and conflict are neither ascriptive nor foregone as our only choice or means to build solidarity.

To borrow from the history related here, only if a mutual interest in peace and prosperity inspires a global Edict of Nantes can we escape further civilizational conflict. Amid ongoing diversity and inequality, now experienced on the global scale, the temptation to use exclusion and conflict as a basis for selective popular cohesion remains yet also aggravates further conflict. If the populace wearies of this conflict and its costs and has more pragmatic and less cynical or impassioned leadership akin to Henri IV, the alternative path to civic inclusion and coexistence may emerge. Even then it will remain vulnerable to attacks by assassins or mass passions inflamed by memories of past antagonisms. In that sense, memory of the past can be interpreted and turned into an enemy of resolving conflict. But rather than try to expunge such memory, my hope is that cognizance of the cost of past and ongoing conflicts will instead inspire efforts to resolve it.

But we should not be premature or naïve in hoping for this outcome. Certainly it is hard to replicate a leader like Henri IV, the product of a particular personal history of attachments on both sides of a pressing conflict. And even he as an absolutist ruler found it difficult to ensure coexistence of factions and was in the end killed for his efforts, with conflict and exclusions later reemerging. More generally, Europe paid the price of centuries of conflict before fitfully embracing liberal tolerance and inclusion. Only extended violence itself forged the ideal of liberalism and taught the benefits of tolerant coexistence. The world we inhabit may still have to pay the price of further conflict, as again the basis of cohering solidarities and fitfully extending rights and benefits to a political community now expanded. As in our past, such a conflictual process may be the way forward, imposing terrible costs before the world learns to avoid the temptations of exclusionary cohesion and of hypocritical pretensions of toleration not actually observed. Only then might we be able to embrace the more difficult path of forging cohesion of an inclusive "us" without an "other." Only then might we become truly modern and liberal.

Early modern history does still provide a remaining basis of hope for our world, if in the longer term. At first glance, it is depressing to acknowledge the inaccuracy of the self-serving distinction between Western civic nationalism and Eastern ethnic, exclusionary, and violent na-

tionalism; the West's past is as benighted as is the past or present elsewhere. But this recognition has another more positive implication in
demonstrating that an exclusionary and violent founding of nationalism
or related solidarities does not preclude the later emergence of a more
inclusionary or liberal and democratic order. Instead, awful origins may
lead to more positive consolidations. Deconstructing the falsely absolute
distinction of forms of nationalism suggests that the path to a more inclusive politics and a less violent world is still open for us to find, as
it was for our predecessors. This does not mean that the West's currently
consolidated nationalism is perfect—far from it—nor that some teleological process will lead others or all of us together to better outcomes.
But it does mean there are possibilities to learn from our past and to
escape current conflicts. The "path dependence" of history does not lock
us in to continuing tragedy as unavoidable. As before, a clash of civilizations is not the only possibility and may instead lead to or be replaced
by a flowering of coexisting civilizations for mutual benefit.

What then is the image of nationalism that emerges?

In ruminating on historical processes, Walter Benjamin conjured up
an image of the angel of history that Benedict Anderson and others have
likened to nationalism.[7] Contemplating a painting by Paul Klee, Benjamin
saw "an angel looking as though he is about to move away from something he is fixedly contemplating. His eyes are staring, his mouth is open,
his wings are spread. This is how one pictures the angel of history. His
face is turned toward the past. Where we perceive a chain of events, he
sees a single catastrophe which keeps piling wreckage upon wreckage
and hurls it in front of his feet. The angel would like to stay, awaken
the dead, and make whole what has been smashed. But a storm is blowing
from paradise; it has got caught in his wings with such violence that
the angel can no longer close them. This storm irresistibly propels him
into the future to which his back is turned, while the pile of debris before
him grows skyward. This storm is what we call progress."[8]

I am less convinced than Anderson that this angel of history is also
an image of nationalism. Anderson may not intend it, but that building
nationalism is symbolized for him by an angel certainly does suggest a
religious basis of such efforts in history. That much wreckage has been
involved is clear, though the resulting violence may suggest a less angelic
or positive religious image. And nationalism does build on the past to
which it looks and from which it emerges, with that past both divisive
and cohering according to its uses. But I disagree that an image of na-

tionalism is so consistently looking backward to the past, given the prominent role of forgetting that past to ultimately consolidate nationalism and heal past wounds on which it was based. Nor do I think the angel of nationalism is unwillingly pushed backward into the future, given the purposeful efforts of monarchs, fanatics, and revolutionaries to forge nationalism. The powerful poetry of Benjamin's angel may be misplaced as an image of nationalism.

I propose an alternative image, that of Saint Bartholomew as the patron of nationalism. Again the religious basis is made evident. But rather than an angel, we now have the image of man, canonized by faith but having lived in this world. We do not know much about Saint Bartholomew the man, which in itself is symbolic of the disputed past of nationalism. We do know that he was one of the twelve apostles, thereby purposefully involved in both the founding of the Catholic faith and of its secular institution as the church. He thereby symbolizes the merger of other and this-worldly authority, with the two reinforcing each other, though also in tension. Finally, we know he was martyred, with his skin flayed; he is often depicted as holding that skin on his arm. The violence and martyrs to early nationalism are thus conjured, as is the acknowledgment that such violence can reinforce both faith and solidarity of the faithful. Also symbolized is the transformation of identity within one's skin—with that skin still held as a retained link to the past yet peeled off, leaving an uncertain identity.

Bartholomew's relics remained, to be prayed or sacrificed to in modern times, when nationalism emerged with the passion of faith. And as if to cement the applicability of this symbolism, the pivotal moment of the French religious wars that forged early nationalism is the massacre of 1572 on Saint Bartholomew's Day. In England, Charles II finally acceded to demands for imposing religious-based unity with the Act of Uniformity enforced in 1662 also on the day of St. Bartholomew, and many churches there are still dedicated to this apostle.

The early modern era in which nationalism was forged on the basis of religious faith is then the era with Saint Bartholomew as its bloodied patron saint. Servant of God, making a place for faith in and of this world, he was as we have been subjected to the tremendous violence of this process. Uncertain of origin, he was cut off from his own skin and his past so symbolized, as we have been, although as with nations his past has been kept alive, his flayed skin at hand. Icon of belief and prayed to as such, Bartholomeic nationalism has been kept alive in incomplete memory. Relics remain, while the actual body or history has been largely lost, as has been the early history of nationalism. Venerated with violence, he built a church in this world at great cost.

As the patron of nationalism, St. Bartholomew's modern church was constructed not in Rome, Jerusalem, or heaven but in the Western world. Perhaps more than any others, the nations of England and France were his initial legacy, less so Spain. These have provided to the world an image which, for better or, more often, worse, much of the world has sought to emulate, trying to forget or deny its bloody past but destined to still carry that past as its flayed skin. If we seek now a new covering other than nationalism, we do so still carrying that skin and the scars it has left. Retained relics of the past are still prayed to and demand sacrifices, even as we seek another world.

To find a better world, we must build it in this world and not just wait for the next. Rather than deny it, the past can be our guide. The angel of history takes the patron saint of nationalism by the hand. Knowing the terrible wreckage of the past on which progress has been built, the angel must stay, awakening the dead to warn the living. If the bloodied saint of nationalism will heed the awful lessons of history's angel, we may yet "make whole what has been smashed."

NOTES

CHAPTER 1

1. Max Weber, *Economy and Society,* ed. Guenther Roth and Claus Wittich (Berkeley: University of California Press, 1978), vol. 2, 922–3.

2. For related definitions, see Ernst B. Haas, *Nationalism, Liberalism, and Progress,* vol. 1, (Ithaca: Cornell University Press, 1997), 23; Eric J. Hobsbawm, *Nations and Nationalism since 1780* (Cambridge: Cambridge University Press, 1990), 5–8; Craig Calhoun, *Nationalism* (Minneapolis: University of Minnesota Press, 1997), 4.

3. Alexander J. Motyl, *Revolutions, Nations, Empires* (New York: Columbia University Press, 1999), 77–80.

4. John Breuilly, *Nationalism and the State* (Chicago: University of Chicago Press, 1982). See also Calhoun, *Nationalism,* 69.

5. Adrian Hastings, *The Construction of Nationhood* (Cambridge: Cambridge University Press, 1997), 98; David Potter, *A History of France, 1460–1560,* (London: Macmillan, 1995), 17.

6. Michael Hechter, *Containing Nationalism* (Oxford: Oxford University Press, 2000).

7. Hobsbawm, *Nations and Nationalism,* 48.

8. Philip S. Gorski, "The Mosaic Moment: An Early Modernist Critique of Modernist Theories of Nationalism," *American Journal of Sociology* 105:5 (March 2000), 1459; Michael Mann, *The Sources of Social Power,* vol. 2 (Cambridge: Cambridge University Press, 1993), 216–7.

9. Among those who explicitly define nationalism without defining nation, are Hobsbawm, Gellner, and Brubaker.

10. Wayne te Brake, *Shaping History* (Berkeley: University of California Press, 1998), 150.

11. See Charles Tilly, *Coercion, Capital, and European States, AD 990–1992* (Cambridge: Blackwell, 1990), 63.

12. Gorski, "Mosaic Moment," 1429. See also Calhoun, *Nationalism*, 70.

13. See Hastings, *Construction of Nationhood*, 5–10; Eugen Weber, *Peasants into Frenchmen: The Modernization of Rural France, 1870–1914* (Stanford: Stanford University Press, 1976).

14. Hobsbawm, *Nations and Nationalism*; Benedict Anderson, *Imagined Communities* (London: Verso, 1983), 19, 26; Haas, *Nationalism, Liberalism and Progress*, 62–6.

15. Philip S. Gorski, "Calvinism and State-Formation in Early Modern Europe," in George Steinmetz, ed., *State/Culture* (Ithaca: Cornell University Press, 1999), 156–7; Anderson, *Imagined Communities*, 89.

16. See Karen Barkey, *Bandits and Bureaucrats: The Ottoman Route to State Centralization* (Ithaca: Cornell University Press, 1994); Mahmood Mamdani, *Citizen and Subject: Contemporary Africa and the Legacy of Late Colonialism* (Princeton: Princeton University Press, 1996).

17. See Hastings, *The Construction of Nationhood*, 108.

18. See Hastings, *The Construction of Nationhood*, 106; Calhoun, *Nationalism*, 7; Brendan O'Leary, "Ernest Gellner's Diagnosis of Nationalism," in John A. Hall, ed., *The State of the Nation* (Cambridge: Cambridge University Press, 1998), 74.

19. Motyl, *Revolutions, Nations, Empires*, 4.

20. Jean-Jacques Rousseau, *The Social Contract* (Hammondsworth: Penguin, 1968), 61. In other works Rousseau discusses nation-state convergence from the other direction, where a state can and should act to encourage national loyalty, for instance, by reducing its territory to create greater homogeneity. See Jean-Jacques Rousseau, "Considerations on the Government of Poland," in Victor Gourevitch, ed., *The Social Contract and Other Later Writings* (Cambridge: Cambridge University Press, 1997).

21. Isaiah Berlin, *Vico and Herder* (New York: Random House, 1976); Hans Kohn, "Western and Eastern Nationalisms," in John Hutchinson and Anthony D. Smith, eds., *Nationalism* (Oxford: Oxford University Press, 1994); Liah Greenfeld, *Nationalism: Five Roads to Modernity* (Cambridge: Harvard University Press, 1992).

22. Anthony Smith, *The Ethnic Origins of Nation*, (Oxford: Basil Blackwell, 1986); Walker Connor, *Ethnonationalism* (Princeton: Princeton University Press, 1994).

23. Will Kymlicka, *Multicultural Citizenship* (Oxford: Clarendon Press, 1995), 11, 23.

24. Quoted in *Ibid*, 52.

25. See Ernest Renan, "What is a Nation?" in Geoff Eley and Ronald Grigor Suny, eds., *Becoming National* (New York: Oxford University Press, 1996), 42–55.

26. Eric Hobsbawm and Terence Ranger, eds., *The Invention of Tradition* (Cambridge: Cambridge University Press, 1983); Eugen Weber, *Peasants*

into Frenchmen (Stanford: Stanford University Press, 1976); Charles Tilly, "Citizenship, Identity and Social History," in *International Review of Social History*, suppl. 3 (1996), 5.

27. Rogers Brubaker, *Nationalism Reframed* (Cambridge: Cambridge University Press, 1996).

28. Kymlicka, *Multicultural Citizenship*, 10; Connor, *Ethnonationalism*, 22.

29. Greenfeld, *Nationalism*, 3, 7, 14.

30. Greenfeld, *Nationalism*, 51–3, 77, 86, 105, 113.

31. Juan Linz, "State Building and Nation Building," *European Review* 1: 4 (1993), 355, 360–1; Hans Kohn, *The Idea of Nationalism* (New York: Macmillan, 1944), 16; Hans Kohn, *Nationalism: Its Meaning and History* (New York: D. van Nostrand, 1965), 10.

32. Tilly, *Coercion, Capital*, 62–3; Greenfeld, *Nationalism*, 8.

33. Anderson, *Imagined Communities*, 41–2; Homi K. Bhabha, ed., *Nation and Narration* (London: Routledge, 1990); Karl Deutsch, *Nationalism and Social Communication* (New York: MIT Press, 1966); Jurgen Habermas, *Communication and the Evolution of Society* (Boston: Beacon, 1979), 184, 192.

34. Anderson, *Imagined Communities*, 133.

35. See Weber, *Economy and* Society, vol. 2, 922; Hobsbawm, *Nations and Nationalism*, 54–6; Greenfeld, *Nationalism*, 99; Weber, *Peasants into Frenchmen*; Geoffrey Parker, *Europe in Crisis, 1598–1648* (Oxford: Blackwell, 1979), 215; David A. Bell, *The Cult of the Nation in France* (Cambridge: Harvard University Press, 2001), 175.

36. Breuilly, *Nationalism and the State*, 406.

37. Anderson, *Imagined Communities*, 59, 129, 44.

38. Anderson, *Imagined Communities*, 15.

39. Ernest Gellner, *Nations and Nationalism* (Ithaca: Cornell University Press, 1983). See also Michael Hechter, *Internal Colonialism* (Berkeley: University of California Press, 1975), 162.; Montserrat Guibernau, *Nationalisms* (Cambridge: Polity Press, 1996).

40. See Steven Pincus, "To Protect English Liberties: The English Nationalist Revolution of 1688–1689," in Tony Claydon and Ian McBride, eds., *Protestantism and National Identity* (Cambridge: Cambridge University Press, 1998), 79.

41. Tom Nairn, "The Curse of Rurality," in Hall, ed., *The State of the Nation*, 122.

42. Tilly, *Coercion, Capital*, ix; Mann, *The Sources of Social Power, vol. 2*, 214.

43. Gorski, "The Mosaic Moment," 1459.

44. See John Plamenatz, "Two Types of Nationalism," in Eugene Kamenka, ed., *Nationalism* (New York: St. Martins Press, 1976), 23–4; Smith, *Ethnic Origins of Nations*, 14; Renan, "What Is a Nation?"

45. Hobsbawm, *Nations and Nationalism Since 1780*, 56, 63; Anthony D. Smith, *Nationalism and Modernism* (London: Macmillan, 1998). I am here arguing against the view that nationalism emerged only with the spread of state schooling developed to meet the needs of industrialization, as argued by Gellner, *Nations and Nationalism*.

46. Michael Mann, "The Emergence of Modern European Nationalism," in John A. Hall and I. C. Jarvie, eds., *Transition to Modernity* (Cambridge: Cambridge University Press, 1992), 143.

47. Renan, "What Is a Nation?"

48. Tilly, *Coercion, Capital*; Brubaker, *Nationalism Reframed*, 5; Kymlicka, *Multicultural Citizenship*, 13; Anderson, *Imagined Communities*, 54, 77; Hobsbawm and Ranger, eds. *The Invention of Tradition*, 10, 80; and Breuilly, *Nationalism and the State*, 19.

49. Benedict Anderson, *Imagined Communities*, Revised edition (London: Verso, 1991).

50. Parker, *Europe in Crisis*, 231.

51. Greenfeld, *Nationalism*; Joseph Reese Strayer, *On the Medieval Origins of the Modern State* (Princeton: Princeton University Press, 1970); Barnaby Conrad Keeney, *Judgement by Peers* (Cambridge: Harvard University Press, 1952).

52. Barry R. Weingast, "The Political Foundations of Democracy and the Rule of Law," *American Political Science Review* 91:2 (June 1997), 245–63. See also James D. Fearon and David Laitin, "Explaining Interethnic Cooperation," in *American Political Science Review* 90 (1996); 715–35.

53. Charles Taylor, "Nationalism and Modernity," in Hall, ed., *The State of the Nation*, 193, 198.

54. Todd Sandler, *Collective Action* (Ann Arbor: University of Michigan Press, 1992), 63–4.

55. Connor, *Ethnonationalism*, 48.

56. Gellner, *Encounters with Nationalism*, 65.

57. Arthur L. Stinchcombe, "Social Structures and Politics," in Fred I. Greenstein and Nelson Polsby, eds., *Handbook of Political Science*, vol. 3 (Reading: Addison-Wesley, 1975), 600–1.

58. Lewis A. Croser, *The Functions of Social Conflict* (Glencoe: Free press, 1956); John A. Armstrong, *Nations Before Nationalism* (Chapel Hill: University of North Carolina Press, 1982).

59. Carl Schmitt, *The Concept of the Political* (Chicago: University of Chicago Press, 1996), 26–8, 33, 46, 67.

60. Michael Billig and Henri Tajfel, "Social Categorization and Similarity in Intergroup Behavior," *European Journal of Social Psychology* 3:1 (1973), 27–52; Henri Tajfel, "Experiments in Intergroup Discrimination," *Scientific American* 223 (November 1970), 96–102; Henri Tajfel and John C. Turner. "The Social Identity Theory of Intergroup Behavior," in *Psychology of Intergroup Relations*, Stephen Worchel and W. G. Austin, eds. (Chicago: Nelson-Hall, 1986), 7, 16; Henri Tajfel, *Differentiation between Social Groups* (London: Academic Press, 1972), 66, 83.

61. Sigmund Freud, *Civilization and Its Discontents* (New York: Norton, 1961), 61.

62. Pierre Bourdieu, *Distinction* (Cambridge: Harvard University Press, 1984), 478.

63. Rogers Brubaker, "Rethinking Classical Theory: The Sociological Vision of Pierre Bourdieu," in *Theory and Society* 14 (1985), 723–44; Pierre

Bourdieu, *Outline of a Theory of Practice* (Cambridge: Cambridge University Press, 1977); Pierre Bourdieu and Loic Wacquant, *An Invitation to Reflexive Sociology* (Chicago: University of Chicago Press, 1992).

64. Pierre Bourdieu, "Codification," in *In Other Words* (Stanford: Stanford University Press, 1990), 76–82.

65. Brubaker, *Nationalism Reframed*, 16.

66. Quoted in Immanuel Wallerstein, *The Modern World-System* (New York: Academic Press, 1974), 207. See also Hobsbawm, *Nations and Nationalism*, 68; Mann, *Sources of Social Power, vol. 2*, 216.

67. Anderson, *Imagined Communities*, 44.

68. Scmitt, *The Concept of the Political*, 37.

69. David A. Bell, *The Cult of the Nation in France* (Cambridge: Harvard University Press, 2001). See also the work of Dale van Kley.

70. Greenfeld, *Nationalism*, 113.

71. Greenfeld, *Nationalism*, 53, 77.

72. Colin Haydon, "I Love my King and my Country, but a Roman Catholic I Hate," in Tony Claydon and Ian McBride, eds., *Protestantism and National Identity*, 49.

73. *Ibid*, 50; Jeremey Black, "Confessional State or Elect Nation?" in Claydon and McBride, eds., *Protestantism and National Identity*, 55, 59, 72. See Linda Colley, *Britons* (New Haven: Yale University Press, 1992).

74. Tony Claydon and Ian McBride, "The Trials of the Chosen People," in Claydon and McBride, eds., *Protestantism and National Identity*, 25, 27.

75. Quoted in Smith, *Nationalism and Modernism*, 101.

76. Bell, *The Cult of the Nation in France*, 198.

77. Elie Kedourie, *Nationalism* (Oxford: Blackwell, 1993), 70.

78. Renan, "What Is a Nation?" 45.

79. *Ibid*, 52–3; Anderson, *Imagined Communities* (1991 edition), 200–4.

80. David Potter, ed., *The French Wars of Religion: Selected Documents* (London: Macmillan, 1997), 118, 203.

81. "Declaration of Breda, 1660" in Andrew Browning, ed., *English Historical Documents, 1660–1714* (London: Eyre and Spottiswoode, 1953), 57; "Act of Indemnity and Oblivion, 16560" in *Ibid*, 164.

82. Greenfeld, *Nationalism*, 77.

83. Schmitt, *The Conept of the Political*, 70.

84. Barrington Moore, *Social Origins of Dictatorship and Democracy* (Boston: Beacon, 1966), chap. 1. For a related critique, see Hastings, *The Construction of Nationhood*, 5.

CHAPTER 2

1. See Perry Anderson, *Lineages of the Absolutist State* (London: Verso, 1974), 45, 53. Anderson however explicitly denies that nationalism emerged under absolutism, for example p. 38.

2. John H. Elliott, *Europe Divided, 1559–1598* (New York: Harper and Row, 1968), 70–1.

3. Wayne te Brake, *Shaping History* (Berkeley: University of California

Press, 1998), 4; Mack P. Holt, *The French Wars of Religion, 1562–1629* (Cambridge: Cambridge University Press, 1995), 216.

4. Quoted in David Potter, *A History of France, 1460–1560* (London: Macmillan, 1995), 284.

5. Charles Tilly, *Coercion, Capital, and European States* (Cambridge: Blackwell, 1990), chap. 3.

6. H. H. Gerth and C. Wright Mills, eds., *From Max Weber* (New York: Oxford University Press, 1978), 268–71, 280–1, 295; Max Weber, *Economy and Society* (Berkeley: University of California Press, 1978), vol. 1, 399–400, 468. See also Mack P. Holt, "Putting Religion Back into the Wars of Religion," *French Historical Studies* 18:2 (Fall 1993), 527.

7. Philip S. Gorski, "Clavinism and State-Formation in Early Modern Europe," in George Steinmetz, ed., *State / Culture* (Ithaca: Cornell University Press, 1999), 173, 149.

8. *Ibid*, 159; Reinhard Bendix, *Nation-Building and Citizenship* (Berkeley: University of California Press, 1964), 40.

9. Holt, *French Wars of Religion*, 19.

10. Mark Kishlansky, *A Monarchy Transformed: Bratain 1603–1714* (London: Penguin, 1996), 41.

11. Ernst B. Haas, *Nationalism, Liberalism and Progress*, vol. 1, (Ithaca: Cornell University Press, 1997), 53. See also Brendan O'Leary, "Gellner's Diagnosis of Nationalism," in John A. Hall, ed., *The State of the Nation* (Cambridge; Cambridge University Press, 1998), 40; Benedict Anderson, *Imagined Communities* (London: Verso, 1983), chap. 2.

12. Gorski, "Calvinism and State-Formation," 170; Eric Hobsbawm, *Nations and Nationalism since 1780* (Cambridge: Cambridge University Press, 1990), 85.

13. Hans Kohn, *Nationalism: Its Meaning and History* (New York: D. van Nostrand, 1965), 11, 16; Liah Greenfeld, *Nationalism: Five Roads to Modernity* (Cambridge: Harvard University Press, 1992), 108. Greenfeld explicitly denies that France "was far from being a nation . . . Yet in some ways, the sixteenth century anticipated it." *Ibid*. It is the process of this anticipation that I am charting here.

14. See Adrian Hastings, *The Construction of Nationhood* (Cambridge: Cambridge University Press, 1997).

15. Elliott, *Europe Divided*, 93, 390; Geoffrey Parker, *Europe in Crisis, 1598–1648* (Oxford: Blackwell, 2001), 35.

16. Gorski, "Calvinism and State-Formation," 169.

17. Paul Kennedy, *The Rise and Fall of the Great Powers* (New York: Random House, 1987), 35.

18. Elliott, *Europe Divided*, 29–30, 94–5; Holt, "Putting Religion Back," 536.

19. W. B. Yeats, "Leda and the Swan."

20. Henry Charles Lea, *A History of the Inquisition of Spain, volume 1* (New York: AMS Press, 1988), 3, 7. See also Perry Anderson, *Lineages of the Absolutist State* (London: Verso, 1974), 60–7; John H. Elliott, *Imperial Spain, 1469–1716* (London: Penguin, 1963), 41, 86; B. Netanyahu, *The Ori-*

gins of the Inquisition in 15th Century Spain (New York: Random House, 1995), 127, 265.

21. Ramon Menendez Pidal, *The Spaniards in Their History* (New York: Norton, 1950), 75.

22. Elliott, *Imperial Spain*, 22, 83; Netanyahu, *Origins of the Inquisition*, 915–6; Lea, *History of the Inquisition*, 18.

23. Elliott, *Imperial Spain*, 108, 229.

24. J. N. Hillgarth, *The Spanish Kingdoms, 1250–1516, volume 2* (Oxford: Clarendon Press, 1978), 484.

25. Hans Kohn, *The Idea of Nationalism* (New York: Macmillan, 1944), 150. See also Henry Kamen, *The Spanish Inquisition* (London: Weidenfeld and Nicolson, 1997), 2; Hillgarth, *The Spanish Kingdoms*, 367.

26. Elliott, *Imperial Spain*. 46–50.

27. *Ibid*, 109; Lea, *A History of the Inquisition*, 135.

28. Elliott, *Imperial Spain*, 64, 128, 225–6; Kamen, *The Spanish Inquisition*, 103; Adrian Hastings, *The Construction of Nationhood* (Cambrge: Cambridge University Press, 1997), 23–4.

29. Elliott, *Imperial Spain*, 126, 110.

30. Netanyahu, *Origins of the Inquisition*, 997, 1002–3, 1007, 1026, 1046; Hilllgarth, *Spanish Kingdoms*, 396.

31. Menendez Pidal, *The Spaniards*, 70. See also Elliott, *Imperial Spain*, 108; Helmut Koenigsberger, "Spain," in *National Consciousness, History, and Political Culture in Early-Modern Europe*, ed. Orest Ranum (Baltimore: Johns Hopkins University Press, 1975), 146.

32. Karl Brandi, *The Emperor Charles V* (New York: Knopf, 1939), 80. 88, 94.

33. *Ibid*, 102–6; Geoffrey Parker, *Philip II* (Boston: Little, Brown, 1978), 4.

34. Brandi, *The Emperor Charles V*, 125–32, 549, 633.

35. See Anderson, *Lineages*, 86; Greenfeld, *Nationalism*, 98; J. H. M. Salmon, *Society in Crisis: France in the Sixteenth Century* (New York: St. Martin's Press, 1975), 30.

36. Potter, *History of France*, 25, 44, 73; Salmon, *Society in Crisis*, 20, 35; Mack P. Holt, "The Kingdom of France in the Sixteenth Century," in Mack P. Holt, ed., *The Short Oxford History of France, volume 4* (25 January 2002, manuscript), 1–2.

37. Anderson, *Lineages*, 86–90; V. G. Kiernan, *State and Society in Europe, 1550–1650* (Oxford: Basil Blackwell, 1980), 88.

38. Greenfeld, *Nationalism*, 91–4; Holt, *The French Wars of Religion*, 26.

39. Barbara Diefendorf, *Beneath the Cross: Catholics and Hugenots in Sixteenth Century Paris* (New York: Oxford University Press, 1991), 159.

40. J. E. Neale, *The Age of Catherine de Medici* (New York: Barnes and Nobles, 1943), 15; N. M. Sutherland, *Princes, Politics and Religion, 1547–1589* (London: Hambledon Press, 1984), 22; Kohn, *Idea of Nationalism*, 130; Holt, "Kingdom of France," 9–10, 15–6.

41. Neale, *The Age of Catherine de Medici*, 37–38; Davis Bitton, *The French Nobility in Crisis, 1560–1640* (Palo Alto: Stanford University Press, 1969), 2, 27, 42.

42. Neale, *The Age of Catherine de Medici*, 34–6; Salmon, *Society in Crisis*, 50.

43. Diefendorf, *Beneath the Cross*, 50; Sutherland, *Princes, Politics and Religion*, 33.

44. Diefendorf, *Beneath the Cross*, 29, 40; Neale, *The Age of Catherine de Medici*, 13.

45. Charlotte Catherine Wells, "The Language of Citizenship in Early Modern France," Ph.D. dissertation, Department of History, Indiana University, December 1991, 38.

46. Potter, *History of France*, 233–46; R. J. Knecht, *Catherine de' Medici* (London: Longman, 1998), 25, 51.

47. Salmon, *Society in Crisis*, 121, 124, 132; Elliott, *Europe Divided*, 36, 96; Richard S. Dunn, *The Age of Religious Wars, 1559–1715* (New York: Norton, 1979), 32; Anderson, *Lineages of the Absolutist State*, 92; Holt, *The French Wars of Religion*, 30.

48. See Olivier Christin, *Le Paix de Religion* (Paris: Seuil/Collection Liber, 1997).

49. Quoted in Salmon, *Society in* Crisis, 127.

50. *Ibid*, 124; Elliott, *Europe Divided*, 98.

51. Potter, *History of France*, 225; Neale. *The Age of Catherine de Medici*, 16–18, 24; Salmon, *Society in Crisis*, 125, 169.

52. N. M. Sutherland, *The Massacre of St. Bartholomew and the European Conflict, 1559–1572* (London: Macmillan, 1973), 8.

53. Neale, *Age of Catherine*, 102–5.

54. Diefendorf, *Beneath the Cross*, 53. The Guises also had pushed for French forces to help quell a Protestant revolt against the authority of Catholic Mary in Scotland in 1559.

55. *Ibid*, 55; Sutherland, *Princes, Politics and Religion*, 97, 111.

56. Knecht, *Catherine de' Medici*, 65–6.

57. Neale, *Age of Catherine*, 48.

58. *Ibid*, 42–5; Anderson, *Lineages*, 91.

59. Neale, *Age of Catherine*, 47–50; Sutherland, *Princes, Politics and Religion*, 31; Knecht, *Catherine de' Medici*, 72–3.

60. Letter of Chantonnay to Margaret of Parma, 7 May 1562, in David Potter, ed., *The French Wars of Religion: Selected Documents* (New York: St. Martin's Press, 1997), 77.

61. Salmon, *Society in Crisis*, 234. See also Natalie Zemon Davis, *Society and Culture in Early Modern France* (Stanford: Stanford University Press, 1975), 2.

62. Greenfeld, *Nationalism*, 106; Neale, *Age of Catherine*, 49–56.

63. Knecht, *Catherine de' Medici*, 77–86; Elliott, *Europe Divided*, 135; Mark Greengrass, *France in the Age of Henry IV: The Struggle for Stability* (London: Longman, 1984), 3.

64. Sutherland, *Princes, Politics and Religion*, 35.

65. Wells, "The Language of Citizenship in Early Modern France," 296.

66. Lettres de cachet, 28 January 1561, in Potter, ed., *French Wars of Religion*, 26–7; Edict of Saint-Germain, 17 January 1562, in *Ibid*, 31–2.

67. Diefendorf, *Beneath the Cross*, 58, 63.

68. Davis, *Society and Culture*, 158; Neale, *Age of Catherine*, 28; Greengrass, *France in the Age of Henri IV*, 4–5.

69. Neale, *Age of Catherine*, 59–67; Salmon, *Society in Crisis*, 140; Sutherland, *Massacre*, 27, 81; Elliott, *Europe Divided*, 113; Sutherland, *Princes, Politics and Religion*, 73–9; Diefendorf, *Beneath the Cross*, 70–1; Knecht, *Catherine de' Medici*, 87, 91.

70. "The Edict of Amboise," 19 March 1563, in Potter, ed., *French Wars of Religion*, 82–4.

71. Letter from Catherine de Medici to King Charles IX, 8 September 1563, in *Ibid*, 15.

72. Greengrass, *France in the Age of Henri IV*, 22.

73. "Declaration forbidding the Reformed religion at Court," 24 July 1564, in Potter, ed., *French Wars of Religion*, 85; Holt, *French Wars of Religion*, 78.

74. Liah Greenfeld, *Nationalism* (Cambridge: Harvard University Press, 1992), 105; Myriam Yardeni, *La Conscience Nationale en France pendant les Guerres de Religion* (Paris: Sorbonne, 1971); Steven Englund, "The Ghost of Nation Past," in *Journal of Modern History* 64 (June 1992), 299–320.

75. Diefendorf, *Beneath the Cross*, 72.

76. Knecht, *Catherine de' Medici*, 108.

77. Neale, *Age of Catherine*, 72; Sutherland, *Massacre*, 106; David Buisseret, *Sully and the Growth of centralized Government in France, 1598–1610* (London: Eyre and Spottiswoode, 1968), 27; Diefendorf, *Beneath the Cross*, 82, 84.

78. "The Edict of Saint-Germain," August 1570, in Potter, ed., *French Religious Wars*, 118–21.

79. Holt, *French Religious Wars*, 109.

80. Sutherland, *Massacre*, 187; Diefendorf, *Beneath the Cross*, 91.

81. Charles IX speech to Parlement, 12 March 1571, in Potter, ed., *French Religious Wars*, 131.

82. Mack P. Holt, "Conclusion," in Mack P. Holt, ed., *The Short Oxford History of France*, volume 4, author's manuscript, 25 January 2002, 1.

83. *Ibid*, 67; Greengrass, *France in the Age of Henri IV*, 6–7.

84. Elliott, *Europe Divided*, 108; Diefendorf, *Beneath the Cross*, 3, 178.

85. Thomas Ertman, *Birth of the Leviathan* (Cambridge: Cambridge University Press, 1997), 156, 167, 175–9; Adrian Hastings, *The Construction of Nationhood* (Cambridge: Cambridge University Press, 1997), 50.

86. Mark Kishlansky, *A Monarchy Transformed: Britain 1603–1714* (London: Penguin, 1996), 36.

87. Kohn, *Idea of Nationalism*, 156; Anderson, *Lineages*, 113–8; Roger Lockyer, *Tudor and Stuart Britain, 1471–1714* (New York: St. Martin's Press, 1985), 1–7.

88. Barry Coward, *The Stuart Age* (London: Longman, 1980), 94. See also G. R. Elton, *England under the Tudors* (London: Routledge, 1955), 1–4.

89. Lockyer, *Tudor and Stuart Britain*, 20; Linda Colley, *Britons* (New

Haven: Yale University Press, 1992), 41; Christopher Hill, *The English Bible and the Seventeenth Century Revolution* (London: Penguin, 1993), 52.

90. H. R. Trevor-Roper, *Religion, the Reformation and Social Change* (London: Macmillan, 1967), chap. 3.

91. Colley, *Britons*, 6, 17.

92. Elton, *England under the Tudors*, 77; Greenfeld, *Nationalism*, 42.

93. Elton, *England under the Tudors*, 2.

94. *Ibid*, 98–101; J. E. Neale, *Queen Elizabeth I* (London: Jonathan Cape, 1938), 14, 18; Lockyer, *Tudor and Stuart Britain*, 32.

95. G. R. Elton, *England under the Tudors* (London: Routledge, 1955), 110.

96. "An Act for the Submission of the Clergy to the King's Majesty" (1534: 25 Henry VIII, c.19) and "An Act concerning restraint of payment of annates to the see of Rome" (1532, 23 Henry VIII, c.20) in G. R. Elton, ed., *The Tudor Constitution: Documents and Commentary* (Cambridge: Cambridge University Press, 1960), 348–53; John Bossy, *The English Catholic Community, 1570–1850* (London: Darton, Longman and Todd, 1975), 36; Elton, *England under the Tudors*, 108–9.

97. "An Act concerning the King's Highness to be Supreme Head of the Church of England . . . ," (1534: 26 Henry VIII, c.1), in Elton, *Tudor Constitution*, 364–5.

98. John Miller, *Popery and Politics in England, 1660–1688* (Cambridge: Cambridge University Press, 1973), 70–1; Elton, *England under the Tudors*, 102–6, 142, 149, 188–9; Lockyer, *Tudor and Stuart Britain*, 19, 21, 55, 68.

99. te Brake, *Shaping History*, 24.

100. Lockyer, *Tudor and Stuart England*, 58–63.

101. Kishlansky, *A Monarchy Transformed*, 41; te Brake, *Shaping History*, 24; Lockyer, *Tudor and Stuart Britain*, 37.

102. Elton, *England under the Tudors*, 114–5, 159–60, 216; William Haller, *Foxe's Book of Martyrs and the Elect Nation* (London: Jonathan Cape, 1963), 21.

103. Carol Z. Weiner, "The Beleaguered Isle: A Study of Elizabethan and Early Jacobean Anti-Catholicism," *Past and Present* 51 (1971), 33; Christopher Hill, *Anti-Christ in Seventeenth Century England* (London: Oxford University Press, 1971), 154.

104. See Hastings, *The Construction of Nationhood*, chap. 2.

105. Quoted in Elton, *England under the Tudors*, 161.

106. Brendan Bradshaw, "The English Reformation," in Brendan Bradshaw and Peter Roberts, eds., *British Consciousness and Identity* (Cambridge: Cambridge University Press, 1998), 48.

107. Elton, *England under the Tudors*, 202–4; Lockyer, *Tudor and Stuart Britain*, 88.

108. Elton, *England under the Tudors*, 214–222; Lockyer, *Tudor and Stuart Britain*, 99–102; Greenfeld, *Nationalism*, 55–8; Haller, *Foxe's Book of Martyrs and the Elect Nation*, 40, 50.

109. "An Act repealing all statutes," (1554: I and 2 Philip and Mary, c.8), in Elton, ed., *The Tudor Constitution*, 368.

110. Neale, *Queen Elizabeth I*, 39–41, 252.

111. Philip Gorski, "The Mosaic Moment," *American Journal of Sociology* 105:5 (March 2000), 1452; Hastings, *The Construction of Nationhood*, 58.

112. W. Grinton Berry, ed., *Foxe's Book of Martyrs* (Grand Rapids: Baker Book House, 1998), 200, 285–7. See also Haller, *Foxe's Book of Martyrs*, 110, 122, 171.

113. Haller, *Foxe's Book of Martyrs*, 250. See also 124–7.

114. "An Act restoring to the crown the ancient jurisdiction . . ." (Act of Supremacy, 1559: I Elizabeth I, c.1), in Elton, *Tudor Constitution*, 372.

115. Anderson, *Lineages*, 128; Haller, *Foxe's Book of Martyrs*, 247; Lockyer, *Tudor and Stuart Britain*, 169; Elton, *England Under the Tudors*, 264.

116. Elton, *England Under the Tudors*, 270; Dunn, *Age of Religious Wars*, 47.

117. "Triplici nodo," 1606, in Johann P. Sommerville, ed., *King James VI and I: Political Writings* (Cambridge: Cambridge University Press, 1994), 91.

118. Elton, *England under the Tudors*, 307; Lockyer, *Tudor and Stuart Britain*, 169–71; Miller, *Popery and Politics in England*, 55, 76–8.

119. "An Act against Jesuits . . ." (1585: 27 Elizabeth I, c.2) in Elton, *Tudor Constitution*, 434.

120. "An Act for the uniformity of common prayer . . ." (Act of Uniformity 1559: I Elizabeth I, c.2), in Elton, *Tudor Constitution*, 410.

121. "An Act Against Popish Recusants" (1593: 35 Elizabeth I, c.2), in *Ibid*, 437–42.

122. Michael Walzer, *The Revolution of the Saints* (Cambridge: Harvard University Press, 1965), 113, 97, 121, 104.

123. *Ibid*, 18, 28, 2.

124. Miller, *Popery and Politics*, 54–5, 76; John D. Brewer and Gareth I. Higgins, *Anti-Catholicism in Northern Ireland, 1600–1998* (London: Macmill, 1998), 16; Lockyer, *Tudor and Stuart Britain*, 172.

125. "Papal Bull against Elizabeth, 1570," in Elton, *Tudor Constitution*, 425–8.

126. Greenfeld, *Nationalism*, 63; Elton, *England under the Tudors*, 303–4, 421; Kiernan, *State and Society in Europe*, 109.

127. Carol Z. Wiener, "The Beleaguered Isle," 27.

128. Elton, *England under the Tudors*, 278, 288.

129. Neale, *Elizabeth*, 320–4.

130. Neale, *Elizabeth*, 107–8, 161, 174, 258, 265–6, 273–5.

131. Neale, *Elizabeth*, 154, 242.

132. John Dryden, *Religio Laici* (1682), quoted in Hill, *The English Bible*, 196.

CHAPTER 3

1. W. B. Yeats, "Among School Children," in M. L. Rosenthal, ed., *Selected Poems and Two Plays of William Butler Yeats* (New York: Macmillan, 1962), 117.

2. David Laitin, "Hegemony and Religious Conflict," in Peter Evans, Dietrich Rueschemeyer, and Theda Skocpol, eds., *Bringing the State Back In* (Cambridge: Cambridge University Press, 1985), 311.

3. See Steven Lukes, *Power: A Radical View* (London: Macmillan, 1974), 16; Russell Hardin, *One for All* (Princeton: Princeton University Press, 1995).

4. William H. Riker, *The Theory of Political Coalitions* (New Haven: Yale University Press, 1962). See also Steven J. Brams, *Rational Politics* (Washington: CQ Press, 1985), 175.

5. Steven J, Brams, *Game Theory and Politics* (New York: Free Press, 1975), 228–32; Kenneth A. Shepsle, "Studying Institutions," *Journal of Theoretical Politics* 1:2 (1989), 131–47.

6. Edwin Wilmsen, "Introduction," in Edwin N. Wilmsen and Patrick MacAllister, eds., *The Politics of Difference* (Chicago: University of Chicago Press, 1996), 3.

7. Ernest Gellner, *Nations and Nationalism* (Ithaca: Cornell University Press, 1983), 18.

8. See Peter A. Hall, *Governing the Economy* (Oxford: Oxford University Press, 1986), 19; Walter W. Powell and Paul J. DiMaggio, eds., *The New Institutionalism in Organizational Analysis* (Chicago: University of Chicago Press, 1991); Mark Granovetter and Richard Swedberg, eds., *The Sociology of Economic Life* (Boulder: Westview, 1992).

9. Robert K. Merton, *Social Theory and Social Structure* (New York: Free Press, 1968), 475–77.

10. Wilmsen, "Introduction," in Wilmsen and MacAllister, eds., *The Politics of Difference*, 2.

11. Abner Cohen, *Two Dimensional Man* (Berkeley: University of California Press, 1974), 15, 31.

12. John Comaroff, "Ethnicity, Nationalism, and the Politics of Difference in the Age of Revolution," in Wilmsen and MacAllister, eds., *The Politics of Difference*, 164, 174.

13. Paul R. Brass, *Ethnicity and Nationalism* (New Delhi: Sage, 1991), 16, 74.

14. Richard D. Ashmore, "The Problem of Intergroup Prejudice," in Barry E. Collins, ed., *Social Psychology* (Reading: Addison-Wesley, 1970), 270.

15. Marshall Sahlins, *Culture and Practical Reason* (Chicago: University of Chicago Press, 1976), 206.

16. Karl Marx, "The Eighteenth Brumaire of Louis Bonaparte," in David McLellan, ed., *Karl Marx: Selected Writings* (Oxford: Oxford University Press, 1977). p. 300.

17. David Laitin, *Hegemony and Culture* (Chicago: University of Chicago Press, 1986). p. 99, 180–2; Jan N. Pieterse, "Varieties of Ethnic Politics and Ethnicity Discourse," in Wilmsen and MacAllister, eds., *The Politics of Difference*, 27.

18. Cohen, *Two Dimensional Man*, 3.

19. Hardin, *One for All*, 70. See also Michael Hechter, *Principles of Group Solidarity* (Berkeley: University of California Press, 1987), 30.

20. Ian S. Lustik, "Culture and the Wager of Rational Choice," *APSA Comparative Politics Newsletter* 8:2 (Summer 1997), 11–14; John Ferejohn, "Rationality and Interpretation," in Kristen Renwick Moore, ed., *The Economic Approach to Politics* (New York: Harper Collins, 1991), 298.

21. Hardin, *One for All*, 17, 21.

22. Thomas Schelling, *The Strategy of Conflict* (Cambridge: Harvard University Press, 1960), 57. See also Carol A. Heimer, "Comment," in Karen Shweers Cook and Margaret Levi, eds., *The Limits of Rationality* (Chicago: University of Chicago Press, 1990), 380.

23. Kipling quoted in Hans Kohn, *The Idea of Nationalism* (New York: Macmillan, 1944), 5. Wordsworth is quoted in Yael Tamir, *Liberal Nationalism* (Princeton: Princeton University Press, 1993), 85.

24. See Linda Colley, *Britons* (New Haven: Yale University Press, 1992); Steven Pincus, "Nationalism, Universal Monarchy, and the Glorious Revolution," in George Steinmetz, ed., *State/Culture* (Ithaca: Cornell University Press, 1999), 182–210; Tim Harris, "The British Dimension . . . ," in Tony Claydon and Ian McBride, eds., *Protestantism and National Identity* (Cambridge: Cambridge University Press, 1998), 138–47.

25. Roger Brubaker's path-breaking work on exclusive citizenship focuses on externally based "other," though his arguments can be applied to insiders as well.

26. B. Netanyahu, *The Origins of the Inquisition* (New York: Random House, 1995), 995–8, 1046; J. H. Elliott, *Imperial Spain* (London: Penguin, 1963), 220.

27. Henry Kamen, *The Spanish Inquisition* (London: Weidenfeld and Nicolson, 1997), 8–9; Netanyahu, *Origins*, 56.

28. Kamen, *Spanish Inquisition*, 11–12; Netanyahu, *Origins*, 65; Americo Castro, *The Structure of Spanish History* (Princeton: Princeton University Press, 1954), 496.

29. Henry Charles Lea, *A History of the Inquisition of Spain* (New York: AMS Press, 1988), 96; Netanyahu, *Origins*, 147, 159.

30. David Nirenberg, *Communities of Violence* (Princeton: Princeton University Press, 1996), chap. 3; Lea, *History of the Inquisition*, 81, 69.

31. Elliott, *Imperial Spain*, 106–7.

32. *Ibid*, 106; Netanyahu, *Origins*, 127, 171, 178, 296–317; Kamen, *Spanish Inquisition*, 14; Lea, *History of the Spanish Inquisition*, 126; Helmut Koenigsberger, "Spain," in *National Consciousness, History, and Political Culture in Early-Modern Europe*, ed. Orest Ranum (Baltimore: Johns Hopkins University Press, 1975), 149.

33. Elliott, *Imperial Spain*, 21, 107; Kamen, *Spanish Inquisition*, 16, 26.

34. Lea, *History of the Inquisition*, 5.

35. Lea, *A History of the Inquisition of Spain*, 172.

36. *Ibid*, 173, 215; Kamen, *Spanish Inquisition*, 104, 137. Kamen adds that the Inquisition itself only developed a fully organized bureaucracy in 1561. See *Ibid*, 139, 154.

37. B. Netanyahu, *Toward the Inquisition* (Ithaca: Cornell University Press, 1997), 185, 187.

38. Lea, *History of the Inquisition*, 291, 152, 28.

39. Niccolo Machiavelli, *The Prince* (Middlesex: Penguin, 1961), chap. xxi, 119–20.

40. Kamen, *Spanish Inquisition*, 7, 45–6, 52, 55, 165, 178, 193, 282.

41. Kamen, *Spanish Inquisition*, 44, 137; V. G. Kiernan, *State and Society in Europe, 1550–1650* (Oxford: Basil Blackwell, 1980), 29, 54–5; Netanyahu, *Origins*, 3, 1164–72.

42. Salo W. Baron, *A Social and Religious History of the Jews* (New York: Columbia University Press, 1969), 62; Hans Kohn, *The Idea of Nationalism* (New York: Macmillan, 1944), 151.

43. Netanyahu, *Toward the Inquisition*, 184; Juan Antonio Llorente, *A Critical History of the Inquisition of Spain* (Williamstown: John Lilburne, 1967), 31; Netanyahu, *Origins*, 1019; Kamen, *Spanish Inquisition*, 68, 149–50; J. N. Hillgarth, *The Spanish Kingdoms 1250–1516*, volume 2 (Oxford: Clarendon Press, 1978), 460.

44. Baron, *Social and Religious History*, 28, 32, 44; Hillgarth, *The Spanish Kingdoms*, volume 2, 460–2; Kamen, *Spanish Inquisition*, 49–50.

45. Netanyahu, *Origins*, xvi, 292, 381, 405, 950; Netanyahu, *Toward the Spanish Inquisition*, 197; Lea, *History of the Inquisition*, 130; Kamen, *Spanish Inquisition*, 28–30, 34. N.B. Many Jews did think of the conversos as linked to them, and indeed many conversos did return to Judaism.

46. Netanyahu, *Origins*, 1002, 1028; Elliott, *Imperial Spain*, 102; Kamen, *Spanish Inquisition*, 137, 157, 165; Lea, *History of the Inquisition*, 154, 172.

47. Netanyahu, *Origins*, 1007, 1026; Kamen, *Spanish Inquisition*, 61, 256.

48. Kamen, *Spanish Inquisition*, 23; Lea, *History of the Spanish Inquisition*, 139–40.

49. Quoted in Kamen, *Inquisition*, 21; Elliott, *Imperial Spain*, 109; Lea, *History of the Inquisition*, 135.

50. Elliott, *Imperial Spain*, 110; Lea, *History of the Spanish Inquisition*, 143.

51. Elliott, *Imperial Spain*, 135; Kamen, *Inquisition*, 139.

52. Baron, *Social and Religious History*, 43; Kamen, *Inquisition*, 217; Elliott, *Imperial Spain*, 221.

53. N. M. Sutherland, *The Massacre of St. Bartholomew and the European Conflict, 1559–1572* (London: Macmillan, 1973), 21; N. M. Sutherland, *Princes, Politics and Religion 1547–1589* (London: Hambledon Press, 1984), 49.

54. Natalie Zemon Davis, *Society and Culture in Early Modern France* (Stanford: Stanford University Press, 1975), 153, 156, 162, 174, 179, 181; Mark Greengrass, *France in the Age of Henri IV* (London: Longman, 1984), 12.

55. "Coligny's memorandum on war" June–July 1572, in David Potter, ed., *The French Wars of Religion: Selected Documents* (Hampshire: Macmillan, 1997), 134.

56. Sutherland, *Princes, Politics and Religion*, 177; J. E. Neale, *The Age of Catherine de Medici* (New York: Barnes and Nobles, 1957), 75.

57. Greengrass, *France in the Age of Henri IV.* 14–6; Sutherland, *Princes, Politics and Religion,* 51; Sutherland, *Massacre,* 128, 163, 217.

58. Sutherland, *Massacre,* 14, 304, 308; Sutherland, *Princes, Politics and Religion,* 178; J. H. M. Salmon, *Society in Crisis: France in the Sixteenth Century* (New York: St. Martins Press, 1975), 186.

59. "Charles IX to Louis of Nassau, 27 April 1572," in Potter, ed., *French Wars of Religion,* 133; Sutherland, *Princes, Politics and Religion,* 173–4.

60. Potter, ed., *French Wars of Religion,* 124; Barbara B. Diefendorf, *Beneath the Cross* (New York: Oxford University Press, 1991), 82.

61. "Charles IX to Fenelon, 22 August 1572," in Potter, ed., *French Wars of Religion,* 138.

62. R. J. Knecht, *Catherine de' Medici* (London: Longman, 1998), 162.

63. "Tamasso Sassetti's account," and "De Thou account, 1659," in Potter, ed., *French Wars of Religion,* 141, 145.

64. Sutherland, *Princes, Politics and Religion,* 44; Neale, *The Age of Catherine,* 78; Davis, *Society and Culture,* 155; Diefendorf, *Beneath the Cross,* 86, 98.

65. Salmon, *Society in Crisis,* 189.

66. Mack P. Holt, *The French Wars of Religion, 1562–1629* (Cambridge: Cambridge University Press, 1995), 85.

67. Neale, *Age of Catherine,* 79; Salmon, *Society in Crisis,* 187; Potter, ed., *French Wars of Religion,* 126.

68. Diefendorf, *Beneath the Cross,* 98–105.

69. Salmon, *Society in Crisis,* 190; Neale, *Age of Catherine,* 78, 82.

70. "Charles IX to Fenelon, 24 August 1572," in Potter, ed., *French Wars of Religion,* 145.

71. "Royal Declaration of 28 August 1572," in *Ibid,* 147.

72. Holt, *French Wars of Religion,* 95, 102, 121.

73. Neale, *Age of Catherine,* 83–7; Sutherland, *Princes, Politics and Religion,* 44; J. H. Elliott, *Europe Divided 1559–1598* (New York: Harper and Row, 1968), 221; Perry Anderson, *Lineages of the Absolutist State* (London: Verso, 1974), 93; Potter, ed., *French Wars of Religion,* 153.

74. Knecht, *Catherine de' Medici,* 172.

75. Elliott, *Europe Divided,* 228–38.

76. Charlotte Catherine Wells, "The Language of Citizenship in Early Modern France," Ph.D. dissertation, Department of History, Indiana University, December 1991, 113.

77. "Edict of Beaulieu, 6 May 1576," in Potter, ed., *French Wars of Religion,* 164.

78. Wells, "Language of Citizenship," 131.

79. "Damville's memorandum to the King, 1577," in Potter, ed., *French Wars of Religion,* 175. See also Elliott, *Europe Divided,* 253–4; Neale, *Age of Catherine,* 90.

80. Salmon, *Society in Crisis,* 206; Elliott, *Europe Divided,* 309; David Buisseret, *Henry IV* (London: George Allen and Unwin, 1984), 41; Roland

Mousnier, *The Assassination of Henry IV* (London: Faber and Faber, 1973), 110, 138; Potter, ed., *French Wars of Religion*, 181.

81. "Royal Edict revoking religious toleration, 15 July 1585," in Potter, ed., *French Wars of Religion*, 194.

82. Salmon, *Society in Crisis*, 240; V. G. Kiernan, *State and Society in Europe* (Oxford: Basil Blackwell, 1980), 94–5.

83. Holt, *French Wars of Religion*, 132.

84. "Royal Edict of Union, Rouen, July 1588," in Potter, ed., *French Wars of Religion*, 203. See also Salmon, *Society in Crisis*, 276; Buisseret, *Henry IV*, 15; Neale, *Age of Catherine*, 98.

85. Quoted in Salmon, *Society in Crisis*, 239.

86. Sutherland, *Massacre*, 16; Salmon, *Society in Crisis*, 309.

87. See Hans Kohn, *The Idea of Nationalism* (New York: Macmillan, 1944), 133.

88. Linda Colley, *Britons: Forging the Nation, 1707–1837* (New Haven: Yale University Press, 1992), 53–4; 35, 52. See also Norman Davies, *The Isles* (London: Macmillan, 1999).

89. John Miller, *Popery and Politics in England, 1660–1688* (Cambridge: Cambridge University Press, 1973), 56.

90. Carol Z. Wiener, "The Beleaguered Isle: A Study of Elizabethan and Early Jacobean Anti-Catholicism," in *Past and Present* 51 (1971), 33, 41; Christopher Hill, *The Anti-Christ in Seventeenth Century England* (London: Oxford University Press, 1971), 154.

91. Weiner, "Beleaguered Isle," 60, 35; Miller, *Popery and Politics*, 67; Barry Coward, *The Stuart Age* (London: Longman, 1980), 106, 109; Colley, *Britons*, 18.

92. John Kenyon, *The Popish Plot* (London: Heinemann, 1972), 4; Coward, *Stuart Age*, 70; Robin Clifton, "Fear of Popery," in Conrad Russell, ed., *The Origins of the English Civil War* (New York: Harper and Row, 1973), 153; Miller, *Popery and Politics*, 12.

93. Mark Kishlansky, *A Monarchy Transformed: Britain 1603–1714* (London: Penguin, 1996), 49, 122; Adrian Hastings, *The Construction of Nationhood* (Cambridge: Cambridge University Press, 1997), 81.

94. J. R. Jones, *The First Whigs* (London: Oxford University Press, 1961), 20.

95. Coward, *Stuart Age*, 272; Miller, *Popery and Politics*, 58.

96. Robin Clifton, "The Popular Fear of Catholics During the English Revolution," in *Past and Present* 52 (1971), 24–5; H. R. Trevor-Roper, *Religion, the Reformation and Social Change* (London: Macmillan, 1967), 108–110, 163.

97. J. H. Plumb, *The Growth of Political Stability in England, 1675–1725* (London: Macmillan, 1967), 27.

98. Roger Lockyer, *Tudor and Stuart Britain* (New York: St Martins, 1985), 208.

99. "King's Speech to Parliament, 1610," in J. R. Tanner, ed., *Constitutional Documents of the Reign of James I* (Cambridge: Cambridge University Press, 1930), 15.

100. "The Trew Law of Free Monarchies," 1598 in Johann P. Sommerville, ed., *King James VI and I: Political Writings* (Cambridge: Cambridge University Press, 1994), 63.

101. Lockyer, *Tudor and Stuart Britain*, 210; Christopher Hill, *The Century of Revolution, 1603–1714* (New York: Norton, 1961), 8; Coward, *The Stuart Age*, 137; Miller, *Popery and Politics*, 81.

102. "Speech to Parliament, 1604" in Tanner, ed., *Constitutional Documents*, 29.

103. Wiener, "Beleaguered Isle," 30.

104. Kishlansky, *A Monarchy Transformed*, 77.

105. "An Act for the better discovering and repressing of Popish recusants, 1606," in J. P. Kenyon, ed., *The Stuart Constitution, 1603–1688* (Cambridge: Cambridge University Press, 1966), 456; Coward, *The Stuart Age*, 111.

106. "King's Speech to the Judges, 1616," in Tanner, ed., *Constitutional Documents*, 22.

107. Robin Clifton, "Fear of Popery," in Conrad Russell, ed., *The Origins of the English Civil War* (New York: Harper and Row, 1973), 154; Miller, *Popery and Politics*, 7, 50–4.

108. "Proclamation for the establishing of the peace and quiet of the Church of England, 16 June 1626," in Kenyon, ed., *Stuart Constitution*, 154.

109. "King's Declaration Prefixed to the Articles of Religion," 1628, in Samuel R. Gardiner, ed., *The Constitutional Documents of the Puritan Revolution, 1625–1660* (Oxford: Oxford University Press, 1962), 75–6.

110. "King's Declaration Showing the Causes of the Late Dissolution, March 10, 1628–9," in *Ibid*, 88–9.

111. "Commons Petition, 3 December 1621," in Kenyon, *Stuart Constitution*, 43–6.

112. "Resolution on Religion Drawn by a Sub-Committee of the House of Commons, February 24, 1628–9," in Gardiner, *Constitutional Documents*, 77–80.

113. "Protestation of the House of Commons, March 2, 1628–9," in *Ibid*, 82–3.

114. Kishlansky, *A Monarchy Transformed*, 103–4; John D. Brewer and Gareth I. Higgins, *Anti-Catholicism in Northern Ireland, 1600–1998* (London: Macmillan, 1998), 18; Hill, *The Century of Revolution*, 48, 8.

115. Coward, *Stuart Age*, 110; Kenyon, *The Popish Plot*, 8; J. P. Kenyon, *The Stuart Constitution, 1603–1688* (Cambridge: Cambridge University Press, 1966), 449.

116. Clifton, "Fear of Popery," 161, 165; Lockyer, *Tudor and Stuart Britain*, 245; Christopher Hill, *The English Bible and the Seventeenth Century Revolution* (London: Penguin, 1993), 69.

117. Lockyer, *Tudor and Stuart Britain*, 266.

118. Steven Pincus, "Nationalism, Universal Monarchy, and the Glorious Revolution," in George Steinmetz, ed., *State/Culture* (Ithaca: Cornell University Press, 1999), 182–210.

119. Clifton, "Fear of Popery," 155–6, 161; Lockyer, *Tudor and Stuart Britain,* 255; Brian Manning, *The English People and the English Revolution* (London: Bookmarks, 1991), 72.

120. Lockyer, *Tudor and Stuart Britain,* 243–5; Coward, *Stuart Age,* 148–52; Clifton, "Fear of Popery," 150–2; Kishlansky, *A Monarchy Transformed,* 128; Hill, *The Century of Revolution,* 50, 70; Manning, *English People and the English Revolution,* 87; Wayne te Brake, *Making History* (Berkeley: University of California Press, 1998), 139.

121. Hill, *Century of Revolution,* 63–4.

122. "Irish Act of Settlement, 1662," in Andrew Browning, ed., *English Historical Documents, 1660–1714* (London: Eyre and Spottiswoode, 1953), 709; Lockyer, *Tudor and Stuart Britain,* 262; Brewer and Higgins, *Anti-Catholicism in Northern Ireland,* 27.

123. Coward, *Stuart Age,* 170; Lockyer, *Tudor and Stuart Britain,* 403; Kishlansky, *A Monarchy Transformed,* 145.

124. Clifton, "Fear of Popery," 164. See also Kenyon, *Stuart Constitution,* 449.

125. William Haller, *Foxe's Book of Martyrs and the Elect Nation* (London: Jonathan Cape, 1963), 227.

126. Clifton, "Popular Fear," 27, 29; Richard S. Dunn, *The Age of Religious Wars, 1559–1715,* (New York: Norton, 1979), 169.

127. Christopher Hibbert, *King Mob* (London: Longmans, Green, 1959), 32; Clifton, "Fear of Popery," 162.

128. Miller, *Popery and Politics,* 84.

129. Michael Walzer, *The Revolution of the Saints* (Cambridge: Harvard University Press, 1965), 257.

130. "The Root and Branch Petition, December 11, 1640," in Gardiner, ed., *The Constitutional Documents,* 137–44; Kishlansky, *A Monarchy Transformed,* 143.

131. Manning, *English People and the English Revolution,* 88.

132. "The Ten Propositions, June 24, 1641," in Gardiner, *Constitutional Documents,* 163–6.

133. "The Act for the Abolition of the Court of the Star Chamber, July 5, 1641" and "The Act for the Abolition of the Court of the High Commission, July 5, 1641" in *Ibid,* 179–89.

134. "The Protestation, 3 May 1641," in Gardiner, ed., *Constitutional Documents,* 155.

135. "The Grand Remonstrance, 1 December 1641" in Kenyon, *The Stuart Constitution,* 228–40.

136. "The Grand Remonstrance, 1 December 1641" full text in Gardiner, ed., *Constitutional Documents,* 202–32.

137. Hill, *English Bible,* 18.

138. "The King's Answer to the Petition Accompanying the Grand Remonstrance, 23 December 1641," in Gardiner, ed., *Constitutional Documents,* 233–6.

139. "The King's Proclamation on Religion, 10 December 1641," in *Ibid,* 232.

140. "The Nineteen Propositions sent by the two Houses of Parliament to the King at York, 1 June 1642," in *Ibid*, 249–54.

141. "Letter to James I, 17 March 1623," in Sir Charles Petrie, ed., *The Letters, Speeches and Proclamations of King Charles I* (New York: Funk and Wagnalls, 1968), 13; "Proclamation, 10 March 1629," in *Ibid*, 69; "Letter to Mr. Nicholas, 18 October 1641," in *Ibid*, 117; "To the Lords and Commons, 4 July 1644," in *Ibid*, 145–6.

142. "To the Earl of Mar, 21 April 1643," in *Ibid*, 138.

143. Manning, *English People and the English Revolution*, 360.

144. Clifton, "Popular Fear," 31; Lockyer, *Tudor and Stuart Britain*, 266; Kenyon, *Popish Plot*, 32; Hill, *Century of Revolution*, 104–6.

145. "The Propositions Presented to the King at the Treaty of Oxford, 1 February 1642/3," in Gardiner, *Constitutional Documents*, 262

146. "The Heads of the Proposals Offered by the Army, 1 August 1647," in *Ibid*, 316–26.

147. "The King's Answer to the Propositions of Parliament, 9 September 1647," in *Ibid*, 326–7.

148. Hill, *Century of Revolution*, 52.

149. Clifton, "Popular Fear," 35–9; Clifton, "Fear of Popery," 144–9, 156; Kenyon, *Popish Plot*, 8.

150. Quoted in Dunn, *Age of Religious Wars*, 173.

151. Hill, *Century of Revolution*, 151.

152. Kishlansky, *A Monarchy Transformed*, 160.

153. Hill, *A Century of Revolution*, 103, 125, 129; Dunn, *Age of Religious Wars*, 172; Michael Walzer, *The Revolution of the Saints* (Cambridge: Harvard University Press, 1965), 114; Keith Lindley, "Part Played by the Catholics," in Brian Manning, ed., *Politics, Religion and the English Civil War* (London: Edward Arnold, 1973), 131–2; Kishlansky, *A Monarchy Transformed*, 152–60.

154. "The Charge against the King, 20 January 1648/9," in Gardiner, ed., *Constitutional Documents*, 371–4.

155. Lockyer, *Tudor and Stuart Britain*, 289; Dunn, *Age of Religious Wars*, 176; Miller, *Popery and Politics*, 85, 91, 155; Hill, *Century of Revolution*, 161.

156. Geoffrey Parker, *Philip II* (Boston: Little, Brown, 1978), 100–1; Geoffrey Parker, *Europe in Crisis, 1598–1648* (Oxford: Blackwell, 1979), 35–6.

CHAPTER 4

1. See Hans Kohn, *The Idea of Nationalism* (New York: Macmillan, 1944), 3–4; Anthony D. Smith, *Nationalism and Modernism* (London: Routledge, 1998), 1; Rogers Brubaker, *Citizenship and Nationhood in France and Germany* (Cambridge: Harvard University Press, 1992), 8; Eric Hobsbawm, *Nations and Nationalism since 1780* (Cambridge: Cambridge University Press, 1990), 3; Brendan O'Leary, "Ernest Gellner's Diagnosis of Nationalism," in John A. Hall, ed., *The State of the Nation* (Cambridge: Cambridge University Press, 1998), 45.

2. Ernst B. Haas, *Nationalism, Liberalism and Progress*, volume 1 (Ithaca: Cornell University Press, 1997), 68.

3. Yael Tamir, *Liberal Nationalism* (Princeton: Princeton University Press, 1993), 90.

4. For discussions of this East versus West model of nationalism, see John Plamenatz, "Two Types of Nationalism," in Eugene Kamenka, ed., *Nationalism: The Nature and Evolution of an Idea* (New York: St. Martin's Press, 1976), 23–36; Liah Greenfeld, *Nationalism: Five Roads to Modernity* (Cambridge: Harvard University Press, 1992). For critiques, see Bernard Yack, "The Myth of the Civic Nation," and Nicholas Xeros, "Civic nationalism: Oxymoron?" in *Critical Review* 10:2 (Spring 1996).

5. Brubaker, *Citizenship and Nationhood in France and Germany*.

6. Alfred Lord Tennyson, "Ulysses."

7. J. H. Elliott, *Richelieu and Olivares* (Cambridge: Cambridge University Press, 1984), 64; J. H. Elliott, *The Count-Duke of Olivares* (New Haven: Yale University Press, 1986), 86–7.

8. Henry Kamen, *Philip of Spain* (New Haven: Yale University Press, 1997), 13, 21.

9. *Ibid*, 87, 109, 285–8; H. R. Trevor-Roper, *Religion, the Reformation, and Social Change* (London: Macmillan, 1967), 46.

10. J. H. Elliott, *Europe Divided, 1559–1598* (New York: Harper and Row, 1968), 87, 184; V. G. Kiernan, *State and Society in Europe, 1550–1650* (Oxford: Basil Blackwell, 1980), 23.

11. Kamen, *Philip of Spain*, 25, 35; J. H. Elliott, *Imperial Spain* (London: Penguin, 1963), 226, ff. 3.

12. Ramon Menendez Pidal, *The Spanish in their History* (New York: Norton, 1950), 116; Elliott, *Richelieu and Olivares*, 68; Elliott, *Count-Duke of Olivares*, 147.

13. Kamen, *Philip of Spain*, 11, 24, 31, 45, 73, 82, 84; Elliott, *Imperial Spain*, 212, 229.

14. Elliott, *Europe Divided*, 180; Elliott, *Imperial Spain*, 235.

15. Kamen, *Philip of Spain*, 131; Elliott, *Imperial Spain*, 305.

16. Kiernan, *State and Society in Europe*, 30; Immanuel Wallerstein, *The Modern World-System* (New York: Academic Press, 1974), 194–5.

17. Kamen, *Philip of Spain*, 22, 64, 243.

18. *Ibid*, 39–40, 69, 72, 109; Wallerstein, *Modern World-System*, 178–9; Elliott, *Europe Divided*, 24.

19. Elliott, *Richelieu and Olivares*, 74.

20. Elliott, *Count-Duke of Olivares*, 10–11, 117, 298–303, 63–4, 590.

21. *Ibid*, 87, 197; Elliott, *Richelieu and Olivares*, 70.

22. Roland Mousnier, *The Assassination of Henry IV* (London: Farber and Farber, 1964), 111; Mark Greengrass, *France in the Age of Henri IV* (London: Longman, 1984), 122.

23. David Buisseret, *Henry IV* (London: George Allen and Unwin, 1984), 17; Greengrass, *France in the Age of Henri IV*, 77.

24. Mack P. Holt, *The French Wars of Religion, 1562–1629* (Cambridge:

Cambridge University Press, 1995), 153; Michael Wolfe, *The Conversion of Henri IV* (Cambridge: Harvard University Press, 1993), 1, 29.

25. David Potter, ed., *The French Wars of Religion: Selected Documents* (London: Macmillan, 1997), 241.

26. Holt, *French Wars of Religion*, 160.

27. Elliott, *Europe Divided*, 356; Wolfe, *Conversion of Henri IV*, 115.

28. Elliott, *Europe Divided*, 351–4; Buisseret, *Henry IV*, 49–55; Perry Anderson, *Lineages of the Absolutist State* (London: Verso, 1974), 93.

29. Jean Francois Marie Arouet de Voltaire, *The Age of Louis XIV* (New York: Dutton, 1961), 397.

30. Mousnier, *Assassination of Henry IV*, 112, 120, 125, 154; David Buisseret, *Sully and the Growth of Centralized Government in France, 1598–1610* (London: Eyre and Spottiswoode, 1968), 35.

31. "Edict of Nantes" in Mousnier, *Assassination of Henry IV*, 316–7.

32. Paul Hay du Chatelet, "Traitte de la politique de France, 1666," in Orest and Patricia Ranum, eds., *The Century of Louis XIV* (New York: Harper and Row, 1972), 354.

33. "Edict of the King, 1685," in *Ibid*, 359.

34. "Edict of Nantes," in Mousnier, *Assassination of Henry IV*, 320, 324, 325, 330.

35. "Royal Warrant, 3 April 1598," and "Secret Articles, 30 April 1598," in *Ibid*, 358–63.

36. Voltaire, *Age of Louis XIV*, 398.

37. "Edict of Nantes," in Mousnier, *Assassination of Henry IV*, 318–9.

38. "Henry's admonition to the Presidents of the Parlement, 5 January 1599" in Potter, ed., *French Wars of Religion*, 250–1.

39. "Speech made by Henri IV to the Parlement Requesting the Registration of the Edict of Nantes, January 1599," in Mousnier, *Assassination of Henry IV*, 367.

40. Buisseret, *Henry IV*, 73.

41. Mousnier, *Assassination of Henry IV*, 148; Elliott, *Europe Divided*, 364–5.

42. Richard S. Dunn, *The Age of Religious Wars, 1559–1715* (New York: Norton, 1979), 40; Greengrass, *France in the Age of Henri IV*, 241.

43. Buisseret, *Sully*, 29, 39–41, 49; Anderson, *Lineages*, 94; Dunn, *Age of Religious Wars*, 155; Mousnier, *Assassination of Henry IV*, 184–5, 195; Greengrass, *France in the Age of Henri IV*, 138, 144, 175, 186, 258.

44. Buisseret, *Henri IV*, 77; Mournier, *Assassination of Henry IV*, 152, 184; Greengrass, *France in the Age of Henri IV*, 138; Buisseret, *Sully*, 36.

45. Mousnier, *Assassination of Henry IV*, 132, 152, 156; Buisseret, *Sully*, 35.

46. Mousnier, *Assassination of Henry IV*, 21, 34, 37, 43, 116, 231; Buisseret, *Henry IV*, 56; Greengrass, *France in the Age of Henri IV*, 252.

47. Mousnier, *Assassination of Henry IV*, 22, 236–8; Greengrass, *France in the Age of Henri IV*, 257; Liah Greenfeld, *Nationalism* (Cambridge: Harvard University Press, 1992), 113, 119; Trevor-Roper, *Religion, the Reformation and Social Change*, 39.

48. Voltaire, *Age of Louis XIV*, 398.

49. Peter Sahlins, "Fictions of a Catholic France: The Naturalization of Foreigners, 1685–1787," *Representations* 47 (Summer 1994), 93.

50. Mark Kishlansky, *A Monarchy Transformed: Britain 1603–1714* (London: Penguin, 1996), 168, 251.

51. Roger Lockyer, *Tudor and Stuart Britain, 1471–1714* (New York: St. Martin's, 1985), 294, 298–9; Barry Coward, *The Stuart Age* (London: Longman, 1980), 229–30; Christopher Hill, *The Century of Revolution* (New York: Norton, 1961), 64–5; John Miller, *Popery and Politics in England, 1660–1688* (Cambridge: Cambridge University Press, 1973), 87; "The Humble Petition and Advice, May 25, 1657," in Samuel Rawson Gardiner, ed., *The Constitutional Documents of the Puritan Revolution, 1625–1660* (Oxford: Clarendon Press, 1889), 449.

52. Dunn, *Age of Religious Wars*, 176; John D. Brewer and Gareth I. Higgins, *Anti-Catholicism in Northern Ireland, 1600–1998* (London: Macmillan, 1998), 29.

53. "Act for the Settlement of Ireland, August 12, 1652," in Gardiner, *Constitutional Documents*, 395.

54. "Declaration of Breda, 1660," in Andrew Browning, ed., *English Historical Documents: 1660–1714, volume 8* (London: Eyre and Spottiswoode, 1953), 57–8.

55. "Act of indemnity and oblivion, 1660," in *Ibid*, 164–5.

56. "Worcester House Declaration, 1660," in *Ibid*, 365.

57. J. H. Plumb, *The Growth of Political Stability in England, 1675–1725* (London: Macmillan, 1967), 15; Coward, *Stuart Age*, 252; "Figures Disclosed by the Census," in Browning, *English Historical Documents*, 413–4.

58. "Act for the preservation of the king, 1661," in Browning, *English Historical Documents*, 64.

59. "Declaration in favour of toleration, 1662," in *Ibid*, 371–4.

60. Corporation Act, 1661" *Ibid*, 375–6; "Act of Uniformity, 116," in *Ibid*, 377–82; "Five Mile Act, 1665," in *Ibid*, 382–4; "Conventicle Act, 1670," in *Ibid*, 384–6.

61. James Shapiro, *Shakespeare and the Jews* New York: Columbia University Press, 1996), 190.

62. "Triennial Act, 1664," in Browning, *English Historical Documents*, 153; Coward, *The Stuart Age*, 263.

63. Lockyer *Tudor and Stuart Britain*, 321.

64. John Kenyon, *The Popish Plot* (London: Heinemann, 1972), 13; Linda Colley, *Britons* (New Haven: Yale University Press, 1992), 20.

65. "Newsletter account of Thomas Blood's theft of the crown and globe, 1671" in Browning, *English Historical Documents*, 508–9.

66. Quoted in Coward, *The Stuart Age*, 271.

67. Quoted in David Ogg, *England in the Reign of Charles II* (Oxford: Clarendon Press, 1934), 345.

68. *Ibid*, 340.

69. *Ibid*, 345; Kenyon, *Popish Plot*, 14, 147; Lockyer, *Tudor and Stuart*

Britain, 332–3; Coward, *Stuart Age*, 263; Kishlansky, *A Monarchy Transformed*, 234–6, 246.

70. "Declaration of Indulgence, 1672" in Browning, *English Historical Documents*, 387.

71. "Speech of Charles II in support of his declaration of indulgence, 5 and 24 February 1673," in *Ibid*, 77–8.

72. *Ibid*, 14 February, 24 February, 3 March, 8 March 1673, 78–81; Coward, *Stuart Age*, 265.

73. Quoted in Kishlansky, *A Monarchy Transformed*, 255.

74. "First Test Act, 1673," in Browning, *English Historical Documents*, 389–91; Miller, *Popery and Politics*, 127.

75. Miller, *Popery and Politics*, 148–9; Ogg, *England in the Reign of Charles II*, 327.

76. Miller, *Popery and Politics*, 172; J. P. Kenyon, *The Stuart Constitution, 1603–1688* (Cambridge: Cambridge University Press, 1966), 450.

77. "Articles of impeachment against the earl of Danby, 1678," in Browning, *English Historical Documents*," 198–9.

78. Christopher Hill, *The Century of Revolution* (New York: Norton, 1961), 198; Kenyon, *Stuart Constitution*, 451.

79. "Second Test Act, 1678," in Browning, *English Historical Documents*, 391–4; Ogg, *England in the Reign of Charles II*, 588. A similar Test Act was enacted for Scotland in 1681. See "Test Act, 1681," in Browning, *English Historical Documents*, 631–4.

80. "Anonymous account of the Popish Plot, 1678," in Browning, *English Historical Documents*, 111.

81. Ogg, *England in the Reign of Charles II*, 575; Miller, *Popery and Politics*, 143, 151; J. R. Jones, *The First Whigs* (London: Oxford University Press, 1961), 70; Kenyon, *The Popish Plot*, 96, 114–6.

82. "Articles of impeachment against the earl of Danby, 1678" in Browning, *English Historical Documents*, 199.

83. John Dryden, "Absalom and Achitophel," in *Ibid*, 113.

84. Ogg, *England in the Reign of Charles II*, 595; Miller, *Popery and Politics*, 125; Coward, *Stuart Age*, 283; "An appeal from the country to the city, 1679" in Kenyon, *Stuart Constitution*, 467.

85. Miller, *Popery and Politics*, 178.

86. "The judgement and decree of the University of Oxford, passed at their Convocation, July 21, 1683," in Kenyon, *Stuart Constitution*, 471–4.

87. Miller, *Popery and Politics*, 131, 184; Ogg, *England in the Reign of Charles II*, 595.

88. Tim Harris, "The British Dimension . . . ," in Tony Claydon and Ian McBride, eds., *Protestantism and National Identity* (Cambridge: Cambridge University Press, 1998), 143–4, 147.

89. *Ibid*, 138; Toby Barnard, "Protestantism, Ethnicity and Irish Identities, 1660–1760," in Claydon and McBride, eds., *Protestantism and National Identities*, 207–8.

90. "An appeal from the country to the city, 1679" in Kenyon, *Stuart Constitution*, 467–9.

91. Coward, *Stuart Age,* 267; Kenyon, *Popish Plot,* 16, 56; Jones, *First Whigs,* 81.

92. Miller, *Popery and Politics,* 154.

93. "Exclusion Bill, 1680," in Browning, *English Historical Documents,* 113; Ogg, *England in the Reign of Charles II,* 618.

94. Ogg, *England in the Reign of Charles II,* 606, 615; Jones, *First Whigs,* 8, 18, 115.

95. "Report of the French ambassador to Louis XIV on the death of Charles II, 1685," in Browning, *English Historical Documents,* 116–20.

96. Kenyon, *Stuart Constitution,* 448.

CHAPTER 5

1. Alfred Lord Tennyson, "Ulysses," in Alfred Tennyson, *Idylls of the King and a Selection of Poems* (New York: Penguin, 1961), 284.

2. J. H. Elliott, *The Count-Duke of Olivares* (New Haven: Yale University Press, 1986), 182, 180; J. H. Elliott, *Richelieu and Olivares* (Cambridge: Cambridge University Press, 1984), 156.

3. Elliott, *Richelieu and Olivares,* 161, 64; Max Weber, *The Protestant Ethic and the Spirit of Capitalism* (New York: Charles Scribner's Sons, 1958).

4. Paul Kennedy, *The Rise and Fall of the Great Powers* (New York: Random House, 1987), 43–54.

5. Elliott, *Count-Duke of Olivares,* 157–61, 432, 70, 439; Wayne te Brake, *Shaping History* (Berkeley: University of California Press, 1998), 122, 125.

6. Elliott, *Count-Duke of Olivares,* 191, 194, 244; Juan Linz, "Early State-Building and Late Peripheral Nationalisms against the State," In *Building States and Nations,* ed. S. N. Eisenstadt and Stein Rokkan (Beverly Hills: Sage, 1973), volume 2, 43.

7. Helmut Koenigsberger, "Spain," in *National Consciousness, History, and Political Culture in Early-Modern Europe* (Baltimore: Johns Hopkins University Press, 1975), 168; Elliott, *Count Duke of Olivares,* 246, 252.

8. Elliott, *Richelieu and Olivares,* 72.

9. Kennedy, *Rise and Fall,* 36.

10. Ramon Menendez Pidal, *The Spanish in Their History* (New York: Norton, 1950), 117; V. G. Kiernan, *State and Society in Europe, 1550–1650* (Oxford: Basil Blackwell, 1980), 70–1.

11. J. H. Elliott, *Europe Divided, 1559–1598* (New York: Harper and Row, 1968), 135, 165, 170–1, 211, 255, 259, 262; Henry Kamen, *Philip of Spain* (New Haven: Yale University Press, 1997), 93, 116, 132.

12. Kamen, *Philip of Spain,* 160.

13. Elliott, *Count-Duke of Olivares,* 51, 65.

14. Elliott, *Europe Divided,* 367.

15. Geoffrey Parker, *Europe in Crisis, 1598–1648* (Oxford: Blackwell, 1976), 107.

16. Immanuel Wallerstein, *The Modern World-System* (New York: Academic Press, 1974), 179.

17. Elliott, *Europe Divided,* 93–4.

18. Hans Kohn, *The Idea of Nationalism* (New York: Macmillan, 1944), 154–5.

19. A. D. Lublinskaya, *French Absolutism: the Crucial Phase, 1620–1629* (Cambridge: Cambridge University Press, 1968), 150, 161, 175, 211–2.

20. *Ibid*, 214, 219; Richard S. Dunn, *The Age of Religious Wars, 1559–1715* (New York: Norton, 1979), 159; Charles Tilly, *The Contentious French* (Cambridge: Harvard University Press, 1986), 87; Peter Sahlins, "Fictions of a Catholic France: The Naturalization of Foreigners, 1685–1787," in *Representations* 47 (Summer 1994), 89.

21. Dale K. Van Kley, *The Religious Origins of the French Revolution* (New Haven: Yale University Press, 1996), 5, 33.

22. Orest Ranum, *The Fronde: A French Revolution, 1648–1652* (New York: Norton, 1993), 55.

23. Voltaire, *The Age of Louis XIV* (New York: Dutton, 1961), 32, 48.

24. Dunn, *Age of Religious Wars*, 163.

25. David A. Bell, *The Cult of the Nation in France* (Cambridge: Harvard University Press, 2001), 52. I am indebted to Dale van Kley for this point.

26. Dunn, *Age of Religious Wars*, 163, 185; John Stoye, *Europe Unfolding, 1648–1688* (New York: Harper and Row, 1969), 105.

27. Dunn, *Age of Religious Wars*, 183; Liah Greenfeld, *Nationalism* (Cambridge: Harvard University Press, 1992), 127.

28. Van Kley, *Religious Origins of the French Revolution*, 50–73.

29. "Edict of the King, October 22, 1685," in Orest and Patricia Ranum, eds., *The Century of Louis XIV* (New York: Harper and Row, 1972), 359–63.

30. Dunn, *Age of Religious Wars*, 186; Burdette C. Poland, *French Protestantism and the French Revolution* (Princeton: Princeton University Press, 1957), 24; Charles Tilly, *The Contentious French* (Cambridge: Harvard University Press, 1986).

31. "Edict of the King, October 22, 1685," in Ranum, eds., *Century of Louis XIV*, 360.

32. Paul Hay du Châtelet, "Traitté de la politique de France," 1666, in Ranum, eds., *Century of Louis XIV*, 350–8.

33. Barrington Moore, Jr., *Social Origins of Dictatorship and Democracy* (Boston: Beacon, 1966), 44.

34. Greenfeld, *Nationalism*, 129–31; Sahlins, "Fictions of a Catholic France," 85.

35. William L. Sacshe, "The Mob and the Revolution of 1688," *Journal of British Studies* 4:1 (November 1964); 24.

36. Barry Coward, *The Stuart Age* (London: Longman, 1980), 297; Linda Colley, *Britons* (New Haven: Yale University Press, 1992), 20.

37. Coward, *Stuart Age*, 294; John Miller, *Popery and Politics in England, 1660–1688* (Cambridge: Cambridge University Press, 1973), 197; Christopher Hill, *The Century of Revolution, 1603–1714* (New York: Norton, 1961), 202.

38. Kenyon, *The Popish Plot*, 33; Miller, *Popery and Politics*, 198, 200, 214; J. R. Jones, *The Revolution of 1688 in England* (New York: Norton, 1972), 52;

Mark Kishlansky, *A Monarchy Transformed: Britain 1603–1714* (London: Penguin, 1996), 274.

39. J. P. Kenyon, *The Stuart Constitution, 1603–1688* (Cambridge: Cambridge University Press, 1966), 453; Miller, *Popery and Politics,* 255; David Ogg, *England in the Reigns of James II and William III* (Oxford: Clarendon Press, 1955), 206–7; Coward, *Stuart Age,* 296; Jones, *Revolution of 1688,* 113.

40. "Report of the French Ambassador to Louis XIV on the death of Charles II, 1685," in Browning, ed., *English Historical Documents,* 116.

41. Steven Pincus, "To Protect English Liberties," inTony Claydon and Ian McBride, eds., *Protestantism and National Identity,* (Cambridge: Cambridge University Press, 1998), 80, 90, 93.

42. Quoted in Steven Pincus, "Nationalism, Universal Monarchy, and the Glorious Revolution," in George Steinmetz, ed., *State/Culture* (Ithaca: Cornell University Press, 1999), 196.

43. "Speech of James II in support of the standing army and the Catholic officers, and the address of the Commons in reply, 1685," in Browning, *English Historical Documents,* 81–2; "Chief Justice Herbert in the case of Godden v. Hales, 1686," in *Ibid,* 83.

44. Ogg, *England in the Reigns of James II and William III,* 168, 179, 187; Roger Lockyer, *Tudor and Stuart Britain, 1471–1714* (New York: St. Martin's Press, 1985), 356; Miller, *Popery and Politics,* 219, 222; Hill, *Century of Revolution,* 170.

45. Coward, *Stuart Age,* 297; Jones, *Revolution of 1688,* 120; "Sir William Petty's enumeration of the royal powers, 1685," in Browning, *English Historical* Documents, *1660–1714,* 73; Ogg, *England in the Reigns of James II and William III,* 183; Kishlansky, *A Monarchy Transformed,* 273.

46. "Declaration of Indulgence, 1687" and "Declaration of Indulgence, 1688," in Browning, *English Historical Documents, 1660–1714,* 395–9.

47. "Order in Council requiring James II's declaration of indulgence to be read in churches, 1688," "Petition of the Seven Bishops, 1688," "Summing up of Chief Justice Wright and opinion of Justice Holloway in the Seven Bishop's Case, 1688," in Browning, *Ibid,* 83–5.

48. Kenyon, *Stuart Constitution,* 455; Coward, *Stuart Age,* 300; Lockyer, *Tudor and Stuart Britain,* 357–8; Dunn, *Age of Religious Wars,* 194.

49. "Letter of Invitation to William of Orange, 1688," in Browning, *English Historical Documents, 1660–1714,* 120–2.

50. Hill, *Century of Revolution,* 171; Ogg, *England in the Reign of James II and William III,* 215, 223; Miller, *Popery and Princes,* 199; Kishlansky, *A Monarchy Transformed,* 279–80.

51. Hill, *Century of Revolution,* 206; Jones, *Revolution of 1688,* 100, 326.

52. "Anonymous account of the death of James II, 1701," in Browning, *English Historical Documents, 1660–1714,* 137.

53. Colin Haydon, "I Love My King and My Country," in Tony Claydon and Ian McBride, eds., *Protestantism and National Identity,* 36.

54. J. H. Plumb, *The Growth of Political Stability in England, 1675–1725* (London: Macmillan, 1967), 61.

55. Pincus, "To Protect English Liberties," 86.

56. Sachse, "Mob and the Revolution of 1688," 25, 28, 34, 40; Lockyer, *Tudor and Stuart Britain*, 360; Kishlansky, *A Monarchy Transformed*, 282.

57. Kishlansky, *A Monarchy Transformed*, 284; Colley, *Britons*, 47; Ogg, *England in the Reigns of James II and William III*, 235–6.

58. "Bill of Rights, 1689," in Browning, *English Historical Documents*, 122–8.

59. *Ibid*, 124, 127. See also Tony Claydon and Ian McBride, "The Trials of the Chosen People," in Claydon and McBride, eds., *Protestantism and National Identity*," 3.

60. Ogg, *England in the Reigns of James II and William III*, 225; Colley, *Britons*, 46.

61. Claydon, "I Love my King and my Country," 37.

62. "Toleration Act, 1689," in Browning, *English Historical Documents*, 400–3; Kishlansky, *A Monarchy Transformed*, 292, 313.

63. "Act against Popery, 1700," in Browning, *English Historical Documents*, 404–6.

64. "Proposed Penal Taxation of Catholics, 1722," in D. B. Horn and Mary Ransome, eds., *English Historical Documents, 1714–1783* (London: Routledge, 1957), 399.

65. Pincus, "To Protect English Liberties," 95–6.

66. Kishlansky, *A Monarchy Transformed*, 287, 295; Dunn, *Age of Religious Wars*, 197; Hill, *Century of Revolution*, 220.

67. "Act excluding papists from public trust in Ireland, 1691," in Browning, *English Historical Documents*, 773; "Act to prevent the growth of popery, 1704," in *Ibid*, 783; David Hempton, *Religion and Political Culture in Britain and Ireland* (Cambridge: Cambridge University Press, 1996), 72.

68. "Act of Union, 1707," in Browning, *English Historical Documents*, 680.

69. Plumb, *Growth of Political Stability*, 108–16; Dunn, *Age of Religious Wars*, 196; Hill, *Century of Revolution*, 220, 244; Kishlansky, *A Monarchy Transformed*, 308, 339.

70. Colley, *Britons*, 19–20.

71. *Ibid*, 53; Kohn, *The Idea of Nationalism*, 210.

72. Liah Greenfeld, *Nationalism* (Cambridge: Harvard University Press, 1992), chapter 1.

CHAPTER 6

1. Dankwart Rustow, "Transitions to Democracy: Toward a Dynamic Model," *Comparative Politics* (April 1970), 350–1; Robert A. Dahl, *Democracy and Its Critics* (New Haven: Yale University Press, 1989), 207. See also Alfred Stepan, *Arguing Comparative Politics* (Oxford: Oxford University Press, 2001), 185.

2. Rustow, "Transitions to Democracy," 352, 351.

3. *Ibid*, 352, 359, 355, 348.

4. *Ibid*, 361, 363.

5. Barrington Moore, Jr., *Social Origins of Dictatorship and Democracy* (Boston: Beacon, 1966), 3.

6. Rustow, *"Transitions to Democracy,"* 355.

7. W. H. Auden, "In Memory of Sigmund Freud," in Edward Mendelson, ed., *W. H. Auden: Selected Poems* (New York: Vintage, 1979), 92.

8. Ernest Renan, "What Is a Nation?" in Geoff Eley and Ronald Grigor Suny, eds., *Becoming National* (Oxford: Oxford University Press, 1996).

9. David Potter, *A History of France, 1460–1560* (London: Macmillan, 1995), 290.

10. Peter Sahlins, "Fictions of a Catholic France: The Naturalization of Foreigners, 1685–1787," *Representations* 47 (Summer 1994), 102–3; John McManners, *The French Revolution and the Church* (Westport: Greenwood, 1969), 1, 6; Burdette C. Poland, *French Protestantism and the French Revolution* (Princeton: Princeton University Press, 1957), 99.

11. Dale K. Van Kley, *The Religious Origins of the French Revolution* (New Haven: Yale University Press, 1996), 43, 47.

12. *Ibid*, 249, 303; David A. Bell, *The Cult of the Nation in France* (Cambridge: Harvard University Press, 2001), 58.

13. Reinhard Bendix, *Nation-Building and Citizenship* (Berkeley: University of California Press, 1977), 114.

14. David A. Bell, "Lingua Populi, Lingua Dei: Language, Religion, and the Origins of French Revolutionary Nationalism," *American Historical Review* 100:5 (December 1995), 1419.

15. Poland, *French Protestantism*, 105, 117–8, 136, 142, 172, 201, 255.

16. "Edict of Toleration, November 1787," in Lynn Hunt, ed., *The French Revolution and Human Rights* (New York: St. Martin's Press, 1996), 41–3.

17. Dale Van Kley, notes to author, 3 April 2002.

18. Van Kley, *The Religious Origins of the French Revolution*, 25, 58, 63, 67.

19. "Letter from Rabaut Saint Étienne on the Edict of Toleration, December 6, 1787," in Hunt, *The French Revolution and Human Rights*, 46.

20. "Declaration of the Rights of Man and Citizen, August 26, 1789," in *Ibid*, 79.

21. Van Kley, *The Religious Origins of the French Revolution*, 1.

22. *Ibid*, 367.

23. See Bell, "Lingua Populi, Lingua Dei", 1405, 1412–5.

24. Charlotte Catherine Wells, "The Language of Citizenship in Early Modern France," Ph.D. dissertation, Department of History, Indiana University, December 1991, 368–9.

25. Poland, *French Protestantism*, 276.

26. Roger Brubaker, *Citizenship and Nationhood in France and Germany* (Cambridge: Harvard University Press, 1992).

27. Eugen Weber, *Peasants into Frenchmen: The Modernization of Rural France, 1870–1914* (Stanford: Stanford University Press, 1976).

28. Andrew McLaren Carstairs, *A Short History of Electoral Systems in Western Europe* (London: George Allen & Unwin, 1980), 175.

29. See Erik Bleich, "Anti-Racism without Races," *French Politics, Culture and Society* 18:3 (Fall 2000).

30. Dietrich Rueshemeyer, Evelyne Huber Stephens, and John D. Stephens, *Capitalist Development and Democracy* (Chicago: University of Chicago Press, 1992), 88; William H. Sewell, Jr., "Artisans, Factory Workers and the Formation of the French Working Class, 1789–1848," in Ira Katznelson and Aristide R. Zolberg, eds., *Working Class Formation* (Princeton: Princeton University Press, 1986), 45, 62–4; Alain Cottereau, "The Distinctiveness of Working Class Cultures in France, 1848–1900," in *Ibid*, 111. See also Ronald Aminzade, *Ballots and Barricades* (Princeton: Princeton University Press, 1993); Reinhard Bendix, *Nation-Building and Citizenship* (Berkeley: University of California Press, 1964), chapter 3.

31. B. R. Mitchell, *European Historical Statistics, 1750–1975* (New York: Facts on File, 1980), 163, 171, 182, 185.

32. John Locke, *A Letter Concerning Toleration*, Patrick Romanell, ed. (New York: Macmillan, 1950), 13.

33. *Ibid*, 17–18, 20, 24.

34. *Ibid*, 56.

35. *Ibid*, 27.

36. *Ibid*, 51, 56.

37. *Ibid*, 51–2.

38. Colin Claydon, "Anti-Catholicism and Xenophobia," in Tony Claydon and Ian McBride, eds., *Protestantism and National Identity* (Cambridge: Cambridge University Press, 1998), 39.

39. Craig Calhoun, *Nationalism* (Minneaplois: University of Minnesota Press, 1997), 76.

40. John Locke, *A Letter Concerning Toleration*, ed. Patrick Romanell, 45; P. J. Kelly, "John Locke: Authority, Conscience and Religious Toleration," in John Horton and Susan Mendus, eds., *John Locke: A Letter Concerning Toleration in Focus* (London: Routledge, 1991), 132.

41. J. W. Gough, "The Development of Locke's Belief in Toleration," in Horton and Mendus, eds., *John Locke . . . in Focus*, 63, 71.

42. John Locke, *A Letter Concerning Toleration*, ed. Patrick Romanell, 26.

43. Susan Mendus and John Horton, "Locke and Toleration," in Horton and Mendus, eds., *John Locke . . . in Focus*, 1; James H. Tully, "Introduction," in John Locke, *A Letter Concerning Toleration*, James H. Tully, ed. (Indianapolis: Hackett, 1983), 6.

44. Maurice Cranston, "John Locke and the Case for Toleration," in Horton and Mendus, eds., *John Locke . . . in Focus*, 82, 89.

45. Mendus and Horton, "Introduction," in Horton and Mendus, eds. *John Locke . . . in Focus*, 5; Cranston, "John Locke and the Case for Toleration," in *Ibid*, 79; Tully, "Introduction," in John Locke, *A Letter Concerning Toleration*, ed. John H. Tully, 11.

46. Gough, "The Development of Locke's Belief in Toleration," in Horton and Mendus, eds., *John Locke . . . in Focus*, 61.

47. Ernst B. Haas, *Nationalism, Liberalism, and Progress* (Ithaca: Cornell University Press, 1997), volume 1, 68; Brian Downing, *The Military*

Revolution and Political Change (Princeton: Princeton University Press, 1992).

48. Liah Greenfeld, *Nationalism* (Cambridge: Harvard University Press, 1992), chapter 1.

49. Frank O'Gorman, *The Long Eighteenth Century* (London: Arnold, 1997), 60, 163, 296.

50. David Hempton, *Religion and Political Culture in Britain and Ireland* (Cambridge: Cambridge University Press, 1996), 146.

51. See J. Paul de Castro, *The Gordon Riots* (London: Oxford University Press, 1926); Christopher Hibbert, *King Mob* (London: Longmans, Green and Co., 1959).

52. Charles Tilly, *Popular Contention in Great Britain, 1758–1834* (Cambridge: Harvard University Press, 1995), 278, 311, 275, 360, 384; Norman Davies, *The Isles* (London: Macmillan, 1999), 725; Tony Claydon and Ian McBride, "The Trials of the Chosen People," in Tony Claydon and Ian McBride, eds., *Protestanism and National Identity* (Cambridge: Cambridge University Press, 1998), 3.

53. Linda Colley, *Britons* (New Haven: Yale University Press, 1992), 19.

54. Adrian Hastings, *The Construction of Nationhood* (Cambridge: Cambridge University Press, 1997), 65.

55. E. P. Thompson, *The Making of the English Working Class* (New York: Random House, 1963), 429–34; Hempton, *Religion and Political Culture,* 148.

56. James Vernon, *Politics and the People* (Cambridge: Cambridge University Press, 1993), 326; Ian S. Lustick, *Unsettled States; Disputed Lands* (Ithaca: Cornell University Press, 1993), 162.

57. Colin Haydon, "Anti-Catholicism and Xenophobia," in Claydon and McBride, eds., *Protestantism and National Identity,* 35; Hempton, *Religion and Political Culture,* 146–7.

58. Barry Coward, *The Stuart Age* (London: Longman, 1986), 418, 319.

59. Quoting J. R. R. Tolkien, in Colin Haydon, "Anti-Catholicism and Xenophobia," in Claydon and McBride, *Protestantism and National Identity,* 49.

60. Christopher Hill, *The Century of Revolution, 1663–1714* (New York: Norton, 1961), 267; J. P. Kenyon, *The Stuart Constitution,* (Cambridge: Cambridge University Press, 1966), 456.

61. Michael Walzer, *The Revolution of the Saints* (Cambridge: Harvard University Press, 1965), 303, 319, 310.

62. Gough, "The Development of Locke's Belief in Toleration," in Horton and Mendus, eds., *John Locke . . . in focus,* 73.

63. Juan Linz, "Early State-Building and Late Peripheral Nationalisms against the State: The Case of Spain," in *Building States and Nations,* volume 2, ed. S. N. Eisenstadt and Stein Rokkan (Beverly Hills: Sage, 1973), 42.

64. *Ibid,* 47, 99. See Ramón Menéndez Pidal, *The Spaniards in Their History* (New York: Norton, 1950), 89.

65. Helmut Koenigsberger, "Spain," in *National Consciousness, History,*

and Political Culture in Early-Modern Europe, ed. Orest Ranum (Baltimore: Johns Hopkins University Press, 1975), 171.

66. Menenedez Pidal, *The Spaniards,* 96; Linz, "Early State-Building," 50, 61, 63.

67. Koenigsberger, "Spain," 155–6.

68. Linz, "Early State-Building," 102.

69. Rustow, "Transitions to Democracy," 361.

CHAPTER 7

1. Benedict Anderson, *Imagined Communities* (London: Verso, 1983), p. 122.

2. Ernest Gellner, *Nations and Nationalism* (Ithaca: Cornell University Press, 1983), p. 39, 65, 82.

3. T. H. Marshall, *Citizenship and Social Class* (London: Pluto, 1992); Reinhard Bendix, *Nation-Building and Citizenship* (Berkeley: University of California Press, 1964).

4. Alfred Stepan, *Arguing Comparative Politics* (Oxford: Oxford University Press, 2001), 214, 219, 221–2.

5. Uday Singh Mehta, *Liberalism and Empire* (Chicago: University of Chicago Press, 1999), 5, 46. See also Edward W. Said, *Orientalism* (New York: Random House, 1978); Hannah Arendt, *The Origins of Totalitarianism* (New York: Harcourt Brace Jovanovich, 1951); Gayatri Spivak, *In Other Worlds* (New York: Methuen, 1987).

6. Samuel P. Huntington, *The Clash of Civilizations and the Remaking of World Order* (New York: Simon and Shuster, 1996).

7. Anderson, *Imagined Communities,* chapter 9.

8. Walter Benjamin, *Illuminations* (New York: Schocken Books, 1969), 257–8.

BIBLIOGRAPHY

Aminzade, Ronald. *Ballots and Barricades*. Princeton: Princeton University Press, 1993.

Anderson, Benedict. *Imagined Communities*. London: Verso, 1983.

———. *Imagined Communities*. Revised, London: Verso, 1991.

Anderson, Perry. *Lineages of the Absolutist State*. London: Verso, 1974.

Arendt, Hannah. *The Origins of Totalitarianism*. New York: Harcourt Brace Jovanovich, 1951.

Armstrong, John A. *Nations Before Nationalism*. Chapel Hill: University of North Carolina Press, 1982.

Ashmore, Richard D. "The Problem of Intergroup Prejudice." In *Social Psychology*, ed. Barry E. Collins, 245–96. Reading: Addison-Wesley, 1970.

Barkey, Karen. *Bandits and Bureaucrats: The Ottoman Route to State Centralization*. Ithaca: Cornell University Press, 1994.

Barnard, Toby. "Protestantism, Ethnicity and Irish Identities, 1660–1760." In *Protestantism and National Identities*, ed. Tony Claydon and Ian McBride, 206–35. Cambridge: Cambridge University Press, 1998.

Baron, Salo W. *A Social and Religious History of the Jews*. New York: Columbia University Press, 1969.

Bell, David A. *The Cult of the Nation in France*. Cambridge: Harvard University Press, 2001.

———. "Lingua Populi, Lingua Dei: Language, Religion, and the Origins of French Revolutionary Nationalism." *American Historical Review* 100: 5 (December 1995): 1403–37.

Bendix, Reinhard. *Nation-Building and Citizenship*. Berkeley: University of California Press, 1964.

Benjamin, Walter. *Illuminations*. New York: Schocken Books, 1969.

Berlin, Isaiah. *Vico and Herder*. New York: Random House, 1976.

Berry, W. Grinton, ed. *Foxe's Book of Martyrs*. Grand Rapids: Baker Book House, 1998.

Bhabha, Homi K., ed. *Nation and Narration*. London: Routledge, 1990.

Billig, Michael and Henri Tajfel. "Social Categorization and Similarity in Intergroup Behavior." *European Journal of Social Psychology* 3:1 (1973): 27–52.

Bitton, Davis. *The French Nobility in Crisis, 1560–1640*. Palo Alto: Stanford University Press, 1969.

Black, Jeremey. "Confessional State or Elect Nation?" In *Protestantism and National Identity*, ed. Tony Claydon and Ian McBride, 53–74. Cambridge: Cambridge University Press, 1998.

Bleich, Erik. "Antiracism without Races." *French Politics, Culture and Society* 18:3 (Fall 2000): 48–74.

Bossy, John. *The English Catholic Community, 1570–1850*. London: Darton, Longman, and Todd, 1975.

Bourdieu, Pierre. *Distinction*. Cambridge: Harvard University Press, 1984.

———. *Outline of a Theory of Practice*. Cambridge: Cambridge University Press, 1977.

———. *In Other Words*. Palo Alto: Stanford University Press, 1990.

Bourdieu, Pierre and Loic Wacquant. *An Invitation to Reflexive Sociology*. Chicago: University of Chicago Press, 1992.

Bradshaw, Brendan. "The English Reformation." In *British Consciousness and Identity*, ed. Brendan Bradshaw and Peter Roberts. Cambridge: Cambridge University Press, 1998.

Brake, Wayne Te. *Shaping History*. Berkeley: University of California Press, 1998.

Brams, Steven J. *Game Theory and Politics*. New York: Free Press, 1975.

———. *Rational Politics*. Washington: CQ Press, 1985.

Brandi, Karl. *The Emperor Charles V*. New York: Knopf, 1939.

Brass, Paul R. *Ethnicity and Nationalism*. New Delhi: Sage, 1991.

Breuilly, John. *Nationalism and the State*. Chicago: University of Chicago Press, 1982.

Brewer, John D. and Gareth I. Higgins. *Anti-Catholicism in Northern Ireland, 1600–1998*. London: Macmillan, 1998.

Browning, Andrew, ed. *English Historical Documents, 1660–1714*. Vol. 8. London: Eyre and Spottiswoode, 1953.

Brubaker, Roger. *Citizenship and Nationhood in France and Germany*. Cambridge: Harvard University Press, 1992.

———. *Nationalism Reframed*. Cambridge: Cambridge University Press, 1996.

———. "Rethinking Classical Theory: The Sociological Vision of Pierre Bourdieu." *Theory and Society* 14 (1985): 745–75.

Buisseret, David. *Sully and the Growth of Centralized Government in France, 1598–1610*. London: Eyre and Spottiswoode, 1968.

———. *Henry IV*. London: George Allen and Unwin, 1984.

Calhoun, Craig. *Nationalism.* Minneapolis: University of Minnesota Press, 1997.

Carstairs, Andrew McLaren. *A Short History of Electoral Systems in Western Europe.* London: George Allen & Unwin, 1980.

Castro, Americo. *The Structure of Spanish History.* Princeton: Princeton University Press, 1954.

Christin, Olivier. *Le Paix de Religion.* Paris: Seuil/Collection Liber, 1997.

Claydon, Tony and Ian McBride. "The Trials of the Chosen People." In *Protestantism and National Identity,* ed. Tony Claydon and Ian McBride, 3–32. Cambridge: Cambridge University Press, 1998.

Clifton, Robin. "Fear of Popery." In *The Origins of the English Civil War,* ed. Conrad Russell, 144–67. New York: Harper and Row, 1973.

———. "The Popular Fear of Catholics during the English Revolution." *Past and Present,* 52 (1971): 23–55.

Cohen, Abner. *Two Dimensional Man.* Berkeley: University of California Press, 1974.

Colley, Linda. *Britons: Forging the Nation.* New Haven: Yale University Press, 1992.

Comaroff, John. "Ethnicity, Nationalism, and the Politics of Difference in the Age of Revolution." In *The Politics of Difference,* ed. Edwin N. Wilmsen and Patrick MacAllister, 162–84. Chicago: University of Chicago Press, 1996.

Connor, Walker. *Ethnonationalism.* Princeton: Princeton University Press, 1994.

Cottereau, Alain. "The Distinctiveness of Working-Class Cultures in France, 1848–1900." In *Working-Class Formation,* ed. Ira Katznelson and Aristide R. Zolberg, 111–56. Princeton: Princeton University Press, 1986.

Coward, Barry. *The Stuart Age.* London: Longman, 1980.

Cranston, Maurice. "John Locke and the Case for Toleration." In *John Locke: A Letter Concerning Toleration in Focus,* ed. John Horton and Susan Mendus, 78–97. London: Routledge, 1991.

Dahl, Robert A. *Democracy and Its Critics.* New Haven: Yale University Press, 1989.

Davies, Norman. *The Isles.* London: Macmillan, 1999.

Davis, Natalie Zemon. *Society and Culture in Early Modern France.* Stanford: Stanford University Press, 1975.

de Castro, J. Paul. *The Gordon Riots.* London: Oxford University Press, 1926.

Deutsch, Karl. *Nationalism and Social Communication.* New York: MIT Press, 1966.

Diefendorf, Barbara. *Beneath the Cross: Catholics and Hugenots in Sixteenth-Century Paris.* New York: Oxford University Press, 1991.

Downing, Brian. *The Military Revolution and Political Change.* Princeton: Princeton University Press, 1992.

Dunn, Richard S. *The Age of Religious Wars, 1559–1715.* New York: Norton, 1979.

Eisenstadt, S. N. and Stein Rokkan, eds. *Building States and Nations.* Beverly Hills: Sage Publications, 1973.

Elliott, John H. *The Count-Duke of Olivares.* New Haven: Yale University Press, 1986.

———. *Europe Divided, 1559–1598.* New York: Harper and Row, 1968.

———. *Imperial Spain, 1469–1716.* London: Penguin, 1963.

———. *Richelieu and Olivares.* Cambridge: Cambridge University Press, 1984.

Elton, G. R. *England under the Tudors.* London: Routledge, 1955.

———, ed. *The Tudor Constitution: Documents and Commentary.* Cambridge: Cambridge University Press, 1960.

Englund, Steven. "The Ghost of Nation Past." *Journal of Modern History* 64 (June 1992): 299–320.

Ertman, Thomas. *Birth of the Leviathan.* Cambridge: Cambridge University Press, 1997.

Fearon, James D. and David Laitin. "Explaining Interethnic Cooperation," *American Political Science Review* 90 (1996): 715–35.

Ferejohn, John. "Rationality and Interpretation: Parliamentary Elections in Early Stuart England." In *The Economic Approach to Politics,* ed. Kristen Renwick Moore, 279–305. New York: Harper Collins, 1991.

Freud, Sigmund. *Civilization and Its Discontents.* New York: Norton, 1961.

Gardiner, Samuel R., ed. *The Constitutional Documents of the Puritan Revolution, 1625–1660.* Oxford: Oxford University Press, 1962.

Gellner, Ernest. *Nations and Nationalism.* Ithaca: Cornell University Press, 1983.

Gerth, H. H. and C. Wright Mills, eds. *From Max Weber.* New York: Oxford University Press, 1978.

Gorski, Philip S. "The Mosaic Moment: An Early Modernist Critique of Modernist Theories of Nationalism." *American Journal of Sociology* 105: 5 (March 2000): 1428–68.

———. "Calvinism and State-Formation in Early Modern Europe." In *State/Culture,* ed. George Steinmetz, 147–81. Ithaca: Cornell University Press, 1999.

Gough, J. W. "The Development of Locke's Belief in Toleration." In *John Locke: A Letter Concerning Toleration in Focus,* ed. John Horton and Susan Mendus, 57–77. London: Routledge, 1991.

Granovetter, Mark and Richard Swedberg, eds. *The Sociology of Economic Life.* Boulder: Westview, 1992.

Greenfeld, Liah. *Nationalism: Five Roads to Modernity.* Cambridge: Harvard University Press, 1992.

Greengrass, Mark. *France in the Age of Henry IV: The Struggle for Stability.* London: Longman, 1984.

Guibernau, Montserrat. *Nationalisms.* Cambridge: Polity Press, 1996.

Haas, Ernst B. *Nationalism, Liberalism, and Progress.* Vol. 1. Ithaca: Cornell University Press, 1997.

Habermas, Jurgen. *Communication and the Evolution of Society.* Boston: Beacon, 1979.

Hall, Peter A. *Governing the Economy.* Oxford: Oxford University Press, 1986.

Haller, William. *Foxe's Book of Martyrs and the Elect Nation.* London: Jonathan Cape, 1963.

Hardin, Russell. *One for All.* Princeton: Princeton University Press, 1995.

Harris, Tim. "The British Dimension . . ." In *Protestantism and National Identity,* ed. Tony Claydon and Ian McBride, 131–56. Cambridge: Cambridge University Press, 1998.

Hastings, Adrian. *The Construction of Nationalism.* Cambridge: Cambridge University Press, 1997,

Haydon, Colin. "I Love My King and My Country, but a Roman Catholic I Hate." In *Protestantism and National Identity,* ed. Tony Claydon and Ian McBride, 33–52. Cambridge: Cambridge University Press, 1998.

Hechter, Michael. *Containing Nationalism.* Oxford: Oxford University Press, 2000.

———. *Internal Colonialism.* Berkeley: University of California Press, 1975.

———. *Principles of Group Solidarity.* Berkeley: University of California Press, 1987.

Heimer, Carol A. "Comment." In *The Limits of Rationality,* ed. Karen Shweers Cook and Margaret Levi, 378–82. Chicago: University of Chicago Press, 1990.

Hempton, David. *Religion and Political Culture in Britain and Ireland.* Cambridge: Cambridge University Press, 1996.

Hibbert, Christopher. *King Mob.* London: Longmans, Green, 1959.

Hill, Christopher. *The English Bible and the Seventeenth Century Revolution.* London: Penguin, 1993.

———. *Anti-Christ in Seventeenth Century England.* London: Oxford University Press, 1971.

———. *The Century of Revolution, 1603–1714.* New York: Norton, 1961.

Hillgarth, J. N. *The Spanish Kingdoms, 1250–1516.* Vol. 2. Oxford: Clarendon Press, 1978.

Hobsbawm, Eric J. *Nations and Nationalism since 1780.* Cambridge: Cambridge University Press, 1990.

Hobsbawm, Eric and Terence Ranger, eds. *The Invention of Tradition.* Cambridge: Cambridge University Press, 1983.

Holt, Mack P. *The French Wars of Religion, 1562–1629.* Cambridge: Cambridge University Press, 1995.

———. "Putting Religion Back into the Wars of Religion." *French Historical Studies* 18:2 (Fall 1993): 524–51.

———, ed. *The Short Oxford History of France.* Vol. 4. From revised manuscript edition of 25 January 2002.

Horn, D. B. and Mary Ransome, eds. *English Historical Documents, 1714–1783.* London: Routledge, 1957.

Hunt, Lynn, ed. *The French Revolution and Human Rights.* New York: St. Martin's Press, 1996.

Huntington, Samuel P. *The Clash of Civilizations and the Remaking of World Order.* New York: Simon and Schuster, 1996.

Jones, J. R. *The First Whigs*. London: Oxford University Press, 1961.

———. *The Revolution of 1688 in England*. New York: Norton, 1972.

Kamen, Henry. *The Spanish Inquisition*. London: Weidenfeld and Nicolson, 1997.

———. *Philip of Spain*. New Haven: Yale University Press, 1997.

Kedourie, Elie. *Nationalism*. Oxford: Blackwell, 1993.

Keeney, Barnaby Conrad. *Judgement by Peers*. Cambridge: Harvard University Press, 1952.

Kelly, P. J. "John Locke: Authority, Conscience and Religious Toleration." In *John Locke: A Letter Concerning Toleration in Focus*, ed. John Horton and Susan Mendus, 125–46. London: Routledge, 1991.

Kennedy, Paul. *The Rise and Fall of the Great Powers*. New York: Random House, 1987.

Kenyon, John. *The Popish Plot*. London: Heinemann, 1972.

Kenyon, J. P. *The Stuart Constitution, 1603–1688*. Cambridge: Cambridge University Press, 1966.

Keohane, Robert O. "International Institutions: Two Approaches." *International Studies Quarterly* 32 (1988): 379–96.

Kiernan, V. G. *State and Society in Europe, 1550–1650*. Oxford: Basil Blackwell, 1980.

Kishlansky, Mark. *A Monarchy Transformed: Britain, 1603–1714*. London: Penguin Press, 1996.

Knecht, R. J. *Catherine de' Medici*. London: Longman, 1998.

Koenigsberger, Helmut. "Spain." In *National Consciousness, History, and Political Culture in Early-Modern Europe*, ed. Orest Ranum, 144–72. Baltimore: Johns Hopkins University Press, 1975.

Kohn, Hans. *The Idea of Nationalism*. New York: Macmillan, 1944.

———. *Nationalism: Its Meaning and History*. New York: D. van Nostrand, 1965.

———. "Western and Eastern Nationalisms." In *Nationalism*, ed. John Hutchinson and Anthony D. Smith, 162–4. Oxford: Oxford University Press, 1994.

Kymlicka, Will. *Multicultural Citizenship*. Oxford: Clarendon Press, 1995.

Laitin, David. *Hegemony and Culture*. Chicago: University of Chicago Press, 1986.

———. "Hegemony and Religious Conflict." In *Bringing the State Back In*, ed. Peter Evans, Dietrich Rueschemeyer, and Theda Skocpol, 285–316. Cambridge: Cambridge University Press, 1985.

Lea, Henry Charles. *A History of the Inquisition of Spain*. Vol. I. New York: AMS Press, 1988.

Lindley, Keith. "Part Played by the Catholics." In *Politics, Religion, and the English Civil War*, ed. Brian Manning, 127–78. London: Edward Arnold, 1973.

Linz, Juan. "Early State-Building and Late Peripheral Nationalisms against the State: The Case of Spain." In *Building States and Nations*. Vol. 2, ed. S. N. Eisenstadt and Stein Rokkan, 32–116. Beverly Hills: Sage Publications, 1973.

————. "State Building and Nation Building." *European Review* 1:4 (1993): 355–69.

Llorente, Juan Antonio. *A Critical History of the Inquisition of Spain.* Williamstown: John Lilburne, 1967.

Locke, John. *A Letter Concerning Toleration.* ed. Patrick Romanell. New York: Macmillan, 1950.

Lockyer, Roger. *Tudor and Stuart Britain, 1471–1714.* New York: St. Martin's Press, 1985.

Lublinskaya, A. D. *French Absolutism: the Crucial Phase, 1620–1629.* Cambridge: Cambridge University Press, 1968.

Lukes, Steven. *Power: A Radical View.* London: Macmillan, 1974.

Lustik, Ian S. "Culture and the Wager of Rational Choice." *APSA Comparative Politics Newsletter* 8:2 (Summer 1997): 11–14.

————. *Unsettled States; Disputed Lands.* Ithaca: Cornell University Press, 1993.

Machiavelli, Niccolo. *The Prince.* Middlesex: Penguin, 1961.

Mamdani, Mahmood. *Citizen and Subject: Contemporary Africa and the Legacy of Late Colonialism.* Princeton: Princeton University Press, 1996.

Mann, Michael. *The Sources of Social Power.* Vol. 2. Cambridge: Cambridge University Press, 1993.

————. "The Emergence of Modern European Nationalism," in *Transition to Modernity*, ed. John A. Hall and I. C. Jarvie, 137–66. Cambridge: Cambridge University Press, 1992.

Manning, Brian. *The English People and the English Revolution.* London: Bookmarks, 1991.

Marshall, T. H. *Citizenship and Social Class.* London: Pluto, 1992.

Marx, Karl. "The Eighteenth Brumaire of Louis Bonaparte." In *Karl Marx: Selected Writings*, ed. David McLellan, 300–25. Oxford: Oxford University Press, 1977.

McManners, John. *The French Revolution and the Church.* Westport: Greenwood, 1969.

Mehta, Uday Singh. *Liberalism and Empire.* Chicago: University of Chicago Press, 1999.

Mendus, Susan and John Horton, "Locke and Toleration." In *John Locke: A Letter Concerning Toleration in Focus*, ed. Susan Horton and John Mendus, 1–11. London: Routledge, 1991.

Menéndez Pidal, Ramón. *The Spaniards in Their History*, trans. Walter Starkie. New York: Norton Library, 1966.

Merton, Robert K. *Social Theory and Social Structure.* New York: Free Press, 1968.

Miller, John. *Popery and Politics in England, 1660–1688.* Cambridge: Cambridge University Press, 1973.

Mitchell, B. R. *European Historical Statistics, 1750–1975.* New York: Facts on File, 1980.

Moore, Barrington. *Social Origins of Dictatorship and Democracy.* Boston: Beacon, 1966.

Motyl, Alexander J. *Revolutions, Nations, Empires.* New York: Columbia University Press, 1999.

Mousnier, Roland. *The Assassination of Henry IV*. London: Faber and Faber, 1973.

Nairn, Tom. "The Curse of Rurality." In *The State of the Nation*, ed. John A. Hall, 107–34. Cambridge: Cambridge University Press, 1998.

———. *The Break-up of Britain*. London: New Left Books, 1977.

Neale, J. E. *Queen Elizabeth I*. London: Jonathan Cape, 1938.

———. *The Age of Catherine de Medici*. New York: Barnes and Noble, 1943.

Netanyahu, B. *The Origins of the Inquisition in 15th Century Spain*. New York: Random House, 1995.

———. *Toward the Inquisition*. Ithaca: Cornell University Press, 1997.

Nirenberg, David. *Communities of Violence*. Princeton: Princeton University Press, 1996.

O'Gorman, Frank. *The Long Eighteenth Century*. London: Arnold, 1997.

O'Leary, Brendan. "Ernest Gellner's Diagnosis of Nationalism." In *The State of the Nation*, ed. John A. Hall, 40–90. Cambridge: Cambridge University Press, 1998.

Ogg, David. *England in the Reign of Charles II*. Oxford: Clarendon Press, 1934.

———. *England in the Reigns of James II and William III*. Oxford: Clarendon Press, 1955.

Parker, Geoffrey. *Europe in Crisis 1598–1648*. 2d Edition. Oxford: Blackwell Publishers, 2001.

———. *Philip II*. Boston: Little, Brown, and Co., 1978.

Petrie, Sir Charles, ed. *The Letters, Speeches and Proclamations of King Charles I*. New York: Funk and Wagnalls, 1968.

Pincus, Steven. "To Protect English Liberties: The English Nationalist Revolution of 1688–1689." In *Protestantism and National Identity*, ed. Tony Claydon and Ian McBride, 75–104. Cambridge: Cambridge University Press, 1998.

———. "Nationalism, Universal Monarchy, and the Glorious Revolution." In *State/Culture*, ed. George Steinmetz, 182–210. Ithaca: Cornell University Press, 1999.

Plamenatz, John. "Two Types of Nationalism." In *Nationalism*, ed. Eugene Kamenka, 23–36. New York: St. Martins Press, 1976.

Plumb, J. H. *The Growth of Political Stability in England, 1675–1725*. London: Macmillan, 1967.

Pocock, J. G. A., ed. *The British Revolution: 1641, 1688, 1776*. Princeton: Princeton University Press, 1980.

Poland, Burdette C. *French Protestantism and the French Revolution*. Princeton: Princeton University Press, 1957.

Potter, David. *A History of France, 1460–1560*. London: Macmillan Press, 1995.

———, ed. *The French Wars of Religion: Selected Documents*. London: Macmillan, 1997.

Powell, Walter W. and Paul J. DiMaggio, eds. *The New Institutionalism in Organizational Analysis*. Chicago: University of Chicago Press, 1991.

Ranum, Orest. *The Fronde: A French Revolution, 1648–1652*. New York: Norton, 1993.

————, ed. *National Consciousness, History and Political Culture in Early-Modern Europe*. Baltimore: Johns Hopkins University Press, 1975.

Ranum, Orest and Patricia Ranum, eds. *The Century of Louis XIV*. New York: Harper and Row, 1972.

Renan, Ernest. "What Is a Nation?" In *Becoming National*, ed. Geoff Eley and Ronald Grigor Suny, 42–55. New York: Oxford University Press, 1996.

Riker, William H. *The Theory of Political Coalitions*. New Haven: Yale University Press, 1962.

Rousseau, Jean-Jacques. *The Social Contract*. Hammondsworth: Penguin, 1968.

————. "Considerations on the Government of Poland." In *The Social Contract and Other Later Writings*, ed. Victor Gourevitch, 177–260. Cambridge: Cambridge University Press, 1997.

Rueshemeyer, Dietrich, Evelyne Huber Stephens and John D. Stephens. *Capitalist Development and Democracy*. Chicago: University of Chicago Press, 1992.

Rustow, Dankwart. "Transitions to Democracy: Toward a Dynamic Model." *Comparative Politics* (April 1970): 337–63.

Sacshe, William L. "The Mob and the Revolution of 1688." *Journal of British Studies* 4:1 (November 1964): 24–40.

Sahlins, Marshall. *Culture and Practical Reason*. Chicago: University of Chicago Press, 1976.

Sahlins, Peter. "Fictions of a Catholic France: The Naturalization of Foreigners, 1685–1787." *Representations* 47 (Summer 1994): 85–110.

Said, Edward W. *Orientalism*. New York: Random House, 1978.

Salmon, J. H. M. *Society in Crisis: France in the Sixteenth Century*. New York: St. Martin's Press, 1975.

Sandler, Todd. *Collective Action*. Ann Arbor: University of Michigan Press, 1992.

Sandler, Todd and John T. Tschirhart. "The Economic Theory of Clubs." *Journal of Economic Literature* 27 (December 1980): 1481–1521.

Schelling, Thomas. *The Strategy of Conflict*. Cambridge: Harvard University Press, 1960.

Sewell, William H. Jr., "Artisans, Factory Workers and the Formation of the French Working Class, 1789–1848." In *Working-Class Formation*, ed. Ira Katznelson and Aristide R. Zolberg, 45–70. Princeton: Princeton University Press, 1986.

Shepsle, Kenneth A. "Studying Institutions." *Journal of Theoretical Politics* 1: 2 (1989): 131–47.

Smith, Anthony. *The Ethnic Origins of Nation*. Oxford: Basil Blackwell, 1986.

————. *Nationalism and Modernism*. London: Macmillan, 1998.

Sommerville, Johann P., ed. *King James VI and I: Political Writings*. Cambridge: Cambridge University Press, 1994.

Spivak, Gayatri. *In Other Worlds*. New York: Methuen, 1987.

Stepan, Alfred. *Arguing Comparative Politics*. Oxford: Oxford University Press, 2001.

Stinchcombe, Arthur L. "Social Structures and Politics." In *Handbook of Political Science*. Vol. 3, ed. Fred I. Greenstein and Nelson Polsby, 557–622. Reading: Addison-Wesley, 1975.

Stoye, John. *Europe Unfolding, 1648–1688*. New York: Harper and Row, 1969.

Strayer, Joseph Reese. *On the Medieval Origins of the Modern State*. Princeton: Princeton University Press, 1970.

Sutherland, N. M. *The Massacre of St. Bartholomew and the European Conflict, 1559–1572*. London: Macmillan, 1973.

———. *Princes, Politics and Religion, 1547–1589*. London: Hambledon Press, 1984.

Tajfel, Henry. "Experiments in Intergroup Discrimination." *Scientific American* 223 (November 1970): 96–102.

———. *Differentiation between Social Groups*. London: Academic Press, 1972.

Tajfel, Henri and John C. Turner. "The Social Identity Theory of Intergroup Behavior." In *Psychology of Intergroup Relations*, ed. Stephen Worchel and W. G. Austin, 7–16. Chicago: Nelson-Hall, 1986.

Tamir, Yael. *Liberal Nationalism*. Princeton: Princeton University Press, 1993.

Tanner, J. R., ed. *Constitutional Documents of the Reign of James I*. Cambridge: Cambridge University Press, 1930.

Taylor, Charles. "Nationalism and Modernity." In *The State of the Nation*, ed. John A. Hall, 191–218. Cambridge: Cambridge University Press, 1998.

Tennyson, Lord Alfred. "Ulysses." In *Alfred Tennyson, Idylls of the King and a Selection of Poems*. New York: Penguin, 1961.

Thompson, E. P. *The Making of the English Working Class*. New York: Random House, 1963.

Tilly, Charles. *Coercion, Capital, and European States*, AD *990–1992*. Cambridge: Blackwell, 1990.

———. "Citizenship, Identity and Social History." *International Review of Social History*, Supplement 3 (1996): 1–18.

———. *The Contentious French*. Cambridge: Harvard University Press, 1986.

———. *Popular Contention in Great Britain, 1758–1834*. Cambridge: Harvard University Press, 1995.

Trevor-Roper, H. R. *Religion, the Reformation and Social Change*. London: Macmillan, 1967.

Tully, James H. "Introduction." In *John Locke: A Letter Concerning Toleration*, ed. James H. Tully, 1–11. Indianapolis: Hackett, 1983.

Van Kley, Dale K. *The Religious Origins of the French Revolution*. New Haven: Yale University Press, 1996.

Vernon, James. *Politics and the People*. Cambridge: Cambridge University Press, 1993.

Voltaire, Jean François Marie Arouet. *The Age of Louis XIV*. New York: Dutton, 1961.

Wallerstein, Immanuel. *The Modern World-System*. New York: Academic Press, 1974.

Walzer, Michael. *The Revolution of the Saints*. Cambridge: Harvard University Press, 1965.

Weber, Eugen. *Peasants into Frenchmen: The Modernization of Rural France, 1870–1914*. Stanford: Stanford University Press, 1976.

Weber, Max. *Economy and Society*. Vol 1. Berkeley: University of California Press, 1978.

———. *The Protestant Ethic and the Spirit of Capitalism*. New York: Charles Scribner's Sons, 1958.

Weingast, Barry R. "The Political Foundations of Democracy and the Rule of Law." *American Political Science Review* 91:2 (June 1997): 245–63.

Wells, Charlotte Catherine. "The Language of Citizenship in Early Modern France." Ph.D. diss., Department of History, Indiana University, December 1991.

Wiener, Carol Z. "The Beleaguered Isle: A Study of Elizabethan and Early Jacobean Anti-Catholicism," In *Past and Present* 51 (1971): 27–62.

Wilmsen, Edwin N. and Patrick MacAllister, eds. *The Politics of Difference*. Chicago: University of Chicago Press, 1996.

Wolfe, Michael. *The Conversion of Henri IV*. Cambridge: Harvard University Press, 1993.

Xeros, Nicholas. "Civic Nationalism: Oxymoron?" *Critical Review* 10:2 (Spring 1996): 213–32.

Yack, Bernard. "The Myth of the Civic Nation." *Critical Review* 10:2 (Spring 1996): 193–212.

Yeats, W. B. "Leda and the Swan." In M. L. Rosenthal, ed., *Selected Poems and Two Plays of William Butler Yeats*. New York: Macmillan, 1962.

———. "Among School Children." In M. L. Rosenthal, ed., *Selected Poems and Two Plays of William Butler Yeats*. New York: Macmillian, 1962.

INDEX